SOVIET STUDIES GUIDE

Edited by Tania Konn

Bowker-Saur

London • Melbourne • Munich • New Jersey

©Bowker-Saur Ltd, 1992

Published by Bowker-Saur
60 Grosvenor Street, London W1X 9DA
Tel: 071-493 5841 Fax: 071-580 4089

Bowker-Saur is part of the Professional Division of
Reed International Books

British Library Cataloguing-in-Publication Data
Soviet studies guide.
I. Konn, Tania
016.947
ISBN 0862917905

Cover design by John Cole Graphics
Typeset by SunSetters
Printed on acid free paper
Printed and bound in Great Britain by Antony Rowe Ltd, Chippenham, Wiltshire

Contents

Series Foreword

The stimulation of an inter-disciplinary approach, which also emphasises the interrelation between the environment and human history, makes Area Studies particularly appealing. But the plethora of literature can be daunting. The purpose of this Series is to meet the need for authoritative and critical guides to the core texts for a given region or country.

The aim is that a student or researcher should be able to use the critical commentary and bibliographic references to pinpoint the main English-language and key native language academic works, as well as to find an overview of the literature as a whole. Alternatively, an advanced student or lecturer will be able to use titles in the series to provide a quick reference to the key publications in the relevant field.

This book, the *Soviet Studies Guide*, is the first in the series. Other titles, covering major regions in the world, will follow. As with the *Soviet Studies Guide*, the editor of each volume will have substantial experience of the relevant literature and information sources, while the contributors will be specialists in one aspect of the field. Thus the total work will give an integrated and highly expert account of the current literature.

About the Contributors

Robert F. Byrnes
Is Distinguished Professor of History at Indiana University, Bloomington, where he helped found the Russian and East European Institute. He has written on anti-semitism in France, conservative thought in nineteenth-century Russia, American policy toward the Soviet Union and Eastern Europe and the history of Russian studies in the United States. He is now completing a book on the historian, V.O. Kliuchevskii.

Terry Cox
Teaches sociology and politics in the Department of Government at Strathclyde University. His books include *Rural Sociology in the Soviet Union* and *Peasants, Class and Capitalism.* His current research is on the changing position of the private sector in Soviet society.

John Erickson
Is Professor and Director of Defence Studies at the University of Edinburgh. Specialising in Soviet military history and Soviet military political affairs, since the mid-1950s he has produced a number of monographs, edited volumes and studies. These include *The Soviet High Command 1918-1941* and the two-volume history of the 'Great Patriotic War 1941-1945', *The Road to Stalingrad* and *The Road to Berlin.*

Stephen Fortescue
Has a BA and PhD in Soviet politics from the Australian National University. After holding research fellowships at the ANU and the University of Birmingham he now teaches Soviet politics at the University of New South Wales. He has published two monographs and a number of articles on Soviet science management and the state bureaucratic apparatus.

Chauncy D. Harris

Studied geography at Oxford University, the London School of Economics, and the University of Chicago, where he is the Samuel N. Harper Distinguished Service Professor Emeritus of Geography. Among his specialisations are the Soviet Union and bibliography of geography. His publications include *Cities of the Soviet Union, Guide to Geographical Bibliographies and Reference Works in Russian or on the Soviet Union, International List of Geographical Serials* and *Bibliography of Geography*. He was also Editor in Chief of *A Geographical Bibliography for American Libraries*.

Tania Konn

Is Head of the Area Studies Division at Glasgow University. This includes responsibility for the Soviet, Slavonic and East European collections. Since 1986 she has specialised in Soviet business information sources and has been closely associated with the establishment of a Soviet and East European Business Information Service at the university. Her publication list in this area includes USSR Business Information (1990). She is currently Chairman of the Advisory Committee on Slavonic and East European Materials of the Standing Conference for National and University Libraries.

Margot Light

Graduated from the University of Surrey in Russian and International Relations. Since 1988 she has been a lecturer in International Relations at the London School of Economics, London University. She has written articles and chapters on Soviet foreign policy and is coeditor of *International Relations: A Handbook of Current Theory* (1985) and the author of *The Soviet Theory of International Relations* (1988).

Alec Nove

Is Emeritus Professor of Economics at the University of Glasgow. He is author of numerous books and articles, including *The Soviet Economic System, Socialism, Economics and Development, The Economics of Feasible Socialism, Stalinism and After, Political and Soviet Socialism, Glasnost in Action* and *Studies in Economics and Russia*.

Robert C. Stuart

Is Professor of Economics at Rutgers University and visiting Professor of Economics at Princeton University. His main fields of interest are Soviet agriculture and Soviet urban development though he is probably best known for his work (with Paul R. Gregory) entitled *Soviet Economic Structure and Performance*, the fourth edition of which was published by HarperCollins in 1990.

Stephen White
Is Professor of Politics and a member of the Institute of Soviet and East European Studies at the University of Glasgow. A graduate of Dublin, Glasgow and Oxford Universities, his numerous published works on Soviet history and politics include *The Origins of Detente* (1986), *Developments in Soviet Politics* (1990) and *Gorbachev and After* (2nd ed., 1991).

Wojciech Zalewski
Is Curator for Slavic and East European Collections and Lecturer in Slavic bibliography at Stanford University. He was educated at the Catholic University, Lublin (Poland), Gregorianum University, Rome, and San Jose State University. He is active in library and Slavic associations, his publications include *Fundamentals of Russian Reference Work in the Humanities and Social Sciences* (1985).

Foreword

English-language students have long needed a guide through the dense forest represented by the multitude of recent books that deal with the Soviet Union. This volume covers a wide range of subjects: geography, history, culture, politics, economics, society, science and technology... In each of these subjects it points to areas of special interest as well as listing the relevant publications. One hopes that the wide range covered will encourage those who see the disadvantages of too narrow a specialisation: who can understand what has gone wrong with the Soviet economy without background knowledge of history, culture, politics..? We are living in dramatic times. The Soviet Union as we knew it is in process of disintegration, long-familiar assumptions no longer hold good; indeed, this book may not be long on the bookshelves before there will be no more Soviet Union under that name. It is a matter of great interest and importance to understand what has been happening, and why. This review of the literature and of the issues, written by eminent specialists in each of the subjects covered, will surely prove of great help to researchers and students alike.

Professor Alec Nove
University of Glasgow

Introduction

Events of recent years have served to heighten interest in the Soviet Union. One consequence of this reinvigorated concern has been a rapid and sustained increase in the volume of academic and other publications devoted to problems, issues and expectations generated by glasnost and perestroika. This increase in publications has been associated with a sharp qualitative distinction. Post-Gorbachev literature differs in content, style and perspectives from most earlier offerings.

The speed and significance of these developments suggested the utility of a guide, the first in a series of such works, to the literature on the Soviet Union, which would highlight the more important trends occurring over the last decade. Such a guide would prove especially informative if written by acknowledged subject experts. This was the proposal that Bowker-Saur presented to me. I had no reservations about the correctness of the analysis; I had felt the need for such a guide in my own work. However, I did have doubts as to the practicality of the proposal. Experience had taught me that academic eminence was rarely associated with a willingness to engage in bibliographical ventures, however useful the final product. Nonetheless the idea seemed so worthwhile that I agreed to contact a panel of specialists to seek their responses. In the event my initial doubts were dissipated. The scholars I approached enthused over the project and willingly agreed to contribute. The success of this recruiting stage, which involved four American, one Australian, and five British scholars, owed much to the guidance and advice of Professor Stephen White, Department of Politics, Glasgow University.

The brief presented to the contributors was to write a 5,000-word critical essay on literature developments in their fields concentrating particularly, but not exclusively, on the last decade. In addition they were asked to provide an annotated bibliography of roughly 100 titles which, in their opinion, merited notice. For reasons of space, attention was to be concentrated upon English language monographs, except where overwhelming reasons supported mention of Russian (or other) language material. References to periodical literature were allowed on the same limited basis. These constraints obviously presented all contributors with a difficult task, but their responses made light of limitations.

Such a brief allowed scope for individual interpretation and choice of titles: a necessary freedom given the differing characteristics of the various subject areas reviewed. The results are to be seen, for example, in the variations of treatment between geography and history. The events of glasnost have devalued many earlier historical contributions, and there has not been time to fill the gaps so created. The bibliography to the essay on this subject is one of the shortest in the book as a consequence. The same cannot be said of geography which, because of its nature, has had to make less profound adjustments to glasnost and perestroika. The quality of earlier work is less challengeable. The bibliography to the chapter on this area, *Land, Environment and People*, is one of the longest.

A number of the subject divisions unavoidably overlap. Where this has led contributors to cite the same title, no attempt has been made to edit out such repetitions. Indeed, different approaches to individual titles resulted in varying assessments and emphases which it is useful to retain. References to periodical articles and to foreign materials naturally vary.

The encouragement of authorial individuality does not include the arrangement of the bibliographies. Contributors were asked to group their titles in broad categories and, within these, by date (the most recent first) and author. In this way it is hoped to reflect something of chronological developments in each field. Two chapters, because of their particular character, fall outside this pattern. These are Chapters Eight and Ten, on *Business* and on *General Reference* respectively. The divergence may need justifying. During the gestation period it was suggested that, since there had been dramatic changes in business literature relating to the Soviet Union, it would be remiss to neglect the transformation. Accordingly the decision was taken to include such a chapter. However, since business information is so centrally concerned with events of the moment and rapidly changing speculative futures, it was unavoidable that any review would have to reflect this phenomenon. Consequently in this chapter there is a greater emphasis upon periodical sources than in other subject chapters, and the arrangement of entries within categories is different. Within the broad groupings, items are arranged by material types and, under these headings, in alphabetical sequence. The reference emphasis of Chapter 10 also entails a heavy reliance upon periodical publications and broad groupings by bibliographical forms.

Together, the contributors cover a wide range of interests in the Soviet Union. Chapter One, *Land, Environment and People*, by Professor Chauncy D. Harris, gives full expression to the wide sweep of the subject and makes clear that, although certain issues such as the environment are likely to gain in significance as a result of glasnost and perestroika, the literature foundations are sound enough. In Chapter Two, *Soviet History*, by Professor Robert F. Byrnes, inevitably the conclusion is markedly different. Much of the old literature has lost its conviction since hidden documents and suppressed views have come out into the open in recent years. As a consequence, those items which have stood the test of history have acquired a special significance. Soviet sociology has had long recognised limitations. These, together with developments suggesting compensating improvements, are explored by Dr Terry Cox in Chapter Three, *Society and Culture*. During the post-Gorbachev period, an expansion in sociological literature has been noted as researchers have attempted to record and describe social movements arising from perestroika and glasnost. *Government and Politics*, Chapter Four, by Professor Stephen White, reviews an area wholly transformed by the events of the last few years. Sources, personal and formal, are available in unprecedented abundance, but the greatest difficulty in studying current Soviet politics is 'that the change was so rapid and its scope so far-reaching that almost all the work that was being produced was overtaken by events before it had appeared'. A refrain that others echo in heartfelt fashion. In discussing *International Relations*, Chapter Five, Dr Margot Light also draws attention to the difficulty which the literature of her own field has in keeping up with the pace of events, as well as to the significant changes in attitudes and aims which have modified the character of that output. Chapter Six, *Armed Forces*, by Professor John Erickson, examines the seeming paradox that, as the Soviet military threat has apparently receded, so the 'intensity of interest in Soviet military affairs has not only increased but also departed in different directions'. The results for the literature are both significant and highly interesting. In Chapter Seven the literature of *The Economy* is reviewed by Professor Robert C. Stuart. The post-Gorbachev influences upon the economic literature, as might be expected, could not be other than considerable. The main changes are charted and organised so that trends are clearly discernible. Chapter Eight, on *Business*, by Tania Konn, concentrates upon the developments of the last three or four years. Such has been the degree of transformation that little business literature before these years is worth studying. *Science and Technology*, Chapter Nine, by Stephen Fortescue, draws attention to the relative lack of English language material and to the slow, patchy response in this field to events which have transformed other areas of study. Dr Wojciech Zalewski, in Chapter Ten, *GeneralReference*, provides an introduction to the bibliographical system and individual guides that enable enquiring minds further to explore the paths indicated by the other contributors.

A work of this nature places strains upon the enthusiasm and tolerance of many busy individuals. In this respect I must acknowledge the debt I owe each of the contributors. Their willingness to participate in the project, and their punctiliousness once having agreed to contribute, made my task much easier than I could have hoped for. All the first drafts, and any subsequent reformulations, were submitted on time. A rare record indeed for a collaborative venture of this kind. The contribution of Stephen White in helping me over early hurdles has been noted already, but the timing of his assistance was vital to the continuation of the project. I am grateful, too, to Alec Nove for allowing himself to be persuaded to provide the Foreword. I should also like to record my thanks to Mark Hudson, of Bowker-Saur, for his advice and guidance.

All the contributions were in the hands of the publishers well before the dramatic coup events of August, 1991. Much has changed in the Soviet Union as a consequence. However, the force and direction of current change owe much to the influential events of the previous decade. The retrospective nature of the assessments in this book, informed throughout by the expectation of continuing change, therefore serve as a convenient introduction to the various processes that led to such dramatic upheaval. Calculated organisation could not have produced better timing for the appearance of this type of work.

Tania Konn
August 1991

Postscript: January 1992
Events have moved so fast that the Soviet Union has ceased to exist. Nevertheless the territories and peoples of the former USSR will still continue to be of great – if not greater – interest to scholars and researchers worldwide. Since this Studies Guide relates to academic and other works written about the Soviet Union while it was functioning, it seems appropriate to leave the title and contents unchanged.

Norway

Boundary treaty
1947

KALININGRAD OBLAST
Annexed 1945

Finland

Tellinn

Boundary treaty 1920

KARELIAN
A.S.S.R.

Poland

Czecho-
slovakia
Bdy. treaty
1945

Agreement
1944

1 Riga 3

Vilnius 2

Minsk

BELO-
RUSSIAN
S.S.R.

Nenets N.O.

KOMI
A.S.S.R.

Yamal
Nenets
N.O.

Rumania
Boundary
treaty 1947

UKRAINIAN S.S.R.

4

Kishinev

Kiev

Moscow

R U S S I A

Komi-
Permyak
N.O.

15 16 17

19

18

BASHKIR

A.S.S.R.

Khanty-
Mansi N.O.

KRASNODAR
KRAY

20

STAVROPOL KRAY

KALMYK
A.S.S.R.

8

Turkey
Boundary treaty
1921

9 5 10

21 11

22 12

Tbilisi

6 13

Yerevan

7

Baku

KARA-
KALPAK
A.S.S.R.

KAZAKH S.S.R.

ALTAY
KRA
G

Iran

TURKMEN S.S.R.

UZBEK S.S.R.

Ashkhabad

Tashkent

Dushanbe

TADZHIK

Frunze

Alma Ata

KIRGIZ
S.S.R.

Boundary
in dispute

Boundary treaty 1870

24

S.S.R.

China

Afghanistan

Key to Map

S.S.R.
1 Lithuanian
2 Latvian
3 Estonian
4 Moldavian
5 Georgian
6 Armenian
7 Azerbaijan

A.S.S.R.
8 Abkhaz
9 Adzhar
10 Karbardino-Balkar

11 North Osetian
12 Chechen-Ingush
13 Dagestan
14 Nakhichevan
15 Mordovinian
16 Chuvash
17 Mari
18 Tatar
19 Udmurt

A.O. (Autonomous Oblast)
20 *Adyge*
21 *Karachev-Cherkess*
22 *South Osetian*
23 *Nagorno-Karabakh*
24 *Gorno-Badakhshan*

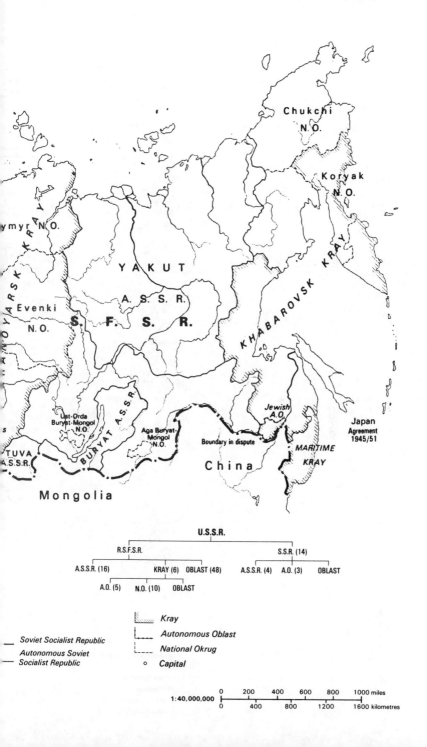

USSR 1990

Chukchi
N.O.

Koryak
N.O.

ymyr N.O.

YAKUT

A. S. S. R.

Evenki

N.O.

S. F. S. R.

KHABAROVSK KRAY

KRASNOYARSK KRAY

Ust-Orda
Buryat-Mongol
N.O.

BURYAT A.S.S.R.

Aga Buryat-
Mongol
N.O.

Boundary in dispute

Jewish
A.O.

Japan
Agreement
1945/51

MARITIME
KRAY

TUVA
A.S.S.R.

China

Mongolia

U.S.S.R.

R.S.F.S.R.   S.S.R. (14)

A.S.S.R. (16)   KRAY (6)   OBLAST (48)   A.S.S.R. (4)   A.O. (3)   OBLAST

A.O. (5)   N.O. (10)   OBLAST

Kray

Autonomous Oblast

National Okrug

○   *Capital*

──   Soviet Socialist Republic

─   Autonomous Soviet
Socialist Republic

1:40,000,000

| 0 | 200 | 400 | 600 | 800 | 1000 miles |
| 0 | 400 | 800 | 1200 | 1600 kilometres |

CHAPTER ONE

Land, Environment and People

Professor Chauncy D. Harris
University of Chicago

First of all it should be noted that the Soviet Union is of continental dimensions with enormous diversity of lands, environments and peoples. Covering an area of 22.4 million square kilometres, it is larger than the United States and Canada together or nearly a hundred times the size of the UK. Within this vast territory lie a great variety of lands and land-scapes, from the tundra and the cold, northern, coniferous forests (taiga) to the semi-arid but agriculturally rich steppes, to the hot deserts of Soviet Middle Asia; and from the plains and lowlands of the European part of the country and Western Siberia to the mountains of the southern and eastern rims in the Caucasus, Central Asia, Eastern Siberia, and the Far East.

Secondly, it should be observed that although the Soviet Union is rich in natural resources, having larger total reserves of many fuels and mine-rals than any other country, deposits often are poorly placed with respect to the centres of population and markets, low in quality, or expensive to develop. Although the Soviet Union is a leading producer of wheat, rye, oats, barley, beet sugar and potatoes, the country in recent years has spo-radically imported large quantities of feedstuffs and foodstuffs.

Thirdly, the Soviet Union is arguably the world's most complex country in its ethnic diversity and in the current intensity of its nationality issues. About half the population are Russians, another 20 per cent are other Slavic groups (Ukrainians and Belorussians) and about 30 per cent are many different non-Slavic peoples. Among the latter are the Baltic na-tionalities (Estonians, Latvians, and Lithuanians), who use the Latin al-phabet and look to the Baltic and Central Europe; the ancient independent Christian groups in the Caucasus (Georgians and Armenians), who have their own alphabets and were Christianised and literate long before the Russians; the Turkic-speaking Muslims of the Caucasus and Soviet

Middle Asia; and many smaller groups. In general the western groups have low birth rates, just enough to maintain a stable population, but the Muslim groups of Middle Asia have very high birth rates typical of Third World countries. These peoples of Soviet Middle Asia are contributing disproportionately to the increase in population and to the age cohorts that in the decades ahead will provide the labour force for the economy and manpower for the military. Generalisations or statistics for the Soviet Union as a whole do not apply equally to all parts of the country or to all its peoples. Neither the Russian imperialism of the nineteenth century nor the Soviet policies or practices of the twentieth have erased these remarkable, persistent, and rich regional differences.

During the 1980s, vigorous political movements arose around three critical issues involving the environment, economy and peoples of the Soviet Union. The first issue involved man's use, misuse and destruction of the environment and his pollution of it. Countrywide, regional and local groups protested vigorously against ecological damage to the environment and the high levels of air and water pollution, caused by factories located and administered by central government ministries in Moscow, without due regard to their impact on the health and lives of peoples in specific regions and cities. The second issue arose out of the deteriorating economy and the need for greater productivity and more efficient distribution. Economic reforms became embroiled in controversies between reformers and hard-liners with resulting compromises that satisfied neither group nor the population at large, and furthermore worked poorly. The third issue centred on the political rights and governance of ethnic groups, particularly the larger nationalities given recognition in the 15 constituent union republics, which have been demanding increased levels of sovereignty and in some cases even complete independence. These environmental, economic and ethnic tensions produced political instability (see chapters on *Government and Politics*, *The Economy*, and *Society and Culture*).

There was plenty to investigate in the Soviet Union in the 1980s. The decade witnessed a swelling stream of publications on the land, the economy, the peoples, and on their complex interrelated problems.

General Geography

Backgrounds for these and similar problems are provided by geographical treatments of the country. Fortunately good recent introductions to the geography of the Soviet Union are available. These generally cover physical geography, economic geography, and human geography. Physical geography provides a foundation for understanding environmental, ecological, and pollution problems. Economic geography furnishes the setting for economic problems. Human geography includes consideration of the national aspirations and ethnic tensions of the country.

Available recent publications range from short general introductions to detailed specialised research studies and reference volumes, too many for individual mention. A few titles will have to exemplify what is available. An individual new to Soviet studies wishing an effective but brief overview in less than a hundred pages can well turn to ZumBrunnen (3). An advanced student probing deeper into the nature of the country can with profit consult Lydolph (1), the most detailed recent systematic treatment in English.

Two highly original works provide quite different insights. Bater (4) discusses selected aspects of the economy and people of the Soviet Union, including original interpretations of modernisation of the Russian Empire as a prelude to present contradictions, management of resources, and the quality of life. He raises fundamental questions about policies and decision-making. Cole (5) provides numerous statistical analyses that illuminate comparisons with other countries and that highlight internal contrasts within the country itself. For example, a diagram of the trend of wheat yields from the 1930s to 1980 reveals that the yields in the Soviet Union have been low and have increased little over half a century while those in Mexico and the United Kingdom have increased dramatically. Why?

In contrast to the above systematic treatments of the country are works that discuss the richly diverse regions. Of particular value is a recent book in French by Radvanyi (2), which provides a perceptive discussion of the regional setting of current nationality problems. Howe (6) treats the 19 economic regions. Since statistical data are sometimes available by these areal units this text serves a valuable function in providing a regional setting for interpretation of such data. Collections of papers often provide a wide range of perspectives on diverse aspects of the geography of the country, for example Holzner (8) and Demko (9).

For detailed regional information on the entire Soviet Union, however, one turns to the massive 22-volume set in Russian, *Sovetskii Soiuz: Geograficheskoe Opisanie* (7), which is the most comprehensive discussion of the regional geography of the entire country. Individual volumes are devoted to each of the union republics, to seven large regions within the Russian Soviet Federated Socialist Republic, and to three within the Ukraine.

Physical Geography

As befits a large country with highly varied natural conditions, physical geography is a well-developed study in the Soviet Union. Soviet physical geographers are among the best in the world. The literature in Russian is voluminous and of high quality. Some of this has been translated into English. General introductions to the physical geography of the Soviet Union in Russian are provided by Gvozdetskii and Mil'kov (10, 12). Berg (16) and Suslov (15) in English translation describe the great natural belts of the entire country and the physical-geographic regions of the Asiatic part. Lydolph (14) is the definitive study of the climate in a land where climatic conditions confine the main agricultural belt to a small triangle in the west. Knystautas in English translation (11) is a striking presentation of the natural history of the country. Velichko (13), also in English translation, synthesises knowledge about the glacial period and its impact on present permafrost (permanently frozen ground that covers nearly half the country), fertile loess soils that underlie the best agricultural land, and even the dispersal of the earliest human cultures.

Resources and the Environment

In a huge country with enormous natural resources owned and administered by the state, much attention has been devoted to their exploration, study and management. Resource use emphasises their active utilisation in the economy whereas conservation lays greater stress on the preservation of the special qualities of environment. Alarm is being increasingly expressed over environmental degradation through pollution. The value of a clear atmosphere, pure water, and the ecological resources of vegetation and animal life are being articulated. Concern for the environment by the Soviet leaders and people has been growing since the first public controversy in the Soviet Union over the status of the environment in the mid-1960s; that controversy was over industrial pollution of Lake Baikal, the world's largest body of fresh water and home to many unique species of animal life. Environmental movements reached unprecedented levels in the 1980s. Environmentalists with support from the media and the public have been pitted against the great industrial ministries and the planning agencies, both of which have focused on expanding material production.

Soviet natural resources have been investigated in detail by a group of scholars in a large volume edited by Jensen, Shabad and Wright (23). The volume reveals the regional dimension of great distances separating resources and markets and the resulting high transportation costs. The book is particularly strong on raw materials located in Siberia and on the role of raw materials in Soviet foreign trade. In my view it is the most valuable single volume devoted to Soviet natural resources and the problems of their utilisation and marketing. Soviet specialists have emphasised the physical characteristics of the resources with respect to their possible use in the economy but with scant attention to cost factors or marketing problems. One particular resource, forests, which cover about half the entire country, has been investigated in detail in a monograph by Barr and Braden (19).

Numerous Western collections of papers have been devoted to environmental use and misuse. Among the more useful are those by Singleton (21), Jackson (26), and Volgyes (27). Ziegler (22) contains a summary of Soviet policy, law, and administration in environmental protection. Gustafson (24) notes the difficulties of reform. Komarov, in English translation (25), catches something of the urgent concern of Soviet citizens for the wasting of resources and for ecological damage.

The journal *Soviet Geography* has published three particularly interesting reports on current Soviet environmental problems. One contains papers of a Soviet conference on the role of scientists in the solution of ecological problems (20), another the views of a panel of Western specialists on the Soviet environment (18), and yet another the concerns expressed in the Soviet parliament (17).

General Economic Geography

General economic geographies provide some background for understanding the problems of the economy. For more recent or more detailed information in this area one must turn to Soviet textbooks such as, for example, those by Khrushchev and Rom (28, 29). Of course one can also utilise some of the more recent, general introductions to the geography of the Soviet Union. But the problems of the Soviet economy in the late 1980s and early 1990s changed so rapidly that one needs to consult current articles in *Soviet Geography* and other periodicals.

Agriculture

Agriculture has been a continuing problem for the Soviet Union with production falling behind plans, behind other sectors of the Soviet economy and behind agriculture in other countries. Because of the high latitudinal position and great longitudinal extent, the USSR has a cool and dry continental climate with more than half the country in the north too cold for agriculture, and great deserts in Soviet Middle Asia too dry. Even the best agricultural land has rather low and irregular yields. But the greatest problem of Soviet agriculture appears to be the centralised management from Moscow that has proved to be inflexible and inefficient. Three works provide special insights into the agricultural problems, Medvedev (30) of its historical background, Johnson and Brooks (31) of its economic aspects, and Symons (32) of its geographical characteristics. The Soviet scholar, Medvedev, is particularly illuminating.

Fuel and Energy

Oil and gas, the twin Cinderellas of the Soviet economy in the 1970s and 1980s, have received much attention recently, as well they should, since the Soviet Union is the world's largest producer of both. Their export in recent years has been earning well over half the foreign exchange of the country. Wilson (34) provides a good overall discussion, and Stern (33, 35) focuses more on natural gas and its export to other countries. Dienes and Shabad (36) provide a comprehensive view of all types of energy and fuel with a richness of maps and tables and with analysis of the planning and administration of the whole Soviet energy system.

Industry

The Soviet government has placed emphasis on industry, especially on heavy industry, to the neglect of light industry, consumer goods, and other sectors of the economy.

The most detailed discussions of Soviet industry are available in Russian by Khrushchev (39). The chemical industry has been examined in detail in a book edited by Sagers and Shabad (37) and in a monograph by Dienes (42), and the wood-processing industry in a study by Barr (41). Two works are devoted to the concept of territorial-production complexes (38, 40), a group of interrelated industries in one area, but the great industrial ministries that determine industrial location may not pay much attention to the concept.

Transportation

Transportation plays a vital role in binding together the enormous territory of the USSR but because of underinvestment the transport system is seriously strained. Monographs in Russian provide an overall treatment of Soviet transportation (53), of railroads (45), and of waterways (51). Recent valuable collections of specialised articles by Western students have been edited by Tismer and others (47), and by Ambler and others (50). The pervasive impact of space friction in the vast distances which separate raw materials and markets in the Soviet Union is well illustrated in the high cost and technical problems of the transport of fuels and industrial raw materials as studied by ZumBrunnen and Osleeb (49) for the iron and steel industry, and by Sagers and Green for energy resources (48).

The most gigantic transport enterprise of the late 1970s and the 1980s, the Baikal-Amur Mainline Railway (BAM), has been described by Shabad and Mote (54) at the time of its highly publicised launching, and in a later phase of neglect by Mote (43). Bergstrand and Doganis (44) analyse the impact of Soviet ocean shipping and North (46), northern transport. North

(52) also presents a detailed study of the role of transport in the development of Western Siberia.

Cities, Housing, and Planning

During the Soviet period the country has been transformed from a predominantly rural society to one dominated by cities. Between 1926 and 1990, the proportion of the urban population increased from about one-sixth to about two-thirds, more exactly from 18 per cent to 67 per cent. This tremendous transformation was not without its costs and problems in investment, in construction and in human lives.

A recent insightful study of Soviet urbanisation is provided by Medvedkov (55). In an examination of the hierarchy of cities, she notes the relatively weak position of Moscow in the far-flung urban network, with an overloaded transportation system. In an analysis of the functional topology of larger cities she concludes that many have the characteristics of company towns. In an analysis of interaction between industrial and social content of cities, she finds deep-seated indications of stagnation and the inadequacy of the service sector. She comes to the conclusion that any measures for improvement must take into account great regional differences.

Collections of articles on Soviet cities have been edited by Morton and Stuart (57), and by French and Hamilton (60). Pallot and Shaw have studied planning (58), Bater (59) decision-making, and Andrusz housing (56). The specific form of the city in Soviet Middle Asia is portrayed by Müller-Wille (61).

Historical Geography

The field of historical geography has been neglected in the Soviet Union. The best works are by Western scholars. Undoubtedly the outstanding publication is the two-volume work, edited by Bater and French (63). Seventeen original scholarly articles by British, Canadian and American authors are grouped by studies on man and the land, the frontier, towns, and the last century of the old regime. Cities in Russian history have received particular attention with two volumes of papers edited by Hamm (62, 65), monographs by Rozman (66) and Fedor (67), and an exemplary case study of St Petersburg by Bater (64).

Peoples

Nationality questions are much in the news because of the aspirations and demands by several ethnic groups for greater autonomy or independence.

Consequently current interest in the diverse peoples of the Soviet Union is very high. The outpouring of literature on nationalities in the 1980s was much greater than in any previous period in history and is perhaps greater than on any other contemporary issue in Soviet studies.

It is important to distinguish two quite distinct types of publications, those devoted to peoples as ethnic groups and those to population in general. The former has as its field of study the characteristics of individual nationalities that make up the complex regional diversity of the Soviet Union, a veritable museum of living peoples. The latter is concerned with demographic aspects, such as birth and death rates, age distributions, marriage rates, population increase, and projections of future population.

Ethnic groups form the basis of the administrative-territorial division of the Soviet Union into 15 union republics, 20 autonomous republics, eight autonomous oblasts, and ten autonomous okrugs. Administrative-territorial units that give recognition to non-Russian ethnic groups are distributed along the western, southern and northern boundaries of the country and in the interior near Kazan at the bend of the Volga river (cf. map to be found at the front of this book). Table 1.1 (below) gives the population of each of the 22 nationalities which counted more than one million members in the 1989 census. Two groups have no such territorial base, the Germans and the Poles. Although the Jews have an area of lower rank (an autonomous oblast) in the Soviet Far East, it is symbolic rather than functional for it contains only a tiny fraction of the Jewish population of the country and is remote from the main concentrations of Jews; furthermore, only a small percentage of the population in this area is Jewish.

Union republics have the theoretical right to secede from the Soviet Union and several wish to exercise that legal right. In particular the three Baltic republics, Estonia, Latvia and Lithuania, separate countries in the years between the First World War and the Second World War, and Georgia aspire to become independent once again. These hopes are complicated, however, by substantial Russian populations in Estonia and Latvia. The Ukraine and Belorussia are composed of Slavs, closely related to Russians. The western parts of these republics, formerly in Poland and with a Catholic tradition, however, pose some special regional problems. Moldavia, formerly largely in Romania and speaking Romanian, has its own ethnic complications. Georgia and Armenia have long, quite distinct histories, religious and national traditions, literatures and cultures. The six republics with Islamic traditions, predominantly Turkic in language, pose yet different types of problems: Azerbaidzhan in the Trans-Caucasus, Kazakhstan (with a very large Russian population), Kirgizia, Uzbekistan, Turkmenistan and Tadzhikistan (speaking a Persian language). Finally the Russian republic itself is the scene of revived nationalist sentiments of many different types.

Table 1.1 Nationalities of the Soviet Union with More than One Million Population According to the 1989 Census

Nationality	Population ('000)
Russians	145,155
Ukrainians	44,186
Uzbeks	16,698
Belorussians	10,036
Kazakhs	8,136
Azerbaidzhans	6,770
Tatars	6,649
Armenians	4,623
Tadzhiks	4,215
Georgians	3,981
Moldavians	3,352
Lithuanians	3,067
Turkmens	2,729
Kirgiz	2,529
Germans	2,039
Chuvash	1,842
Latvians	1,459
Bashkirs	1,449
Jews	1,378
Mordva	1,154
Poles	1,126
Estonians	1,027
All groups	285,743

Source: *Narodnoe Khoziaistvo SSSR v 1989 g.*; *Statisticheskii Ezhegodnik* (1990), p. 30.

Numerous recent Western works discuss in detail the nationality problems of the Soviet Union as a whole. A good review article on the demands and roles of national groups is presented by Lapidus (75), who clearly distinguishes among different types of national self-assertion and admirably summarises the complex economic, political, party, military and language issues of possible federal restructuring. Monographic summaries of nationality problems have been published by, for example, Nahaylo and Swoboda (71), Motyl (82) and Karklins (89). Ethnographic inventories by individual groups have been made by the Soviet scholar, Kozlov in English translation (77), and by American specialists Katz, Rogers and Harned (97) devoted to the large, titular nationalities of the 15 union republics plus the Tatars and Jews, and by Wixman (90), useful for treatment of the many small ethnic groups. Kingkade (78) has made projections of the population by major nationalities to the year 2050. Collections of diverse papers are a publication feature of this field. Recent contributions include Hajda and Beissinger (70), and Conquest (87). There is even a panel discussion (76). A collection of documents and readings has been helpfully assembled and edited by Olcott (73).

Other studies are devoted to individual ethnic groups in the European part of the Soviet Union. For the Slavic core of the country, Dunlop (91) and Allworth (92) examine Russian nationalism. John A. Armstrong (69) recently revised his study of Ukrainian nationalism during the Second World War, enriching the documentation. Special studies have been devoted to the two most populous nationalities without a proper ethnic homeland, to the Jews by Pinkus (80), Levin (79) and Altshuler (81), and to the Germans by Fleischhauer and Pinkus (88). The Baltic peoples, who have received extensive sympathy and interest in the West, have been studied in a collected volume edited by Allworth (96), while the Estonians, the smallest union-republic ethnic group in population in the third smallest union republic in area, are the subject of a monograph by Raun (84). A monograph by Wixman (93) is devoted to the even smaller groups of the ethnically complicated North Caucasus.

By far the largest number of recent studies, however, are devoted to Muslim peoples and Soviet Middle Asia. Examples of the range of treatments are provided by Rywkin (72), Allworth (74), Bennigsen and Wimbush (86, 94) and Akiner (85). McCagg and Silver (95) have studied the peoples located on both sides of international boundaries in Soviet Middle Asia, Mongolia, and the Caucasus. Recent monographs study in depth the two most populous Turkic Muslim peoples. Allworth (68) has investigated the bases of Uzbek group identity and the conflict between old and new modernity. The Kazakhs are effectively treated by Olcott (83).

Population

Soviet population, like other aspects of Soviet life, is subject to Soviet planning and policy, as noted by Desfosses (102) among others, but with only slight results. The indirect and unplanned impacts of other government policies, such as those on capital investments, housing, industrialisation, employment of women and education have been much greater. Studies have been made of fertility by Jones and Grupp (99), and by Coale, Anderson and Harm (106), and of migration by Soboleva (105), Grandstaff (104) and Anderson (103). Lewis and colleagues (107, 108) have studied the evolving regional and national composition of the population since the 1897 census, and Kingkade (98, 100) has made projections of the population to 2025. Clem (101) has edited a guide to Russian and Soviet censuses, particularly useful to anyone engaged in research on population, manpower or nationalities.

Regional Studies

Soviet Asia received special attention in the 1980s. A sharp contrast has been noted between resource-rich but population-poor and distant Siberia, which has trouble attracting labour, and resource-limited but population-rich Soviet Middle Asia, which has substantial underemployment but negligible emigration. Studies have noted the vast size of Siberia, its remoteness from the main economic and political centres of the Soviet Union, its imperfect integration into the economy of the country as a whole, and specifically into its centre. The weak integration reflects long distances and high transport costs in Eastern Siberia and the Soviet Far East. The oil and gas fields of Western Siberia constitute an exception in their close link with the industrial centre.

Ethnic and cultural contrasts between the labour deficient Slavic areas in Europe or Siberia, and the Turkic-speaking Muslim population of Middle Asia impede migration. The rapid population growth of Soviet Middle Asia and its increasing labour surplus underline its need for substantial capital investment to provide employment, but investments in the region are relatively small. Furthermore, the national groups in Middle Asia are not attracted by urban industrial employment even within Middle Asia, exhibiting a tendency to prefer traditional and rural life. This is the only part of the Soviet Union with a rapidly increasing rural population.

A question is raised whether Gorbachev's economic policy represents a possible turning away from Siberian development, long a goal of Soviet raw material development policy and huge capital investment in gigantic projects. Siberian development has been examined by successive meetings of the British Universities Siberian Studies Seminar in volumes edited by Wood and French (109) or Wood alone (112), and in a project of the Association of American Geographers edited by Jensen, Shabad and Wright (23). Dienes has also written an analytical monograph (110). A quite different approach is taken in a series of papers in a volume edited by Swearingen (111), in which a multinational and multidisciplinary group of authors examine strategic dimensions of Siberia and the Soviet Far East.

Atlases

Studies on the Soviet Union are blessed by the availability of many excellent Soviet atlases but hampered by restrictions on public access to accurate large-scale topographic and urban maps. A general purpose atlas in

English by Dewdney (115) is particularly valuable for orientation, since it provides on facing pages lucid text and clear maps and diagrams. Two large-format thematic atlases prepared by the United States Central Intelligence Agency provide graphic and cartographic data: *USSR Energy Atlas* (113) and *USSR Agriculture Atlas* (116). By far the best recent atlas of the Soviet Union, however, is the large-format Russian *Atlas SSSR* (114), which will need to be consulted frequently by anyone doing serious research on the Soviet Union.

Statistics

Statistical data are important in any study of the land, the economy and the peoples of the Soviet Union. The handiest running statistical series in English is *USSR Facts and Figures Annual* (118), published since 1977. Mickiewicz (119) has compiled very useful tables of social science data. The basic Soviet annual statistical volume, *Narodnoe Khoziaistvo SSSR: Statisticheskii Ezhegodnik* (120), has been published annually since 1956. Clem (101) provides a valuable guide to statistics found in the basic censuses of Russia and the Soviet Union from 1897 on. Heleniak (117) inventories more than 2,000 thematic or regional statistical handbooks published 1953-1988.

Biographies

Biographical material on Soviet geographers and other students of the lands and peoples of the USSR may be found in *Directory of Soviet Geographers* (121). It contains information on about 3,700 Soviet scholars, scientists, educators, writers and administrators who have published articles or books in the period since the Second World War.

Bibliographies

Two current running geographical bibliographies are of high value in following new and recent literature. The best Western source is the great French bibliography, *Bibliographie Géographique Internationale* (123), published annually or quarterly since 1891. Of course, the most detailed and authoritative listing and abstracting of Soviet works is the massive bibliography in Russian, *Referativnyi Zhurnal: Geografiia* (122), published monthly since 1954. Works on the Soviet Union are included in Section E, Geography of the USSR.

Bibliography

General Geography

1   Lydolph, Paul E. (1990) *Geography of the USSR*, 5th edn. Elkhart Lake, WI: Misty Valley Publishing

Generally the fullest and best systematic introduction to the geography. Detailed coverage of both physical geography (land, climate, vegetation and water resources) and human geography (population, settlement patterns and the economy). Includes wealth of data in tables and maps. Useful bibliographies by categories and chapters with 668 references.

2   Radvanyi, Jean (1990) *L'URSS: Régions et Nations*. Paris: Masson (Collection Géographie)

Insightful discussion of the regions and the many peoples of the Soviet Union, with their rich diversity, traditions, problems, and aspirations. Helpful in treatment of current nationality problems in their regional setting. Bibliography.

3   ZumBrunnen, Craig (1990) The Soviet Union. In *Europe in the 1990s: A Geographic Analysis*, 6th edn. edited by George W. Hoffman, pp. 635-716. New York; Chichester: John Wiley

Brief but effective introduction to the geography of the country. Bibliography.

4   Bater, James H. (1989) *The Soviet Scene: A Geographical Perspective*. London; New York: Edward Arnold

Readable introduction to selected systematic aspects of the economy and peoples of the Soviet Union. Quite original in treatments of topics selected. Emphasises two themes: (1) an historical perspective is essential to an understanding of the contemporary scene and (2) the gap between stated ideal and actual reality is often enormous. Suggested readings by chapters.

5   Cole, J. P. (1984) *Geography of the Soviet Union*. London; Boston: Butterworths

Distinguished by many ingenious statistical analyses that shed light on comparisons with other countries and on internal contrasts within the Soviet Union. Strong on treatment of the economy, population, regional problems, and quality of life and regional inequalities. Informative fact boxes scattered throughout the text. Original and dramatic maps and diagrams. Bibliography.

6   Howe, G. Melvyn (1983) *The Soviet Union: A Geographical Survey*, 2nd edn. Plymouth: Macdonald and Evans; New York: Halsted

Textbook introduction to the physical framework, economic structure, human resources, and especially to the regional geography, organised by the 19 economic regions. Includes discussion of individual cities in each region. Bibliography.

7   *Sovetskii Soiuz: Geograficheskoe Opisanie (1966-1972)*, edited by S. V. Kalesnik and others. Moscow: Mysl'. 22 vols.

The most detailed treatment of the regional geography of the entire country and therefore a key reference set. Individual volumes are devoted to each of the union republics, to seven large regions within the Russian Soviet Federated Socialist Republic, and to three regions within the Ukraine. One volume is on the Soviet Union as a whole, systematically treated. Bibliographies.

Geography: Collected Works

8   Holzner, Lutz, and Knapp, Jeane M. (1987) Editors. *Soviet Geography Studies in Our Time: A Festschrift for Paul E. Lydolph*. Milwaukee, WI: College of Letters and Science,

American Geographical Society Collection of the Golda Meir Library, University of Wisconsin-Milwaukee

Collection of 14 original Western papers on Siberia, Middle Asia, Soviet cities and towns, population, river-sea transport, earth resource observation by satellite, and geographic information systems. References at end of papers.

9   Demko, George J., and Fuchs, Roland J. (1984) Editors. *Geographical Studies on the Soviet Union: Essays in Honor of Chauncy D. Harris*. Chicago: University of Chicago, Department of Geography. (Research Paper no. 211)

Collection of 13 original Western papers, especially on urban and population phenomena and on Siberian resources. Source footnotes.

Physical Geography

10   Gvozdetskii, N.A., Mil'kov, F.N., and Mikhailov, N.I. (1987) *Fizicheskaia Geografiia SSSR: Aziatskaia Chast'*, 4th edn. Moscow: Vysshaia Shkola

Standard Soviet textbook on the physical geography of the Asiatic part of the Soviet Union with detailed regional treatment. Bibliography.

11   Knystautas, Algirdas (1987). *The Natural History of the USSR*. Foreword by Vladimir Flint. London: Century; New York: McGraw-Hill

Beautifully illustrated presentation of the natural history of the USSR. Depicts the flora and fauna arranged by primary natural regions with emphasis on the nature preserves of the country. Appendix lists of typical animals for each major natural region. Bibliography.

12   Mil'kov, F.N., and Gvozdetskii, N.A. (1986) *Fizicheskaia Geografiia SSSR: Obshchii Obzor, Evropeiskaia Chast' SSR, Kavkaz*, 5th edn. Moscow: Vysshaia Shkola

Standard Soviet textbook on the physical geography of the European USSR. Includes a general systematic overview and then a detailed regional treatment. Bibliography.

13   Velichko, A.A. (1984) Editor. *Late Quaternary Environments in the Soviet Union*, English language edition edited by H.E. Wright, Jr. and C.W. Barnosky. Minneapolis: University of Minnesota Press; London: Longman

English translation of the best collected Soviet work. Many Soviet scientists summarise knowledge on glaciation, permafrost, loess soils, vegetation history, animal populations, inland sea basins, paleoclimatic reconstruction, and the dispersal of human cultures in the Paleolithic, Mesolithic, and Neolithic. Bibliographies at ends of articles.

14   Lydolph, Paul E. (1977) *Climates of the USSR*. Amsterdam; Oxford; New York: Elsevier. (World Survey of Climatology, Vol. 7)

Detailed study of the climate of the Soviet Union, and of its regions and its elements: European USSR and Western Siberia, Eastern Siberia, Far East, Central Asia, the Caucasus, the thermal factor, the moisture factor, wind, and climate distribution. References at ends of chapters. Appendix of climatic tables. Reference, geographical and subject indexes.

15   Suslov, S.P. (1961) *Physical Geography of Asiatic Russia*. San Francisco; London: Freeman

English translation of a standard Soviet work with detailed treatment of the physical geographic regions of the Asiatic part of the country: Soviet Middle Asia, Kazakhstan, Western Siberia, Eastern Siberia, and the Soviet Far East. Bibliography. Indexes of plants, animals, and places.

16   Berg, L.S. (1950) *Natural Regions of the USSR.* New York: Macmillan

English translation of the classic Soviet work treating the great landscape zones (vegetation belts) that extend across the Soviet Union in east-west bands from the Arctic tundra in the north, southward across the forest belt (taiga), the wooded steppe, the steppe, the semidesert, the desert, and the mountains. Glossary. Bibliography.

Resources and the Environment

17   Lavrov, S.B. (1990) Regional and environmental problems of the USSR: a synopsis of views from the Soviet parliament. *Soviet Geography* 31 (7), September 1990, 477-499.

Report on discussions in the Soviet parliament 1989-1990 on imbalanced development in resource frontier regions; the Aral Sea problem; environmental problems exacerbated by decisions concerning location of new productive capacity; nuclear power generation and testing; regional and local environmental problems; administrative measures promoting environmental protection; and environmental spending and legislation.

18   Panel on the state of the Soviet environment at the start of the nineties (1990). *Soviet Geography* 31 (6), June 1990, 401-468.

Discussion of air and water quality; water management issues in Central Asia; farmland conservation and environmental impacts on agriculture; environmental impacts of mineral development; toxic wastes; biotic resources; the environment and perestroika; regional issues; and the aftermath of Chernobyl'.

19   Barr, Brenton M., and Braden, Kathleen E. (1988) *The Disappearing Russian Forest: A Dilemma in Soviet Resource Management.* London: Hutchinson; Totowa, NJ: Rowman and Littlefield

Examination of the timber resources, forest products, international trade and various constraints on their development. Bibliography.

20   Pryde, Philip R. (1988) Editor. Special issue on environmental problems and management in the USSR. *Soviet Geography* 29 (6), June 1988, 555-632.

Papers of a Conference at the Institute of Geography of the Academy of Sciences of the USSR on the role of geography in the solution of ecological problems; nature preserves; forest management; the level of the Caspian Sea; and summary of the Glasgow Conference on Soviet environmental policies and practices.

21   Singleton, Fred (1987) Editor. *Environmental Problems in the Soviet Union and Eastern Europe.* Boulder, CO; London: Lynne Rienner

Ten articles, largely from Third World Congress for Soviet and East European Studies, held in Washington, DC, 1985. Includes Elisabeth Koutaissoff on Soviet materials on environmental problems, Philip R. Pryde on environmental impact analysis, notably of the Kansk-Achinsk energy complex, the Kursk Magnetic Anomaly, and the Pripiat' marshes region, Kathleen E. Braden on the uncoordinated policy on scientific research in nature reserves, Ihor Strebelsky on soil mismanagement, Brenton M. Barr on regional alternatives in Soviet timber management, and Milka Bliznakov on environmental design and planning of new towns along the Baikal-Amur route. Source notes.

22   Ziegler, Charles E. (1987) *Environmental Policy in the USSR.* Amherst, MA: University of Massachusetts Press

Discussion of environmental protection in the Soviet system; Soviet images of the environment; environmental policy, law, and administration; and environmental protection in Soviet foreign policy. Source notes.

23 Jensen, Robert G., Shabad, Theodore, and Wright, A.W. (1983) Editors. *Soviet Natural Resources in the World Economy*. Chicago; London: University of Chicago Press

Detailed examination by an international interdisciplinary group of 28 specialists of Soviet natural resources, especially in Siberia. Particularly good studies on energy policy, petroleum, natural gas, timber and forest products, iron ore, and gold mining. Studies also treat the regional dimension of resource utilisation in Siberia and the Soviet Far East, especially in their severe environmental conditions and great distances to national or international markets. Source notes for each chapter.

24 Gustafson, Thane (1981) *Reform in Soviet Politics: Lessons of Recent Policies on Land and Water*. Cambridge; New York: Cambridge University Press

Well-documented investigation of the interrelationships of programmes on the environment, especially of agricultural land and water power and the effects of policy, dogma, technology, economics, politics and the difficulties of reform. Bibliographical notes.

25 Komarov, Boris (1980) *The Destruction of Nature in the Soviet Union*. Foreword by Marshall I. Goldman. White Plains, NY: M. E. Sharpe; London: Pluto

English translation of a Soviet cry of anguish at the destruction of nature in the Soviet Union. Source notes.

26 Jackson, W. A. Douglas (1978) Editor. *Soviet Resource Management and the Environment*. Columbus, OH: American Association for the Advancement of Slavic Studies

Thirteen papers by Western scholars on Soviet resources, their development, management, and environmental impact. Source footnotes by papers.

27 Volgyes, Ivan (1974) Editor. *Environmental Deterioration in the Soviet Union and Eastern Europe*. New York; London: Praeger

A collection of Western papers on Soviet response to environmental disruption by Keith Bush, air pollution by Victor L. Mote, soil erosion by Ihor Strebelsky, the falling level of the Caspian Sea by Philip P. Micklin, and the pollution of Lake Baikal and the controversy surrounding it by Craig ZumBrunnen. Source notes.

General Economic Geography

28 Khrushchev, A.T., Kalashnikova, T.M., and Nikol'skii, I.V. (1989) Editors. *Ekonomicheskaia Geografiia SSSR. Chast' II*, 2nd edn. Moscow: Izdatel'stvo Moskovskogo Universiteta

Standard Soviet economic geography for use in universities, part 2, economic regions, one for each union republic, except for the RSFSR with eleven regions and the Ukraine with three regions. Economic maps of industry, agriculture, and minerals by regions.

29 Rom, V. Ia (1986-1987) Editor. *Ekonomicheskaia i Sotsial'naia Geografiia SSSR*. 2 vols. Vol.1, General, 1986. Vol. 2, Regional, 1987. Moscow: Prosveshchenie

Soviet textbook for economic and social geography, systematic and regional, for use in pedagogical institutes.

Agriculture

30 Medvedev, Zhores A. (1987) *Soviet Agriculture*. New York; London: W. W. Norton

A well-informed and insightful analysis of the historical evolution of Soviet agriculture, of contemporary problems, and of proposed solutions. References and notes.

31   Johnson, D. Gale, and Brooks, Karen McConnell (1983) *Prospects for Soviet Agriculture in the 1980s.* Bloomington, IN: Indiana University Press

Published in association with the Center for Strategic and International Studies, Georgetown University, Washington, DC. Policies and performance in Soviet agriculture, particularly in the 1970s with prospects for the 1980s for livestock and crop production noting the role of climate and weather but emphasising the negative impact of Soviet central planning. Source notes.

32   Symons, Leslie (1972) *Russian Agriculture; A Geographic Survey.* London: G. Bell; New York: John Wiley

Somewhat dated but still the fullest discussion of the geographic patterns of agricultural resources and production. Bibliography.

Fuel and Energy

33   Stern, Jonathan P. (1987) *Soviet Oil and Gas Exports to the West: Commercial Transaction or Security Threat?* Aldershot, Hants.; Brookfield, VT: Gower. Joint Energy Programme. Policy Studies Institute. Royal Institute of International Affairs. (Energy Papers, no. 21)

Focus on oil and gas exports to the West.

34   Wilson, David (1982) *Soviet Oil and Gas to 1990.* Cambridge, MA: Abt Books. (EIU Special Series 2). Originally published by the Economic Intelligence Unit as Special Report no. 90.

Discussion of the resource base, location of production, transport, refining, markets, problems, and regional patterns. Bibliography.

35   Stern, Jonathan P. (1980) *Soviet Natural Gas Development to 1990: The Implications for the CMEA and the West.* Lexington, MA: Lexington Books, D. C. Heath; Farnborough, Hants.: Gower

Reserves, production, transportation and marketing of natural gas with special attention to its potential impact on world and regional markets. Bibliography.

36   Dienes, Leslie, and Shabad, Theodore (1979) *The Soviet Energy System: Resource Use and Policies.* New York; London: John Wiley

Comprehensive view of Soviet energy and fuels, especially of the distribution of production, transport, and marketing. Discussion of petroleum and natural gas; coal, lignite, oil shale, and peat; hydroelectric power; nuclear power; and electric power. Analysis of modelling, planning, and administration of the Soviet energy system. Especially valuable are the 12 maps and 53 tables. Source notes.

Industry

37   Sagers, Matthew J., and Shabad, Theodore (1990) Editors. *The Chemical Industry in the USSR: An Economic Geography.* Boulder, CO: Westview Press; Washington, DC: American Chemical Society. (ACS Professional Reference Book)

Detailed studies of the geography of the chemical industry of the Soviet Union. Bibliographical references.

38   De Souza, Peter (1989) *Territorial Production Complexes in the Soviet Union – With Special Focus on Siberia.* Göteborg, Sweden: Department of Geography, University of Gothenburg. Meddelanden från Göteborgs Universitets Geografiska Institutioner. (Serie B. Nr. 80)

Examines the concept of territorial production complexes.

39   Khrushchev, A.T. (1986) *Geografiia Promyshlennosti*, 3rd edn. Moscow: Mysl'

Most detailed discussion of the geography of Soviet industry. Discusses functional characteristics of industry, the economic and resource factors in its location, its territorial characteristics, the basic branches of industry and their interrelations and regional concentrations. Bibliography.

40   *Territorial Industrial Complexes: Optimisation Models and General Aspects* (1980) Moscow: Progress

English translation of theoretical discussion of the formation of territorial industrial complexes and their planning, economic mathematical models of their structure, location, and interrelations and applied studies of individual problems.

41   Barr, Brenton M. (1970) *The Soviet Wood-Processing Industry: A Linear Programming Analysis of the Role of Transportation Costs in Location and Flow Patterns.* Toronto: University of Toronto Press. (University of Toronto Department of Geography Research Publication no. 5)

Linear programming analysis of the role of transportation costs in location of the Soviet wood-processing industry and in flow patterns of wood products. Bibliography.

42   Dienes, Leslie (1969) *Locational Factors and Locational Developments in The Soviet Chemical Industry.* Chicago: The University of Chicago, Department of Geography. (Research Paper no. 119)

Locational factors, developments and regional patterns in the Soviet chemical industry. Source footnotes. Bibliography.

Transportation

43   Mote, Victor L. (1990) BAM, boom, bust: analysis of a railway's past, present, and future, *Soviet Geography*, 31 (5), May 1990, 321-331.

Story of the Baykal-Amur-Mainline (BAM) railway, a gigantic pet project of Leonid Brezhnev to construct a parallel and more northern route to the Trans-Siberian railway, and an orphan under Mikhail Gorbachev. Bibliography.

44   Bergstrand, Simon, and Doganis, Rigas (1987) *The Impact of Soviet Shipping.* London; Boston, MA: Allen and Unwin

Detailed study of demand for and supply of Soviet shipping, its fleet movements, its competition in the liner market, bulk trades, and cruise markets, its economic and commercial basis and its impact. Bibliography.

45   Kazanskii, N.N. (1987) Editor. *Geografiia Putei Soobshcheniia*, 4th edn. Moscow: Transport

General discussion of all forms of transport but particularly detailed on railroad routes.

46   North, Robert N. (ca 1987) *An Annotated Bibliography on Soviet Northern Transport 1975-1986.* Vancouver, BC: University of British Columbia. Department of Geography. (Departmental Paper no. 38)

1,400 entries, briefly annotated, in alphabetical order of names of authors. Includes mainly works in Russian and English. Subject and geographical index.

47   Tismer, Johannes F., Ambler, John, and Symons, Leslie (1987). Editors. *Transport and Economic Development: Soviet Union and Eastern Europe.* Berlin: In Kommission bei Verlag Duncker & Humblot. Osteuropa-Institut an der Freien Universität Berlin. (Wirtschaftswissenschaftliche Veröffentlichungen, Band 42)

Contains significant articles by Holland Hunter on demands on the Soviet transport system, by John Ambler on performance, by John N. Westwood on inland waterways, by Paul E. Lydolph on maritime transport, by Terence Armstrong on shipping in the

Central Arctic Basin, by David Wilson on consumption of automotive oil products in road transport, by Jörg Stadelbauer on transport in Soviet Caucasia, and by Robert N. North on transport and traffic between the Soviet Union and Eastern Europe. Bibliographies.

48   Sagers, Matthew J., and Green, Milford B. (1986) *The Transportation of Soviet Energy Resources.* Totowa, NJ: Rowman and Allenheld; London: Croom Helm

Analysis of transportation of Soviet natural gas, petroleum, refined petroleum products, coal, and electricity. Bibliography.

49   ZumBrunnen, Craig, and Osleeb, Jeffrey P. (1986) *The Soviet Iron and Steel Industry.* Totowa, NJ: Rowman and Allanheld

Examination of commodity flow patterns within the Soviet ferrous metallurgy industry, which faces high costs in the transport of raw materials and products. Theoretical models are used to economise flows, compare them with actual distributions in the industry and make projections for the future. Bibliography.

50   Ambler, John, Shaw, Denis J.B., and Symons, Leslie (1985) Editors. *Soviet and East European Transport Problems.* London: Croom Helm; New York: St. Martin's Press

Includes articles by Denis J. B. Shaw on branch and regional problems in Soviet transportation, by John Ambler, Holland Hunter, and John N. Westwood on Soviet railways, by David Wilson on transport of fuel, by Paul E. Lydolph on Soviet shipping, by Leslie Symons on air transport, and by Martin Crouch on road transport. Bibliographies and notes.

51   Nikol'skii, I.V., Toniaev, V.I., Krasheninnikov, V.G. (1983) *Geografiia Vodnogo Transporta SSSR,* 2nd edn. Moscow: Transport

Divided into two parts. The first is a consideration of the unified transport system of the USSR and each of its components: railways, internal water transport, ocean transport, and automobile, air and pipeline transport. The second is a more detailed study of the geography of water transport by river basins. Bibliography.

52   North, Robert N. (1979) *Transport in Western Siberia: Tsarist and Soviet Development.* Vancouver, BC: University of British Columbia Press; Centre for Transportation Studies

Role of transportation in the development of Western Siberia organised by successive periods, from before the Siberian Railway to 1975. Bibliography.

53   Nikol'skii, I.V. (1978) *Geografiia Transporta SSSR.* Moscow: Izdatel'stvo Moskovskogo Universiteta

Standard Soviet textbook on geography of transport in the USSR. Divided into three parts: basic geographic factors in transportation, individual types of transport (railroads, rivers, ocean transport, automobile transport, airlines, pipelines), and transport by 12 regions. Particularly interesting in its depiction of freight flows. Extensive bibliography.

54   Shabad, Theodore, and Mote, Victor L. (1977) *Gateway to Siberian Resources (The BAM).* New York; London: John Wiley. (A Halsted Press Book. Scripta Technica, Inc.)

Includes chapters on Siberian resource development in the Soviet period by Theodore Shabad, the Baykal-Amur Railway (BAM) by Victor L. Mote, and translations of Soviet articles on its planning, its design and construction, its economic impact, its economic geography, its region-shaping functions, and its study as a problem in applied geography. Appendix of principal places along the BAM.

Cities, Housing, and Planning

55   Medvedkov, Olga (1990) *Soviet Urbanization.* London; New York: Routledge

Insightful study based on personal experience and statistical analysis of published and unpublished data for 221 cities of more than 100,000 population. Intriguing methodology. Lively and sometimes provocative text. Concrete and illuminating examples. Bibliography.

56 Andrusz, Gregory F. (1985) *Housing and Urban Development in the USSR.* London: Macmillan; Albany, NY: State University Press

Analysis of housing tenure; social, economic and spatial dimensions of housing; and relations of housing to urban growth. Notes and references arranged by chapters.

57 Morton, Henry W., and Stuart, Robert C. (1984) Editors. *The Contemporary Soviet City.* Armonk, NY: M.E. Sharpe

Eleven essays examine labour, family, and crime in contemporary Soviet cities and the problems of urban services in health, education, transport, trade, and the bureaucracy. Notes by chapters. Bibliography.

58 Pallot, Judith, and Shaw, Denis J.B. (1981) *Planning in the Soviet Union.* London: Croom Helm; Athens, GA: University of Georgia Press

Discusses first the ideological, political and economic context of planning, then several aspects of spatial planning, especially population and physical factors in regional planning, industrial location, location of agricultural production, consumer welfare, settlement systems and cities. Bibliography.

59 Bater, James H. (1980) *The Soviet City: Ideal and Reality.* London: Edward Arnold; New York: Holmes and Meier

Examination of decision-making in town planning, patterns of city growth, spatial organisation of the city and life in the city. Effectively portrays the discrepancy between ideal and reality, lack of a single decision-making authority, and conflicts between local town planners and the central industrial ministries. Bibliography.

60 French, R.A., and Hamilton, F.E. Ian (1979) Editors. *The Socialist City: Spatial Structure and Urban Policy.* Chichester; New York: John Wiley

Contains valuable studies on the characteristics of contemporary Soviet cities, their individuality by R.A. French, their housing by Mervyn Matthews, their recreation by Denis J.B. Shaw, and their socialist transformation, as illustrated by the Islamic cities of Soviet Middle Asia by Ernst Giese. Bibliographies.

61 Müller-Wille, Wilhelm (1978) *Stadt und Umland im südlichen Sowjet-Mittelasien.* Wiesbaden: Franz Steiner. (Erdkundliches Wissen, Heft 49)

Considers the city of Soviet Middle Asia in the Oriental-Aral period, Russian tsarist colonial period, and Soviet socialist period. Bibliography. Summary in English.

Historical Geography

62 Hamm, Michael F. (1986) Editor. *The City in Late Imperial Russia.* Bloomington, IN: Indiana University Press

Individual studies of Moscow, St Petersburg, Kiev, Warsaw, Riga, Odessa, Tiflis, and Baku. Source notes for each study. Bibliography of English-language works on the Imperial Russian city and related topics 1860-1917.

63 Bater, James H., and French, R.A. (1983) Editors. *Studies in Russian Historical Geography.* 2 vols. London; New York: Academic Press

Seventeen original, scholarly articles by British, Canadian and American scholars, grouped under four themes: man and the land, the frontier, the towns and the last century of the old regime. Bibliographies.

64   Bater, James H. (1976) *St Petersburg: Industrialization and Change.* London: Edward Arnold; New York: Holmes and Meier; Montreal: McGill-Queen's University Press

Detailed monographic analysis of industrialisation, social characteristics, housing and spatial patterns of St Petersburg during the nineteenth and early twentieth centuries. Bibliographical footnotes. Notes on methods and on sources.

65   Hamm, Michael F. (1976) Editor. *The City in Russian History.* Lexington, KY: University Press of Kentucky

Seventeen original studies of Russian cities from the medieval town up to the 1970s. Bibliographical notes for each study. Bibliography.

66   Rozman, Gilbert (1976) *Urban Networks in Russia, 1750-1800, and Premodern Periodization.* Princeton, NJ; Guildford: Princeton University Press

Discussion of the establishment of urban networks prior to 1750, spatial division in social structure, regional variations in urbanisation in the 1780s, and urban networks of advanced premodern societies. Bibliographic notes and bibliography.

67   Fedor, Thomas Stanley (1975) *Patterns of Urban Growth in the Russian Empire During The Nineteenth Century.* Chicago: University of Chicago. Department of Geography. (Research Paper no. 163)

Research monograph on urban development 1811-1910, its patterns, factors, relation to economic development, industrialisation, and natural increase and migration. Bibliographical footnotes and bibliography.

Peoples

68   Allworth, Edward A. (1990) *The Modern Uzbeks: From the Fourteenth Century to the Present. A Cultural History.* Stanford, CA: Hoover Institution Press. (Studies of Nationalities in the USSR)

Discusses the bases of Uzbek group identity and the conflict between old and new modernity in history, education, culture and religion, homeland, disintegration, intelligentsia, communication and tradition. Bibliographical notes and bibliography.

69   Armstrong, John A. (1990) *Ukrainian Nationalism,* 3rd edn. Englewood, CO: Ukrainian Academic Press, a Division of Libraries Unlimited

A study of Ukrainian nationalism during the Second World War. Source notes. Bibliography.

70   Hajda, Lubomyr, and Beissinger, Mark (1990) Editors. *The Nationalities Factor in Soviet Politics and Society.* Boulder, CO; Oxford: Westview Press

Papers on the role of nationalities in Soviet politics, economy, military, linguistic and ethnic Russification, literature and religion. Regional discussions on the Ukraine, Belorussia and Moldavia; the Baltic Republics; Transcaucasia; and Central Asia. Source footnotes for each paper.

71   Nahaylo, Bohdan and Swoboda, Victor (1990) *Soviet Disunion: A History of the Nationalities Problem in the USSR.* London: Hamish Hamilton; New York: Free Press

Overall historical context for the evolution of ethnic groups in tsarist Russia and the Soviet Union and their current status. Source notes. Bibliography.

72   Rywkin, Michael (1990) *Moscow's Muslim Challenge: Soviet Central Asia,* revised edn. Armonk, NY; London: M.E. Sharpe

Muslims of Soviet Middle Asia in their historical, economic, population, national-religious, cultural, sociopolitical and governmental settings. Terminology of nationality politics. Perestroika in Soviet Middle Asia. Bibliographical notes and bibliography.

73   *The Soviet Multinational State: Readings and Documents* (1990), edited by Martha B.
     Olcott, with Lubomyr Hajda and Anthony Olcott. Armonk, NY; London: M.E. Sharpe

     A selection of key documents, translated into English, covering official Soviet policy,
     studies by Soviet scholars, party politics, economic development, ethnodemographic
     trends, language training, literature, religion, patriotism, and two special areas: the
     Baltic republics, and Nagorno-Karabakh. Bibliography.

74   Allworth, Edward (1989) Editor. *Central Asia: 120 Years of Russian Rule*. Durham, NC;
     London: Duke University Press. (Central Asia Book Series)

     Seventeen studies by Western scholars covering many aspects of the history and current
     population, society, culture and economy. Bibliography of selected works in English.
     Glossary.

75   Lapidus, Gail W. (1989) Gorbachev and the 'National Question': restructuring the Soviet
     federation. *Soviet Economy*, 5 (3), July-September 1989, 201-250.

     Brief but comprehensive analysis of demands and roles of nationalities in possible
     restructuring of the Soviet federation. Bibliography.

76   Panel on Nationalism in the USSR: Environmental and Territorial Aspects. (1989)
     Soviet Geography, 30 (6), June 1989, 441-509.

     Wide-ranging discussion of the political environment, the demographic dimension,
     urban-rural differences, homelands, territorial and cultural claims, nationality-related
     environmental protests, comparative perspectives, and economic strategies for
     territorial and national autonomy. Bibliography.

77   Kozlov, Viktor (1988) *The Peoples of the Soviet Union*. Introduction by Michael Rywkin
     and translation by Pauline M. Tiffen. London: Hutchinson; Bloomington, IN: Indiana
     University Press

     English translation of monograph by a member of the Institute of Ethnography of the
     Academy of Sciences of the USSR. Discusses the history, geography, urbanisation,
     demography and processes of transformation of ethnic groups. Provides much useful
     reference material. Maps and diagrams. Appendix on ethno-linguistic composition and
     ethnic distribution in 1897.

78   Kingkade, W. Ward (1988) *USSR: Estimates and Projections of the Population by Major
     Nationality, 1979 to 2050*. Washington, DC: US Bureau of the Census. Center for
     International Research. Soviet Branch. (CIR Staff Paper no. 41)

     Possible future size of nationality groups in USSR. Bibliography.

79   Levin, Nora (1988) *The Jews in the Soviet Union since 1917. Paradox of Survival*. 2
     vols. New York; London: New York University Press

     Narrative description of the Jewish experience in the USSR, 1917-1986. Source notes.
     Glossary.

80   Pinkus, Benjamin (1988) *The Jews of the Soviet Union: The History of a National
     Minority*. Cambridge; New York: Cambridge University Press

     Presentation of successive stages in the history of Soviet Jews: the years of construction,
     1917-1939; the years of destruction, 1939-1953; and the post-Stalin period, 1953-1983.
     In each period consideration is given to official policy; to ideological, political and
     economic changes; and to relations between Soviet Jews and world Jewry. Source notes.
     Bibliography.

81 Altshuler, Mordechai (1987) *Soviet Jewry since the Second World War: Population and Social Structure.* New York; London: Greenwood. (Studies in Population and Urban Demography, no. 5)

Discusses historical background, size of population, geographic distribution, composition by sex, education, social stratification and economic activity, language and nationality and Communist Party participation. Source notes. Bibliography.

82 Motyl, Alexander J. (1987) *Will the Non-Russians Rebel? State, Ethnicity and Stability in the USSR.* Ithaca, NY; London: Cornell University Press

Discusses stability, ethnicity, ethnic hegemony, prosperity and passivity, ideology, politics and language, coercion and control, and why the non-Russians have not rebelled and are not likely to rebel. Bibliography.

83 Olcott, Martha Brill (1987) *The Kazakhs.* Stanford, CA: Hoover Institution Press. (Studies of Nationalities in the USSR)

The Kazakhs in three periods: in the Kazakh Khanate, in Imperial Russia, and in the Soviet period. The impacts of revolution and civil war, the New Economic Policy, collectivisation, creation of a Soviet apparatus, and the Virgin Lands and industrialisation programmes are discussed. Glossary. Source notes. Bibliography.

84 Raun, Toivo U. (1987) *Estonia and the Estonians.* Stanford, CA: Hoover Institution Press. (Studies in Nationalities in the USSR)

Historical survey in four periods: before 1710, under Imperial Russia, independent, and in the Soviet Union. Source notes. Bibliography.

85 Akiner, Shirin (1986) *Islamic Peoples of the Soviet Union (with an Appendix on the non-Muslim Turkic Peoples of the Soviet Union): An Historical and Statistical Handbook,* 2nd edn London; New York: KPI. Distributed by Routledge and Kegan Paul

Detailed discussion of Islamic peoples who make up large clusters at the bend of the Volga River in the Kazan' region, in Siberia, in the North Caucasus and Transcaucasia, in Kazakhstan, and in Soviet Middle Asia. Especially valuable is its discussion of numerous small ethnic groups. An appendix provides information on 17 non-Muslim Turkic peoples, such as the Yakuts and the Gagauz. Bibliography.

86 Bennigsen, Alexandre, and Wimbush, S. Enders (1986) *Muslims of the Soviet Empire: A Guide.* London: C. Hurst; Bloomington, IN: Indiana University Press

Part 1 is devoted to general questions of the background and practice of Islam in the Soviet Union. Part 2 is devoted the discussions of individual Muslim groups in Central Asia, Transcaucasia and the North Caucasus, and European Russia and Siberia. Glossary. Extensive bibliography.

87 Conquest, Robert (1986) Editor. *The Last Empire: Nationality and the Soviet Future.* Stanford, CA: Hoover Institution Press

Sixteen studies by Western scholars on many characteristics of nationality in the USSR and on several major ethnic groups. Bibliographic notes.

88 Fleischhauer, Ingeborg, and Pinkus, Benjamin (1986) *The Soviet Germans: Past and Present,* edited with an introduction by Edith Rogovin Frankel. London: C. Hurst; New York: St Martin's Press

Historical and contemporary position of the German ethnic group. Source notes. Bibliography.

89 Karklins, Rasma (1986) *Ethnic Relations in the USSR: The Perspective from Below.* London; Boston, MA: Allen and Unwin

Interesting analysis of ethnic relations within the Soviet Union based mainly on in-depth interviews with a structured sample of 200 Soviet Germans who emigrated to the Federal Republic of Germany in 1979. Bibliographic notes and bibliography.

90   Wixman, Ronald. (1984) *The Peoples of the USSR: An Ethnographic Handbook.* Armonk, NY: M.E. Sharpe

Comprehensive listing of ethnic groups, in alphabetical order, with identification and characterisation. Particularly useful for sorting out the many small ethnic groups, some of which have been differently named at various periods.

91   Dunlop, John B. (1983) *The Faces of Contemporary Russian Nationalism.* Princeton, NJ; Guildford: Princeton University Press

Historical background, issues important to spokesmen for Russian nationalism, ideological struggle, the contemporary spectrum of Russian nationalist views. Source footnotes. Appendix of texts of statements by Russian nationalist leaders.

92   Allworth, Edward (1980) Editor. *Ethnic Russia in the USSR: The Dilemma of Dominance.* New York; Oxford: Pergamon

39 papers by specialists on many aspects of the Russian nationality, its leadership role in the Soviet Union, its ethnocentrism, its historical origins, its identity in literature, its relation to religion, its role in integration of the Soviet people, the confusing relation of the RSFSR and the USSR, the ethnic frontier, the Russian language, spatial diffusion of Russians throughout the USSR and leadership quandaries. Bibliographical notes.

93   Wixman, Ronald (1980) *Language Aspects of Ethnic Patterns and Processes in the North Caucasus.* Chicago: University of Chicago, Department of Geography. (Research Paper no. 191)

Study of ethnic processes, nationality policy and practice and assimilation in the North Caucasus, one of the most complex ethnic areas in the Soviet Union, with many small groups in mountain valleys and the foreland of the Caucasus. Source footnotes. Bibliography.

94   Bennigsen, Alexandre A., and Wimbush, S. Enders (1979) *Muslim National Communism in the Soviet Union: A Revolutionary Strategy for the Colonial World.* Chicago; London: University of Chicago Press

Insightful study of the rise of the concept of national communism, the impact of the Revolution and Civil War, Muslim national communism, the struggle for power and the liquidation of the national communists in the late 1920s and early 1930s. Source notes. Bibliography.

95   McCagg, William O., Jr. and Silver, Brian D. (1979) Editors. *Soviet Asian Ethnic Frontiers.* New York; Oxford: Pergamon

Ten papers on peoples of the Caucasus, Middle Asia, and Mongolia, who straddle international boundaries of the Soviet Union with other countries on the south and south-east. Source notes.

96   Allworth, Edward (1977). Editor. *Nationality Group Survival in Multi-ethnic States: Shifting Support Patterns in the Soviet Baltic Region.* New York; London: Praeger

Eight studies of nationality survival in the Baltic republics, the roots of nationality differences, historical interpretations, economic and political leaders, Sovietisation, the Baltic Jews, and social distance among ethnic groups. Source notes. Bibliography.

97   Katz, Zev, Rogers, Rosemarie, and Harned, Frederic (1975) Editors. *Handbook of Major Soviet Nationalities.* London: Collier Macmillan; New York: Free Press

Studies of the 15 nationalities that form the basis of the 15 union republics, plus the Tatars and the Jews, the two largest nationalities in the Soviet Union that lack union-republic status. Appendix of comparative tables for major Soviet nationalities. Bibliographies for each study.

Population

98   Kingkade, W. Ward (1988) Recent and prospective population growth in the USSR, 1979-2025. *Soviet Geography* 29, (4), April 1988, 394-412.

     Textual discussion of the future population of the Soviet Union, which is projected to grow throughout the period to 2025. The working age population, however, will grow very slowly during the 1990s. The pension-age population will increase sharply, doubling by 2025. Bibliography.

99   Jones, Ellen, and Grupp, Fred W. (1987) *Modernization, Value Change and Fertility in the Soviet Union.* Cambridge; New York: Cambridge University Press. (Soviet and East European Studies)

     Outstanding study of population dynamics and fertility decline in the Soviet Union, including social change and fertility transition, demographic modernisation, the social correlates of fertility, and Soviet social and demographic policies as they have affected fertility change. Source notes.

100 Kingkade, W. Ward (1987) *Estimates and Projections of the Population of the USSR by Age and Sex, 1979 to 2025.* Washington, DC: US Bureau of the Census. Center for International Research. Soviet Branch. (CIR Staff Paper no. 33)

     Technical discussion of methodology. Detailed tables of projected population. Bibliography.

101 Clem, Ralph S. (1986) Editor. *Research Guide to the Russian and Soviet Censuses.* Ithaca, NY; London: Cornell University Press. (Studies in Soviet History and Society)

     Eight studies on the history of Russian and Soviet censuses and their utilisation: their use for research by Ralph S. Clem, comparability problems by Robert A. Lewis, their history by Lee Schwartz, ethnic and language dimensions by Brian D. Silver, occupation and work force by Michael Paul Sacks, urbanisation and migration by Richard H. Rowland, marriage, family, and fertility by Barbara A. Anderson, and education and literacy by Ronald D. Liebowitz. Bibliographies at ends of studies. Detailed list of tables in the Russian and Soviet censuses, 1897 to 1979, with keyword cross-index to topics and list of geographic units in each census by Peter R. Craumer. An indispensable reference book for anyone seeking data from Russian or Soviet censuses.

102 Desfosses, Helen (1981) Editor. *Soviet Population Policy: Conflicts and Constraints.* New York; Oxford: Pergamon. Pergamon Policy Studies on International Politics

     Studies on population problems, ageing Soviet society, fertility and female work status, pro-natalism, and Soviet population policy. Source notes.

103 Anderson, Barbara A. (1980) *Internal Migration During Modernization in Late Nineteenth-Century Russia.* Princeton, NJ; Guildford: Princeton University Press

     Study of Russia as a modernising society, outmigration from province of birth, migration to urban centres, migration to the agricultural frontier in Asia, migration to destinations of intermediate modernity in European Russia, migration in the Pale to Odessa and Kiev, and comparison of migration patterns. Bibliography.

104 Grandstaff, Peter J. (1980) *Interregional Migration in the USSR: Economic Aspects, 1959-1970.* Durham, NC: Duke University Press

     Discussion of state policies, 'laws' of migration, estimates, determinants, and economic effects. Bibliography.

105 Soboleva, Svetlana (1980) *Migration and Settlement: 8. Soviet Union.* Laxenburg, Austria: International Institute for Applied Systems Analysis

     Current patterns of spatial population growth, regional population analysis and population policy. Bibliography.

106 Coale, Ansley J., Anderson, Barbara A., and Harm, Erna (1979) *Human Fertility in Russia since the Nineteenth Century*. Princeton, NJ; Guildford: Princeton University Press

Detailed study of human fertility in European Russia, Central Asia, and the Caucasus, variations in nuptiality, and summary of fertility change. Technical appendices. Bibliography.

107 Lewis, Robert A., and Rowland, Richard H. (1979) *Population Redistribution in the USSR: Its Impact on Society, 1897-1977*. New York; London: Praeger

Detailed analysis of changes in population 1897-1977, based on adjustment of census areas to produce comparable areal units. Discussion of regional population distribution and redistribution, urbanisation and urban growth, city size, urban regions and rural population change. Bibliography.

108 Lewis, Robert A., Rowland, Richard H., and Clem, Ralph S. (1976) *Nationality and Population Change in Russia and the USSR: An Evaluation of Census Data, 1897-1970*. New York; London: Praeger

Analysis of changes 1897-1970 in ethnic groups in their urbanisation, regional distribution, population growth, work force and education. Based on Russian and Soviet censuses but with elaborate adjustments to get comparability among the censuses. Source notes. Bibliography.

Regional Studies

109 Wood, Alan, and French, R.A. (1989) Editors. *The Development of Siberia: People and Resources*. London: Macmillan; New York: St Martin's Press

Fourth Meeting of the British Universities Siberian Studies Seminar held at the School of Slavonic and East European Studies, University of London, April, 1986. A dozen papers by an international group of specialists. Papers of particular interest include ones on indigenous peoples by James Forsyth, urbanisation of minority peoples by S.S. Savoskul, the Buryats by Caroline Humphrey, social development by T.I. Zaslavskaya and colleagues, labour by John Sallnow, water transport by Robert N. North, exploration for oil and gas in Eastern Siberia by David Wilson, and Gorbachev's economic policy by the late Theodore Shabad. Bibliographic references.

110 Dienes, Leslie (1987) *Soviet Asia: Economic Development and National Policy Choices*. Boulder, CO; London: Westview Press

Policy issues for Soviet Asia. Population, settlement, and regional planning. Emphasises sharp contrasts between Siberia and the Soviet Far East on one hand and Soviet Middle Asia on the other. Analytical and probing.

111 Swearingen, Rodger (1987) Editor. *Siberia and the Soviet Far East: Strategic Dimensions in Multinational Perspective*. Stanford, CA: Hoover Institution Press

Multinational and multidisciplinary group of authors examine strategic dimensions of Siberia and the Soviet Far East. An excellent introduction to Siberia is provided by Violet Conolly, followed by studies of communications by Victor L. Mote, energy by Thane Gustafson, and technology transfer in relation to trade by Michael J. Bradshaw. Other studies deal with linkages with Europe and Japan, military situation, and strategic dimensions. Patricia Polansky discusses resources for current research on Siberia and the Soviet Far East: a bibliographic profile. Source notes.

112 Wood, Alan (1987) Editor. *Siberia: Problems and Prospects for Regional Development*. London; New York: Croom Helm

Nine studies by specialists, including geographical background by Denis Shaw, history by Alan Wood, economic resources by Theodore Shabad, oil and gas by David Wilson, transport and communication by Robert North, the Baikal-Amur Railway by Violet

Conolly, military and strategic factors by John Erickson, relations to its Far Eastern neighbours by Stuart Kirby, and relations to the world economy by John J. Stephan. Source notes.

Atlases

113 *USSR Energy Atlas* (1985). Washington, DC: Central Intelligence Agency

Large-format thematic atlas. Text. Coloured maps and diagrams. Tables. Coloured and black-and-white photographs. Gazetteer and index.

114 *Atlas SSSR* (1983), edited by V.V. Tochenov. Moscow: Glavnoe Upravlenie Geodezii i Kartografii. Frequently reprinted with minor changes, in 1985 and 1988 for example.

Best and most up-to-date general-reference and thematic atlas of the Soviet Union. Full-colour plates arranged in sections: regional physical-geographic maps, elements of the environment for the country as a whole, socio-economic maps for systematic branches of the economy, and socio-economic maps for economic regions. Coloured satellite images and photographs. Tables. Index of geographical names in four colours: water features in blue; orographic features in brown; political-administrative units in red; and place names and all other features in black.

115 Dewdney, J.C. (1982) *USSR in Maps*. London: Hodder and Stoughton; New York: Holmes and Meier

Good general purpose smaller atlas in English with 49 black-and-white maps illustrating important aspects of physical environment, human geography, economic geography, and regions. Each map plate occupies one page accompanied by text on the facing page, which describes and explains the significant features depicted on each map. The maps and text are exceptionally clear. Most easily obtained atlas of the Soviet Union, it provides an excellent introduction to the country. Charts. Tables. Bibliography. Index.

116 *USSR Agriculture Atlas* (1974). Washington, DC: Central Intelligence Agency

Large-format thematic atlas. Text. Coloured maps and diagrams. Tables. Coloured and black-and-white photographs.

Statistics

117 Heleniak, Timothy E. (1988) *Bibliography of Soviet Statistical Handbooks*. Washington, DC: US Bureau of the Census. Center for International Research. (CIR Staff Paper no. 42)

Inventory of more than 2,000 statistical handbooks published in the Soviet Union during the 35-year period from the death of Stalin in 1953 up to 1988. These are arranged by 29 thematic categories for the Soviet Union as a whole and by 15 union republics, subdivided thematically and regionally. Separate section on international handbooks. Appendices include geographical index and summaries of statistical handbooks by years.

118 *USSR Facts and Figures Annual* (1977-) Annual. Gulf Breeze, FL: Academic International Press

Handiest running series in English of statistics of the USSR. Includes data on demography, the economy, industry, energy, agriculture, foreign trade, health, education and welfare, communications, transportation. Maps. Sources indicated. Bibliography of key works.

119 Mickiewicz, Ellen (1973) *Handbook of the Soviet Social Science Data*. New York: Free Press; London: Collier Macmillan

Basic source of social science data with sections by leading specialists. Now somewhat dated. Chapters on demography, agriculture, production, health, housing, education, elite recruitment and mobilisation, communications and international interactions. Each chapter has a textual introduction followed by many tables. Sources indicated for each table.

120 *Narodnoe Khoziaistvo SSSR: Statisticheskii Ezhegodnik.* (1956-) Annual. Moscow: Finansy i Statistika

Тhe basic annual statistical compilation for the Soviet Union. Coverage differs somewhat from year to year but generally includes basic social, cultural, environmental, and economic data, with some international comparisons.

Biographies

121 *Directory of Soviet Geographers 1946-1987* (1988), compiled by Theodore Shabad; edited and supplemented by Chauncy D. Harris. Silver Spring, MD: V. H. Winston

Part I: Introduction; Sources; Institutions. Part II: Biographies. Also published as Special Issue *Soviet Geography*, 29 (2-3), February-March 1988, 95-274. Information on about 3,700 Soviet geographers active in the period after World War II. It is both current and retrospective in listing those now alive and active and also deceased persons who have published any time over the last two score years. Information is provided on date of birth (if available) and death (if applicable), on advanced academic degrees with names of institution and date, major fields or topics of specialisation and of published contributions, and positions, with titles, institutions and dates. A list of principal institutions with which these individuals have been associated is also provided.

Bibliographies

122 *Referativnyi Zhurnal: Geografiia* (1954-). Monthly. Moscow: Vsesoiuznyi Institut Nauchnoi i Tekhnicheskoi Informatsii

The most detailed and authoritative listing of Soviet works on the lands and peoples of the USSR. Works on the Soviet Union are included in Section E, Geography of the USSR, with sub-sections on general problems in the geography of the USSR, geography of natural resources and physical conditions of production, geography of population and settlements, geography of the economy and its branches, regionalisation of the country and regional planning. Includes abstracts of works listed. Annual index.

123 *Bibliographie Géographique Internationale. International Geographical Bibliography* (1891-). Annual 1891-1976. Quarterly 1977-. Paris: Centre National de la Recherche Scientifique. Laboratoire d'Information et de Documentation en Géographie (INTERGEO)

Best Western running bibliography on geography of Soviet resources, peoples and economy. Includes brief notes on works listed. Annual list of periodicals analysed. Annual indexes of subjects, places and authors.

CHAPTER TWO

Soviet History

Professor Robert F. Byrnes
Indiana University

Historical scholarship published in English in the 1980s about Soviet history since 1917 is relatively weak both in quality and in quantity, compared to work on Soviet economics, politics and military affairs and to the scholarship concerning Russian history in the nineteenth century. It also provides few if any analyses of economic, social, intellectual and institutional developments of the varieties common about more open societies. The biographies that flower in other countries and that help interest men and women in history are almost totally absent. In addition, scholarship concentrates upon particular periods, such as the Revolution, the calamitous famine in the early 1930s, and purges of party leaders in the late 1930s, neglecting the years after Stalin.

If this new era of openness or glasnost survives, which appears doubtful, Soviet historical scholarship in the 1990s may improve. The Soviet media may also provide materials on other periods of Soviet history than the dramatic and dreadful events of the 1930s, on which it has been most rich. If Soviet archives open and other sources of data become available, and if a new generation of Soviet scholars with genuine intellectual curiosity and critical intelligence emerges, Western scholarship may benefit considerably.

Scholarship in English concerning Russian and Soviet history became significant only in the 1950s. Consequently, work in Soviet history has a small and weak foundation. Nevertheless, the basic reasons for the visible shortcomings of the literature of Soviet history lie within the Soviet Union and are the responsibility of the Soviet government. Soviet officials have denied access to archives and other basic sources. The enforced absence over many years of the kinds of rich information in the Soviet press that Western journals and newspapers systematically provide concerning Western societies constitute another substantial cause. Memoirs and biographies are absent from the Soviet scene, except for those of military leaders that surfaced in the 1960s, and for the dull memoirs of Andrei Gromyko that revealed nothing but the state of mind and limited perspective of the late Soviet Foreign Minister. In addition, the Soviet government's failure to provide reliable documentary material on factors as central as population statistics or book production has hampered and even discouraged historical research.

Soviet scholarship on Soviet history, which should be richer and deeper than that of outside observers, has not only provided little guidance or insight to foreign scholars, but has been misleading and often false. When one compares French and British analyses of their national histories in the twentieth century with those Soviet scholars have produced on Soviet society since 1917, the contrast is overwhelming. Soviet scholars have published little and much appears in multi-volume loyalist studies of the party or of the Second World War, compiled by groups of authors. Soviet historians ignore difficult issues, neglect important leaders and, in Gorbachev's phrase, have left many 'blank pages'. Much, perhaps most, Soviet scholarship on Soviet history has been shallow and tendentious. State and party controls, lack of access to primary sources, and the particular distortion nationalist Marxism-Leninism produces have created scholarship that even Soviet leaders and scholars now consider 'useless rubbish'. The low quality of this work and the revelations that have appeared since 1987 have caused such contradictions and confusion that the ministry responsible for secondary education even cancelled school examinations in history in 1988. Recent Soviet decisions to translate work by Western authors on the revolution, Stalin and the disasters of the 1930s also illustrate the incredibly low quality of Soviet historical work and even the absence of research on central issues and men.

Generally, Western specialists of Soviet history have been able to visit the country only since 1957, and then usually in limited numbers and for short periods under cultural exchange agreements between the Soviet government and individual Western governments. Moreover, access to basic sources has been so limited that most historians allowed to study in the Soviet Union chose to concentrate upon the nineteenth century. On this period, and on earlier times as well, Soviet scholars and published work of high merit have provided assistance and intellectual competition. Moreover, archival and published materials have often been accessible.

Even so, one of the reasons for the improved quality of Western research on Russian history, even on Soviet history, has been the establishment of a substantial core of scholars who have studied in the Soviet Union since 1957. Many historians have visited the Soviet Union on a number of occasions and have acquired quite full access to libraries and some access to archives. They have also benefited from living in the society in which they are interested and from working with, and often establishing close relations with, Soviet scholars. In fact, some of the most able research has been the product of young men and women who have worked with Soviet scholars and who are in a sense sons and daughters or even grandchildren of the opportunities that first opened in 1957. Maintenance and expansion of these openings, continued travel abroad by Soviet historians, and the improvement of Soviet scholarship will help improve the quality of Western scholarship.

The stream of revelations from the Soviet media in recent years and readier Soviet permission to Western scholars to enter the Soviet Union and study 'sensitive' Soviet history have stimulated increased interest in the period since 1917. However, opening the doors to more historians and publishing more materials have thus far produced little impact on Western or Soviet research. Moreover, the recently published personal accounts of the 1920s have not yet provided significant new data or insights. Indeed, much of the information new to the Soviet public but not to Western scholars came from published Western research 'recycled' by Soviet publicists for Soviet readers, without attribution. Other information in the Soviet media has consisted of accounts by survivors, relatives or witnesses or has resulted from 'investigative reporting' and excavations that have provided horrifying substantiation of other evidence Western scholars have carefully pieced together. Unfortunately, professional Soviet historians have thus far not taken advantage of the openness and have not developed the sense cf critical inquiry that might lead to published volumes on crucial events, trends and individuals of the Soviet period. Unlike Soviet geneticists, economists and students of military affairs, Soviet historians have proved unprepared for the opportunity openness has at least temporarily provided. Few, except for Yuri Afanas'ev, Academicians Dimitri Likhachev and A.M. Samsonov, and a number of others have been active in criticising the shortcomings of their profession or in demanding access to primary sources.

Similarly, Robert Conquest's 1990 *The Great Terror: A Reassessment* (45) and his 1986 *The Harvest of Sorrow: Soviet Collectivization and the Terror-Famine* (51), proved substantially accurate, so much so that Conquest, long vilified by the Soviet press and Westerners sympathetic to the Soviet system, has twice visited the Soviet Union on invitation and has seen these two volumes published there in Russian. Robert C. Tucker's first volume on Stalin, which appeared in 1972, has also been published in Moscow in Russian, and a Soviet publisher is now considering the second volume as well. These works demolished the foundations of those Western studies that praised Stalin as a humanitarian genius and that suggested that 'only thousands', not millions, had died in the famine between 1931 and 1934. They are now completely destroying the legends Soviet propagandists and scholars have created about Stalinist collectivisation, the purges, and dictatorship over all Soviet life.

Historiography

The information released or made available in the Soviet Union since February 1987 has demonstrated that the horrors of the Soviet past have been even more dreadful, that economic production was lower, and that internal controls and espionage had been even more pervasive than Western scholarship had described. Realists or traditional scholars have therefore emerged with laurels for their careful, objective research and analysis, while those who tended to be uncritical or apologetic concerning Soviet developments have been exposed by the Soviets themselves. This has put a new light upon Stephen Cohen's *Rethinking the Soviet Experience: Politics and History since 1917* (7), which stimulated much controversy. This volume argued that American scholarship since 1945 had been overly political and that much of it, excluding that of George Kennan and Cohen's colleagues at Princeton, had surrendered to the 'containment' argument and had served American policy, not the high goals of scholarship. Cohen's approach has now been discredited. The volume Leo Labedz edited, *The Use and Abuse of Sovietology* (5), contributed a valuable, level-headed series of analyses of the work of prominent scholars and commentators upon the Soviet Union, mostly English, such as Deutscher, Carr, Werth and Orwell.

Political leaders, columnists, intellectuals and newspaper correspondents have published more and exercised greater influence upon public understanding of the Soviet Union than have scholars: the 1976 volume by Hedrich Smith, *The Russians* (published by Times Books), is an outstanding example. S.J. Taylor's study of *Stalin's Apologist. Walter Duranty: The New York Times' Man in Moscow* (4), is therefore of special value and probably the forerunner of critical studies of other newspapermen and scholars who have helped misshape opinion. Taylor demonstrates that the much-honoured Duranty deliberately withheld news concerning the famine and other Soviet atrocities from his reporting, in part because he sympathised with the Soviet regime and in part because he believed he would be expelled from Moscow if he reported honestly.

Glasnost has led to a number of studies of Soviet scholarship. *Facing up to the Soviet Past: Soviet Historiography under 'Perestroika'* (1), consists of a number of essays presented at the meeting of the American Association for the Advancement of Slavic Studies in Honolulu in 1988 by Japanese, American, French and German scholars analysing Soviet historians' reactions to the new opportunity to write more freely. These articles reveal that in some fields, especially early Russian history, Soviet scholarship has improved because of relaxed constraints and controls under Gorbachev, but that work on the twentieth century remains mired in old clichés. They also show that Japanese scholarship on the Soviet Union has made remarkable progress in the past three decades, and that a number of specialists on early Russian history are making important contributions to the knowledge and understanding of Russia. *Soviet Historians and Perestroika: The First Phase* (2), provides a splendid introductory essay by Raleigh to translations of research articles by Soviet scholars that, in his judgment, suggest significant changes are occurring. R.W. Davies' *Soviet History in the Gorbachev Revolution* (3) contributes a more optimistic description of the changes Davies believes are taking place in the perspective of a brief review of Soviet historiography since 1945. Briefly, Davies is far less critical of Soviet scholarship than Cohen is of American research.

Histories of the Soviet Union

Russia Abroad (8) is not a history of the Soviet Union, but studies the Russian emigrants, especially in Western Europe, until 1939. Written by Marc Raeff, a 'son' of that emigration who benefits from personal knowledge of it and acquaintance with some of the outstanding emigrant intellectuals, this is a rich addition to our understanding of the Soviet Union, the immense spiritual and intellectual loss the Soviet Union suffered from the departure of these men and women, and the achievements the emigration has already made to the revival of Russian culture.

General surveys or textbooks exercise a considerable impact upon the English-speaking world because they constitute the most significant source of judgments thousands of college students reach concerning Soviet history. Two of the most significant produced in the 1980s were translated from French: Hélène Carrère d'Encausse, *A History of the Soviet Union* (14) and David Roussett, *The Legacy of the Bolshevik Revolution: A Critical History of the USSR*, Vol. I (16). Perhaps the one providing the most balanced judgment and keenest insight is that by Geoffrey Hosking, *The First Socialist Society: A History of the Soviet Union from Within* (9). This emphasises the economic and political circumstances that have altered Marxist-Leninist ideology and produced changes within the system. The volume by Mikhail Heller and Aleksandr M. Nekrich, *Utopian Power: The History of the Soviet Union from 1917 to the Present* (11), views Soviet history through the eyes of two former Soviet scholars now resident in Paris and Cambridge, Massachusetts, respectively. Their analysis is briskly critical of things Soviet. Recent Soviet revelations suggest that their analyses are far more accurate than those of many Western scholars susceptible to Soviet propaganda and their own hopes and wishes, or so critical of their own countries that their view of the Soviet Union became rosy. Alec Nove's *An Economic History of the USSR* (15) concentrates upon economic development. Nove, an outstanding English specialist on the Soviet economy and the Soviet system as a whole, emphasises the significance played in modern Russian history by their leaders' concentration upon modernisation and achieving an important role in the world economy and in international politics, at the expense of human values.

The most useful books for the ordinary citizen at a less demanding intellectual level than these are Martin McCauley, *The Soviet Union since 1917* (17), John M. Thompson, *Russia and the Soviet Union: An Historical Introduction* (10), and Woodford McClellan, *Russia: A History of the Soviet Period* (12). These are introductory volumes of great merit for those just beginning to study Soviet history.

Analyses of the Soviet Breakdown

Zbigniew Brzezinski's *The Grand Failure: The Birth and Death of Communism in the Twentieth Century* (18) describes an ideology and a system of rules in inexorable decline. Brzezinski's view of Soviet history led him to see with remarkable clarity that if reform and revisionism succeeded, they would erode the one-party state. On the other hand, if they failed, Soviet problems would deepen. Either way, Brzezinski's analysis of the Soviet past and present disarray anticipated the Soviet collapse.

After Brezhnev: Sources of Soviet Conduct in the 1980s (19) edited by Robert F. Byrnes before the visible decay of the Soviet Union, is a scholarly analysis of the Soviet political system, economy, military forces, social system, cultural life and foreign policy by 25 American and British scholars who looked at the 1980s from an historical perspective. Together they designed the study, organised the analyses, reviewed the seven chapters in draft and in revision, and then agreed to the volume and its conclusions. The book represents the agreed judgment of these scholars of the Soviet Union in 1983 of the interrelated problems Brezhnev's successors would face. It has proved an accurate analysis of long-term developments and of the emerging crisis.

Religious and National Problems

Two issues which Soviet scholarship has neglected, and on which Gorbachev in 1991 cannot find accurate information and understanding within the Soviet Union, are those religious and national problems have raised and that are becoming increasingly threatening to Soviet stability. Scholarship and textbooks alike in the English-speaking world have also paid insufficient attention to these factors, in part because most scholars view the Soviet Union from Russian or Moscow point of view and in part because reliance upon Soviet sources has overwhelmed them. Most studies of high quality have been the work of refugees from the Soviet Union, or of scholars whose religious faith or national background has directed research towards these subjects.

The late Alexandre Bennigsen long ago anticipated the unrest that now marks Soviet Central Asia. The volume he and one of his former students, S. Enders Wimbush, now of Radio Free Europe/Radio Liberty, produced, *Muslims of the Soviet Empire* (22) provides the central information about the Muslims of Central Asia and describes the cause of tension, as well as their relationships with Muslims elsewhere. Michael Rywkin's *Moscow's Muslim Challenge: Soviet Central Asia* (20), published in 1989 and in a revised edition in 1990, in more brief compass summarises the same data. Robert Conquest, more alert to the nationality problem than most scholars, edited a volume, *The Last Empire: Nationality and the Soviet Future* (24) that accurately described the problems Russian rule over other national groups was creating. Other volumes concentrated on particular nationalities: James F. Mace, *Communism and the Dilemmas of National Liberation: National Communism in Soviet Ukraine, 1918-1933* (28) and Azade-Ayse Rorlich, *The Volga Tatars: A Profile in National Resilience* (23).

The Russian Orthodox Church, the Ukrainian Catholic Church, and their survival, resurgence and now competition have attracted the attention of many scholars in recent years, leading to several volumes written by men of Ukrainian origin. Years of research by Dmitry V. Pospielovsky have led to several outstanding volumes, two on *The Russian Church under the Soviet Regime, 1917-1982* (27), and two others, *A History of Soviet Atheism in Theory and Practice* (21). Bohdan R. Bociurkiw studied religion in the Ukraine in *Ukrainian Churches under Soviet Rule: Two Case Studies* (26).

The Russian Revolution

The Revolution in 1917 and the Civil War until 1921 continue to attract enormous attention from scholars, outside as well as within the Soviet Union. The most significant volume published recently is the first of a projected two-volume set by Richard Pipes, *The Russian Revolution* (29). This is the result of years of research on the period from 1894 to 1928, and of Pipes' active service in government early in the 1980s that gave new additional insight into the consequences of the Bolsheviks' seizure of power. The volumes promise to influence the view of many scholars concerning the Bolsheviks' preparations and programme and the direct line of descent from Lenin to Stalin and his successors. It is a thoroughly scholarly study.

E.N. Burdzhalov's *Russia's Second Revolution: The February 1917 Rising in Petrograd* (33) brings to the English-reading public the translation of a 1967 volume that caused its author great troubles in the Soviet Union because of its revisionist views. Robert M. Slusser's *Stalin in October: The Man Who Missed the Revolution* (30), published in 1990 and later in Moscow in a Russian translation, describes Stalin's minor role in

1917, an objective analysis that fits into the campaign launched against Stalin by Gorbachev in 1986. Orlando Figes' *Peasant Russia, Civil War: The Volga Countryside in Revolution, 1917-1921* (32) resembles an earlier volume by Raleigh on the Revolution in Saratov and indicates that Western research on the Revolution has expanded beyond Moscow and St. Petersburg and has benefited from these scholars' research in the Soviet Union. Similarly, Diane Koenker's *Moscow Workers and the 1917 Revolution* (36) represents another aspect of the deepening of scholarship. Robert Service's *The Russian Revolution, 1900-1927*, (34) and Sheila Fitzpatrick's *The Russian Revolution, 1917-1932* (35) are brief surveys of the Revolution and its immediate aftermath.

1921-1931

Most research on this period concentrates upon the Soviet economy, particularly the vast transformation of the economy and the country Stalin launched in 1927-1928 and the historical setting behind these revolutionary changes. Dorothy Atkinson and George Yaney provide part of the historical background, with Atkinson's study *The End of the Russian Land Commune, 1905-1930* (43) and George Yaney's *The Urge to Mobilize: Agrarian Reform, 1861-1930* (44). These volumes, both the product of research in the Soviet Union, are fundamental for understanding Russian and Soviet agricultural problems and the fateful decision to collectivise. The Terry Cox volume, *Peasants, Class and Capitalism: The Rural Research of L.N. Kritsman and His School* (41), brings into focus the views of a prominent Soviet specialist on agriculture in the 1920s that Stalin totally ignored. Alan M. Ball's *Russia's Last Capitalists: The Nepmen, 1921-1929* (38) examines the manufacturers and tradesmen who took advantage of Lenin's relaxing of controls over the economy in 1921, brought about economic recovery by 1928, and then were crushed by Stalin.

Michael Reiman, a scholar who left the Soviet Union, explains *The Birth of Stalinism: The USSR on the Eve of the 'Second Revolution'* (40). This translation from Russian constitutes a dissident Soviet view, now popular in the Soviet Union, of the situation before Stalin began the Revolution that many consider more important than 1917 itself.

E.A. Rees' *State Control in Soviet Russia: The Rise and Fall of the Workers' and the Peasants' Inspectorate, 1920-1934* (39) and Hiroaki Kuromiya's *Stalin's Industrial Revolution: Politics and Workers, 1928-1931* (37) both examine in new detail aspects of the 1927-1931 Revolution that had been neglected. Kuromiya suggests that workers' resentment of the NEP provided Stalin with support for the rapid industrialisation policy he launched and that Stalin was not so unpopular and oppressive as most foreign scholars have concluded.

The 1930s

Published research on this decade is probably the richest and most illuminating of all that which appeared in the 1980s. The volumes by Robert Conquest and Robert C. Tucker, both veterans of more than thirty years of research and writing, stand out. Conquest's *The Harvest of Sorrow: Soviet Collectivization and the Terror-Famine* (51) and *The Great Terror: A Reassessment* (45) represent years of painstaking research and have become internationally significant studies exposing the manmade famine of 1931-1933. Conquest, whom the Soviets and scholars sympathetic to the Soviet Union have vilified because of what has proved to be the accuracy of his exposures of these massacres, has had the satisfaction of seeing Soviet statistics and revelations since 1987 support his findings. Conquest also published an interesting analysis, probably correct, of the varieties of fragmentary evidence available to show that Stalin was responsible for the 1934 murder of Kirov, the Leningrad party leader and potential rival, *Stalin and the Kirov Murder* (48) and an analysis of the secret police during the great purges, *Inside Stalin's Secret Police: NKVD Politics, 1936-1939* (53).

The Columbia University Press in 1990 published an expanded edition of the Roy Medvedev companion piece to Conquest's earlier work on the purges, *Let History Judge: The Origins and Consequences of Stalinism* (46). This tome, written by a dissident Soviet historian and published abroad in 1971, was an independent study based on conversations Medvedev held with his late father's associates and other Soviet leaders and upon work Medvedev completed on the Soviet press and in Soviet archives. The original edition reinforced the work of Conquest and others and established Medvedev's reputation in the West. He has since accepted invitations to return to party membership. After being an early Leninist advocate of reform under Gorbachev, he has turned conservative, as have many other critics of the system in Gorbachev's first years.

Tucker, a foremost specialist on Marxism, student of the life of Stalin, and acute interpreter of the Soviet system, in 1990 brought out the second of his three-volume study of Stalin, *Stalin in Power: The Revolution from Above, 1928-1941* (47). This massive volume, a reflection of years of study that emphasised Stalin's psychology, covers the crucial years that have also attracted the attention of many other scholars. Soviet publication in Russian of the first volume in 1989 and consideration of the second volume for translation in 1990 measure the change in the Soviet attitude towards Stalin that has occurred in recent years, as do Soviet translations of Conquest's major books.

The famine in Ukraine in the early thirties has attracted much research. James F. Mace, whose doctorate was on Ukraine, has been an active participant, particularly through *Commission on the Ukraine Famine:*

Report to Congress (50). Personal insights into this massacre come from Miron Dolot, a survivor of the famine who now teaches in the United States: *Execution by Hunger: The Hidden Holocaust* (54) and Ewald Ammende, *Human Life in Russia* (56). The Ammende volume was ignored when published in England in 1936 but fifty years later contributed to exposing the dreadful massacre.

In 1988, the Indiana University Press published Victor P. Danilov's *Rural Russia Under the New Regime* (49). Danilov is an outstanding Soviet historian, specialising in agriculture in the 1920s and 1930s. One of the few Soviet historians who fought for access to archives and objective scholarship as early as the mid-1960s, Danilov has been especially active since 1987, pressing for candid scholarship and trying to obtain permission to publish work prohibited twenty years ago. However, like Medvedev (although he was not expelled from the party), he has remained a loyal Leninist. This volume is a pale version of Western scholarship on the decision to collectivise agriculture and on some of its consequences, especially the famine.

Translations of two memoirs on the 1930s and later periods add further insight into the years of the Terror. Anton Antonov-Ovseyenko, *The Time of Stalin: Portrait of a Tyranny* (58), is the personal story of the son of a Soviet diplomat killed in the purges who himself survived years in the labour camps and returned to active life in Moscow to attack those who continued Stalinism after the great dictator's death. Varlam Shalamov's *Kolyma Tales* (59) supplements this account with a description of life in the labour camp in Kolyma.

The War, the End of Stalin, and Khrushchev

The Second World War, which attracted enormous attention from Soviet and outside observers alike, has yielded its place of honour as a research subject to the 1930s.

Probably the most interesting volumes on the war, although by no means reliable, are translations of works by Oleg Rzheshevsky and Ernst Topitsch. Rzheshevsky, a leading Soviet military historian, produced *World War II: Myths and Realities* (66). This volume is an old-fashioned Soviet effort to assign responsibility to Britain, France and the US for the war and threats to the Soviet Union since 1945. Its lack of intellectual quality is reflected well in statements such as this: 'In November 1939, the reactionary government of Finland, prodded by the imperialist powers, initiated an armed conflict on the Soviet-Finnish border'. Rzheshevsky is a Soviet participant in the joint Polish-Soviet commission to investigate the Katyn massacre. His presence and delaying tactics there reflect Soviet unwillingness to accept responsibility for that massacre of Polish officers and indicate why the commission has not published its report, although Polish members, other Polish scholars, and even General Jaruszelski have correctly placed responsibility upon the Soviets.

The Ernst Topitsch volume, *Stalin's War: A Radical New Theory of the Origins of the Second World War* (63), is just as far-fetched as Rzheshevsky's work. Topitsch argues that Stalin arranged that Japan and Germany confront the Western powers, masterminded the coming of the War, and emerged as the true victor. More responsibly, Catherine Andreev's *Vlasov and the Russian Liberation Movement: Soviet Reality and Emigré Theories* (61) analyses the background and the tragic plight of those Soviet soldiers who, as German prisoners of war, joined the army of General Vlasov, also a prisoner, to fight alongside the Nazis against the Soviets.

The tragic death of N.I. Vavilov, the famed geneticist whom Stalin arrested at Lysenko's instigation and who died in prison of malnutrition in January, 1943, has been explained by a Soviet journalist of science, Mark A. Popovsky, *The Vavilov Affair* (57). Popovsky, who had access to KGB documents and who brought his notes out of the Soviet Union, wrote this volume in 1971-1972. It is a cameo of the Stalinist system. Another cameo is Louis Rapaport, *The Doctor's Plot and the Soviet Solution* (60) on Stalin's last days, in which he launched a campaign charging Kremlin doctors who were Jewish with the deaths of several Soviet leaders. This was to be the prelude to the removal of all Jews from Moscow and European Russia on the grounds that they were Western agents.

Some of the men who surrounded and succeeded Stalin are the subjects of two volumes: Roy Medvedev's *All Stalin's Men* (65), and *Khrushchev and Khrushchevism* (62), edited by McCauley. These tomes indicate how little we know of those who have ruled the Soviet Union.

Some Memoirs

Soviet history produces few memoirs or autobiographies. Those few that exist are especially precious. Perhaps the most valuable is that by the Yugoslav Ambassador between 1956 and 1958, particularly because General Veljko Micunovic was such a close friend of Khruschchev and kept a rich diary. *Moscow Diary* (74) provides a fascinating account of Kremlin political life as the Yugoslav Ambassador witnessed it.

Andrei Sakharov's *Memoirs* (67) is an immensely valuable account of the life and times of a great scientist and citizen, as close to required reading on Soviet history since 1940 as any other single volume. Elena Bonner, Sakharov's wife, provides a supplementary memoir on Sakharov's last years (he died in 1990): *Alone Together* (69).

Raisa Orlova, an emigré, in her *Memoirs* (71) describes the erosion of Communist faith among intellectuals and artists, overwhelmed by the cultural bureaucracy, politics and the 'system'. Dina Kaminskaya's *Final*

Judgment: My Life as a Soviet Defense Attorney (73) provides valuable but still different testimony concerning the Soviet system.

The Gorbachev Years

The fascinating developments since February 1985 have produced many books, most inevitably shallow, but some of great insight. I have listed those by well-known observers and scholars, whose comments on current developments represent years of scholarship as well as careful analysis of the flood of material that has emerged in the past five years.

Bibliography

Historiography

1   Ito, Takayuki (1989) Editor. *Facing up to the Soviet Past: Soviet Historiography under 'Perestroika'*. Sapporo, Japan: Slavic Research Center, Hokkaido University

A collection of essays on Soviet scholarship since 1986 by American, French, German and Japanese authors. Shows considerable improvement on period before 1917, especially on early Russian history, as well as the perils a critical view of the Soviet past raises for the system's stability. Editor is a senior scholar in the Slavic Research Center of Hokkaido University.

2   Raleigh, Donald J. (1989) Editor. *Soviet Historians and Perestroika: The First Phase.* Armonk, NY: M.E. Sharpe

Translations of essays by Soviet scholars on various aspects of Russian and Soviet history, suggesting quality has risen in recent years. Excellent introduction by Raleigh, a well-informed scholar on the Revolution and on Soviet historical scholarship, who is a professor of history at the University of North Carolina.

3   Davies, R.W. (1989) *Soviet History in the Gorbachev Revolution.* Bloomington, IN: Indiana University Press

Analysis with historical perspective concerning Soviet history and Soviet scholarship by a sympathetic British scholar, recently retired from the University of Birmingham, well-known for work on Soviet industrialisation under first five-year plans.

4   Taylor, S.J. (1989) *Stalin's Apologist. Walter Duranty: The New York Times' Man in Moscow*. New York: Oxford University Press

Accurate, devastating analysis of reporting by Walter Duranty of *The New York Times* in Moscow in the late 1920s and 1930s. Taylor shows Duranty concealed evidence of disasters such as the enforced famine in the early 1930s in his dispatches and was a propagandist for the Stalinist regime. Illustrates one aspect of the politicising of reportage and scholarship on the Soviet Union.

5   Labedz, Leopold (1988) *The Use and Abuse of Sovietology.* New Brunswick, NJ: Transaction Publications

Series of essays, many brilliant, by senior British journalist and Soviet specialist who was born in eastern Poland and knows the languages and cultures of the Russian and Soviet people and has resolutely exposed the evils and flaws of the Soviet system. Essays include studies of Solzhenitsyn, Deutscher, Carr, Werth, Orwell, Milosz, Chomsky, Kennan and Kolakowski. Preface by Zbigniew Brzezinski. Labedz is editor and founder of *Survey*.

6   Richardson, William (1988) *Mexico through Russian Eyes*. Pittsburgh, PA: University of Pittsburgh Press

Interesting study by young professor at Wichita State University who spent 1982-1983 in the Soviet Union. Important because it illustrates the importance of the 'glasses' or perspective through which foreign observers look at the Soviet Union and through which Soviets review other peoples, in this case, Mexicans.

7   Cohen, Stephen F. (1985) *Rethinking the Soviet Experience: Politics and History since 1917*. New York: Oxford University Press

Important work that attracted much attention. Passionate argument that American scholarship on the Soviet Union has been marred by cold war, 'containment' philosophy. Cohen is a professor of political science at Princeton University who has studied often in the Soviet Union, known especially for his classic volume on Bukharin and his commenting on American television.

Histories of the Soviet Union

8   Raeff, Marc (1990) *Russia Abroad: A Cultural History of the Russian Emigration, 1919-1939*. New York: Oxford University Press

This learned volume pulls together scattered information on those Russians, especially intellectuals, who fled abroad or were expelled after 1917 and who, in difficult circumstances, preserved Russian culture, passed it to their children, and kept alive values to which the Soviet Union may one day return. Raeff, who spent his early years in this emigration, is an emeritus professor at Columbia University. One of the most learned and original American scholars, he teaches often in Germany and France.

9   Hosking, Geoffrey (1990) *The First Socialist Society: A History of the Soviet Union from Within*, enlarged edn. Cambridge, MA: Harvard University Press

Textbook which first appeared in 1985. Devotes more attention than most texts to the impact of the regime and its policies upon the people and to the circumstances that have gradually weakened ideology. Hosking is a senior British scholar at the School of Slavonic and East European Studies in the University of London.

10   Thompson, John M. (1990) *Russia and the Soviet Union: An Historical Introduction*, 2nd edn. Boulder, CO: Westview Press

This was first published by Macmillan in 1986. Textbook by distinguished specialist who has studied often and travelled frequently in the Soviet Union and has written on Russia at the peace conference after the First World War and on 1905. Now a roving professor after years at Indiana University.

11   Heller, Mikhail and Nekrich, Aleksandr M. (1986) *Utopian Power: The History of the Soviet Union from 1917 to the Present*, translated by P.B. Carlos. New York: Summit Books

Massive textbook, profoundly critical of Soviet system and Soviet policies by two Soviet historians who left the Soviet Union years ago and are now in the West, Heller in Paris and Nekrich at the Russian Research Center at Harvard. Nekrich was expelled from the party in the late 1960s for his book on the origins of the Second World War, a volume that was released, condemned, and then prohibited in the Soviet Union.

12   McClellan, Woodford (1986) *Russia: A History of the Soviet Period*. Englewood Cliffs, NJ: Prentice Hall

Textbook by senior historian at University of Virginia who has studied in the Soviet Union several times since the early 1960s and who is a specialist also on Yugoslavia.

13 Kort, Michael (1985) *The Soviet Colossus: A History of the USSR*. New York: Scribner's

Textbook with a pronounced anti-Soviet point of view by associate professor of history at Boston University.

14 Carrère d'Encausse, Hélène (1982) *Lenin, Revolution and Power: A History of the Soviet Union, 1917-1953*, translated by V. Ionescu. London; New York: Longman

Two-volume textbook on Soviet history up to Stalin's death in 1953, emphasising the roles of Lenin and Stalin. Carrère d'Encausse, an outstanding French specialist at the Sorbonne, foresaw the collapse of the Soviet system long before most observers, assigning responsibility largely to the communist policy towards the various nationalities, especially those in Central Asia. Translated from French.

15 Nove, Alec (1982) *An Economic History of the USSR*. New York; Harmondsworth: Penguin Books

Economic history by eminent retired British professor, a leading specialist on the Soviet economy who believes pressure to give Russia a modern economy and to make Russia a powerful state explains much of the harshness and violence of the Soviet period.

16 Rousset, David (1982) *The Legacy of the Bolshevik Revolution: A Critical History of the USSR*, Vol. 1, translated by A. Freeman. New York: St. Martin's Press

The first volume of a textbook history of the Soviet Union by a prolific French scholar.

17 McCauley, Martin (1981) *The Soviet Union since 1917*. London; New York: Longman

Brief textbook.

Analyses of the Soviet Breakdown

18 Brzezinski, Zbigniew (1989) *The Grand Failure: The Birth and Death of Communism in the Twentieth Century*. New York: Scribner's

Volume intended for informed public that describes what author considers inexorable decline of the Soviet Union, because system has proved ineffective economically and politically and because ideology has lost its attraction. Brzezinski, a professor at Columbia University, has long been a specialist on the Soviet Union and Eastern Europe. Born in Poland, he was President Carter's National Security Advisor on the Soviet Union and is a frequent commentator.

19 Byrnes, Robert F. (1983) Editor. *After Brezhnev: Sources of Soviet Conduct in the 1980s*. Bloomington, IN: Indiana University Press; London: Pinter

This is a scholarly analysis made in the early 1980s of the total Soviet system, including foreign policy and Soviet relations with other states ruled by communists, especially those of Eastern Europe. It emphasises historical perspective with essays by groups of senior British and American scholars on almost every aspect of Soviet life. It identified the massive and above all interrelated problems the Soviet government would face after Brezhnev died. Byrnes is a retired senior historian at Indiana University. The other 24 scholars who worked together on this cooperative volume were from other American and British institutions. The chairs of the sections include Maurice Friedberg of the University of Illinois, Robert Campbell of Indiana University, Gail Lapidus of the University of California, Berkeley, Andrzei Korbonski of the University of California, Los Angeles, Severyn Bialer of Columbia University, and Adam Ulam of Harvard.

Religious and National Problems

20 Rywkin, Michael (1989) *Moscow's Muslim Challenge: Soviet Central Asia*.Rev. edn. 1990. Armonk, NY: M.E. Sharpe

Brief (186 pages) analysis by a senior professor of history at the City College of New York.

21   Pospielovsky, Dmitry V. (1987/1988) *A History of Soviet Atheism in Theory and Practice, and the Believer.* New York: St. Martin's Press; Basingstoke: Macmillan

Two brief volumes which describe Marxist-Leninist atheism and Soviet anti-religious campaigns and persecution.

22   Bennigsen, Alexandre and Wimbush, S. Enders (1986) *Muslims of the Soviet Empire.* Bloomington, IN: Indiana University Press

The late Alexandre Bennigsen, a distinguished specialist on Soviet Central Asia and the Muslim world, completed this book with one of his outstanding former students, now a senior official with Radio Free Europe/Radio Liberty. Bennigsen foresaw eruptions against Soviet rule among Muslims long before others considered it likely. He combined teaching at the Sorbonne and at the University of Chicago.

23   Rorlich, Azade-Ayse (1986) *The Volga Tatars: A Profile in National Resilience.* Stanford, CA: Hoover Institution Press

This analyses the history of one of the national groups that has suffered most under Soviet rule, as well as the small group's continued determination to maintain its culture. Rorlich is a professor of history at the University of Southern California.

24   Conquest, Robert (1986) Editor. *The Last Empire: Nationality and the Soviet Future.* Stanford, CA: Hoover Institution Press

Conquest, a senior fellow at the Hoover Institution of Stanford University, has seen his years of research in his native United Kingdom and at Stanford reach fruition and full recognition in the 1980s with his several books on the enforced famine of 1931-1934, the purges of 1936-1938, and Soviet policy towards national and religious minorities. Once criticised as overly critical of Soviet philosophy and policies, Conquest has now won wide recognition in the Soviet Union and in the West for his painstakingly accurate and objective analyses of subjects on which solid information had been difficult to collect. His books have done as much as those by Solzenitsyn to illuminate the realities of Soviet political life and its impact upon the peasants and nationality groups.

25   Ellis, Jane (1986) *The Russian Orthodox Church: A Contemporary History.* Bloomington, IN: Indiana University Press

A sound history of the Russian Orthodox Church's position since the Soviets took power.

26   Bociurkiw, Bohdan R. (1984) *Ukrainian Churches under Soviet Rule: Two Case Studies.* Cambridge, MA: Harvard University Press

A Canadian scholar of Ukrainian origin, Bociurkiw has published a number of scholarly volumes on various aspects of Ukrainian life. He is a professor of political science at Carleton University.

27   Pospielovsky, Dmitry V. (1984) *The Russian Church under the Soviet Regime, 1917-1982.* 2 vols. Crestwood; New York: St. Vladimir's Seminary Press

These two volumes are a history of the Church under Soviet rule until 1982. Pospielovsky has emerged as one of the outstanding specialists on this increasingly important subject. He is a youngish senior member of the faculty of the University of Western Ontario who received his early training in London.

28   Mace, James F. (1983) *Communism and the Dilemmas of National Liberation: National Communism in Soviet Ukraine, 1918-1933.* Cambridge, MA: Harvard University Press

This is an excellent study, originally a doctoral thesis at Harvard, on the dilemma Ukrainian communists as nationalists faced until Stalin intervened brutally in 1933. Mace has become an outstanding specialist on the Ukraine, especially the enforced famine, as a research scholar in the US government.

The Russian Revolution

29 Pipes, Richard (1990) *The Russian Revolution, 1899-1919.* New York: Knopf; London: Collins Harvill

This is the massive first volume of a two-volume history of the Russian Revolution from 1894 until 1928. Pipes, born in Poland, but like Brzezinski educated in the United States, has combined a productive career as a scholar at Harvard, writing mostly on the nineteenth century and the revolutionary years, with activity as a commentator in leading journals and newspapers on contemporary Soviet developments and two years on the National Security Council early in the first Reagan term. His views and those of Stephen F. Cohen differ greatly. These two deeply-researched volumes will profoundly influence Western and Soviet views.

30 Slusser, Robert M. (1990) *Stalin in October: The Man Who Missed the Revolution.* Baltimore, MD: Johns Hopkins University Press

This appeared in hardback in 1987. One of the outstanding American veterans of the study of Soviet life and politics, Slusser here demonstrates what a minor role Stalin played in the Revolution and how some of his later actions against rivals or potential rivals were designed to conceal that lack of prominence. Slusser is a professor of political science at Michigan State.

31 von Hagen, Mark (1990) *Soldiers in the Proletarian Dictatorship: The Red Army and the Soviet Socialist State, 1917-1930.* Ithaca, NY; London: Cornell University Press

This is an extremely able study of the role the Army and the soldiers played before 1930 and the impact of these years upon the Army and the men who served in it. Von Hagen is one of the most promising youngish American scholars who have benefited from prolonged study and travel in the Soviet Union. He, Orlando Figes (32), and Dorothy Atkinson (43) are among those who have worked closely with Victor P. Danilov in Moscow University and the Institute of History in the USSR. Von Hagen is an associate professor of history at Columbia University.

32 Figes, Orlando (1989) *Peasant Russia, Civil War: The Volga Countryside in Revolution, 1917-1921.* Oxford: Clarendon

An outstanding study by a young scholar who selected the Volga area to illuminate the history of the Civil War outside the major cities, which have received most attention from Soviet and American scholars. Figes spent 1984-1985 in the Soviet Union.

33 Burdzhalov, Eduard N. (1987) *Russia's Second Revolution: The February 1917 Rising in Petrograd,* translated and edited by Donald J. Raleigh. Bloomington, IN: Indiana University Press

This significant volume, which caused Burdzhalov great trouble when published in Moscow in 1967, has been translated and edited by one of the outstanding young American specialists on the Revolution. It demonstrated that the worker disaffection with the pre-revolutionary regime that helped bring about the February 1917 Revolution preceded Bolshevik action. Fortunately, the author survived to enjoy Raleigh's translation and his rehabilitation.

34 Service, Robert (1986) *The Russian Revolution, 1900-1927.* Atlantic Highlands, NJ: Humanities Press; London: Macmillan

A brief textbook.

35 Fitzpatrick, Sheila. (1982) *The Russian Revolution, 1917-1932.* New York: Oxford University Press

A brief textbook history of the 1917-1932 period by an American of Australian origin and British training who is quite sympathetic to Soviet policies. A specialist on Soviet cultural life, especially education, in the 1920s, she is a senior professor of history at the University of Chicago.

36 Koenker, Diane (1981) *Moscow Workers and the 1917 Revolution.* Princeton, NJ: Princeton University Press

A detailed study by a young American scholar, one of those who have benefited from study in the Soviet Union. She is now in the history department in the University of Illinois, Champaign-Urbana.

1921-1931

37 Kuromiya, Hiroaki (1988) *Stalin's Industrial Revolution: Politics and Workers, 1928-1931.* Cambridge; New York: Cambridge University Press

Kuromiya has faced the immensely complicated problem of studying the regime's policies towards the workers during the first five-year plan. His book suggests that Stalin had strong support from the workers. Kuromiya received his college education in Japan and his doctorate from Princeton. He has benefited from study in the Soviet Union and from research opportunities in England. He is an assistant professor of history at Indiana University.

38 Ball, Alan M. (1987) *Russia's Last Capitalists: The Nepmen, 1921-1929.* Berkeley, CA: University of California Press

Ball is an assistant professor at Marquette University trained at North Carolina.

39 Rees, E.A. (1987) *State Control in Soviet Russia: The Rise and Fall of the Workers' and Peasants' Inspectorate, 1920-1934.* New York: St. Martin's Press; Basingstoke: Macmillan

Outlines the role of the People's Commissariat of Workers' and Peasants' Inspectorate as an instrument of state control and form of direct participatory democracy. Extensive bibliography.

40 Reiman, Michael (1987) *The Birth of Stalinism: The USSR on the Eve of the 'Second Revolution',* translated by George Saunders. Bloomington, IN: Indiana University Press

This short essay on the critical turn in 1927-1928 is by a former Soviet scholar.

41 Cox, Terry (1986) *Peasants, Class and Capitalism: The Rural Research of L.N. Kritsman and His School.* Oxford; New York: Clarendon

Interesting in that it concentrates attention upon contemporary approaches to agricultural issues at odds with those favoured by Stalin.

42 Remington, Thomas F. (1984) *Building Socialism in Bolshevik Russia: Ideology and Industrial Organization, 1917-1921.* Pittsburgh, PA: University of Pittsburgh Press

Analyses early efforts to establish institutions for planning and administering industry. Argues that the massive campaigns of economic mobilisation may have prevented the establishment of 'self-sustaining social institutions on which a socialist regime depends' (viii). The analysis has implications for current events. Remington is an associate professor of political science at Emory University trained at Yale.

43 Atkinson, Dorothy (1983) *The End of the Russian Land Commune, 1905-1930.* Stanford, CA: Stanford University Press

This study, which benefited from a year in the Soviet Union and work with Professor Danilov, traces the land commune, which the Russian government had tried to make the base of agricultural arrangements, from 1905, and the Stolypin programme to dismantle it through the 1920s, when collectivisation ended it. Atkinson is Executive Director of the American Association for the Advancement of Slavic Studies.

44 Yaney, George (1982) *The Urge to Mobilize: Agrarian Reform, 1861-1930*. Urbana, IL; London: University of Illinois Press

This large and useful study puts collectivisation into the historical perspective of the efforts to resolve the 'peasant problem' from the abolition of serfdom in 1861 until Stalin imposed collectivisation. Yaney, who has studied in the Soviet Union, is a leading American specialist on Russian and Soviet administration and agriculture over this period. He is a senior scholar in history at the University of Maryland.

The 1930s

45 Conquest, Robert (1990) *The Great Terror: A Reassessment*. London; New York: Hutchinson

See earlier comments on Conquest (24).

46 Medvedev, Roy (1990) *Let History Judge: The Origins and Consequences of Stalinism*, revised and expanded edition. New York: Columbia University Press

Medvedev, twin brother of Zhores Medvedev, prominent in exile in London as a powerful force for revisionism, compiled this important volume, not published in the Soviet Union, from conversations with his late father's associates, other survivors of the purges, press accounts, and some access to archives arranged by protectors among high officialdom. An impressive volume completed inside the Soviet Union, it supports Conquest's work. This is the most important of Medvedev's works. The original edition appeared in 1971.

47 Tucker, Robert C. (1990) *Stalin in Power: The Revolution from Above, 1928-1941*. New York: W. W. Norton

Tucker, one of the most outstanding American scholars on Soviet philosophy and politics, has devoted much of his career to a painstaking biography of Stalin, of which this is the second volume. Tucker worked in the American Embassy in Moscow for ten years, beginning late in the Second World War, and has returned often in recent years for continued research and conversations with survivors of these years and with Soviet scholars. He is an emeritus professor of politics at Princeton.

48 Conquest, Robert (1989) *Stalin and the Kirov Murder*. London; New York: Hutchinson

See earlier comments on Conquest (24).

49 Danilov, Victor P. (1988) *Rural Russia Under the New Regime,* translated and introduced by Orlando Figes. Bloomington, IN: Indiana University Press; London: Hutchinson

This study by an outstanding Soviet specialist on Soviet agriculture, especially collectivisation, is a valuable illustration of the difficulties even resolute Soviet scholars have faced to find and describe the truth about this destructive period. Danilov has been an early 'reformer' among Soviet historians, but is limited by his loyalty to Lenin and Leninism. He has helped train a number of young American scholars.

50 Mace, James F. (1988) *Commission on the Ukraine Famine: Report to Congress*. Washington, DC: Government Printing Office

See earlier (28). This study, commissioned by the American Congress, analyses the famine and reaches the same conclusions on the millions killed as Conquest had, now confirmed by Soviet revelations under glasnost.

51 Conquest, Robert (1986) *The Harvest of Sorrow: Soviet Collectivization and the Terror-Famine*. London; New York: Hutchinson

See earlier comments on Conquest (24).

52   Procyk, Oksana, Heretz, Leonid, and Mace, James F. (1986) *Famine in the Soviet Ukraine, 1932-1933: A Memorial Exhibition*. Cambridge, MA: Harvard University Press

A short collection of photographs by a scholar trained at Harvard and two Harvard librarians.

53   Conquest, Robert (1985) *Inside Stalin's Secret Police: NKVD Politics, 1936-1939*. Stanford, CA: Hoover Institution Press; London: Macmillan

See earlier comments on Conquest (24).

54   Dolot, Miron (1985) *Execution by Hunger: The Hidden Holocaust*. Introduction by Adam Ulam. New York: W. W. Norton

A description of the famine of the early 1930s by a survivor, now a teacher in the United States, with an introduction by one of the most informed and perceptive American specialists.

55   Tucker, Robert C. and Cohen, Stephen F. (1985) Editors. *The Great Purge Trial*, edited and with notes. New York: Grosset and Dunlap

This collection of documents contains an especially helpful introduction by Tucker, explaining Bukharin's 'confession' and the way Bukharin used it to show that Stalin was destroying Bolshevism.

56   Ammende, Ewald (1984) *Human Life in Russia*. Introduction by Rt. Hon. Lord Dickinson; historical introduction by J.F. Mace. Cleveland: Zubal

An early (1936) study ignored then, in part because of the atmosphere Duranty and others like him created, but reprinted in 1984.

57   Popovsky, Mark A. (1984) *The Vavilov Affair*. With a foreword by Andrei Sakharov. Hamden, CN: Archon Books

The geneticist N.I. Vavilov was arrested in 1940 for sabotage in agriculture. Sentenced to 15 years, he died in Saratov prison. A harrowing account based on contemporary accounts.

58   Antonov-Ovseyenko, Anton (1983) *The Time of Stalin: Portrait of a Tyranny*. London; New York: Harper and Row

One of the most vivid memoirs of Stalin's years by a man whose father was executed and who himself spent years in labour camps. Antonov-Ovseyenko argues convincingly that Stalin 'surpassed all the infamous despots of history' and that his successors continue his work. He still struggles against Bolshevism in the Soviet Union.

59   Shalamov, Varlam (1980) *Kolyma Tales*, translated by S. Glad. New York: W. W. Norton

Neglect and cruelty are coped with as a matter of survival.

The War, the End of Stalin, and Khrushchev

60   Rapaport, Louis (1990) *Stalin's War Against the Jews: The Doctors' Plot and the Soviet Solution*. New York: Free Press

Building on Stalin's distrust of his doctors, the security agencies, under Beria, prepared a case against a number of doctors on the grounds that they were shortening the lives of the leadership. Forced confessions were secured and an anti-Semitic campaign whipped up. The affair was ended on Stalin's sudden death. A revealing insight into the high levels of suspicion, distrust and sycophancy in the higher echelons.

61   Andreev, Catherine (1987) *Vlasov and the Russian Liberation Movement: Soviet Reality and Emigré Theories*. Cambridge; New York: Cambridge University Press

Captured Lt-General A.A. Vlasov was persuaded by the Germans to head the Russian Liberation Army with the declared aim of overthrowing Stalin and creating a New

Russia. The rise and fall of the ill-starred venture, and the eventual harsh retribution, are absorbingly delineated.

62 McCauley, Martin (1987) Editor. *Khrushchev and Khrushchevism*. Bloomington, IN: Indiana University Press; Basingstoke: Macmillan

Intended to 'provide an overview of the Khrushchev period for the general reader'. Contributors discuss specific policy areas, such as industry, agriculture, labour, state and ideology, contrasting and comparing the Khrushchev and Stalin years. The innovative aspects of the period form an interesting basis for considering some of the reforming intentions of Gorbachev. A stimulating work.

63 Topitsch, Ernst (1987) *Stalin's War: A Radical New Theory of the Origins of the Second World War*, translated by Arthur Taylor. New York: St. Martin's Press; London: Fourth Estate

A strained interpretation of the facts. Interesting as an example of how uncritical ideology distorts historical balance.

64 Linz, Susan J. (1985) Editor. *The Impact of World War II on the Soviet Union*. Totowa, NJ: Rowan and Allanheld

A collection of essays covering history, politics, economics and social topics from the viewpoint of the influence of World War II.

65 Medvedev, Roy (1984) *All Stalin's Men*, translated by M. Shukman. New York: Doubleday

First published in 1983 by Blackwell. This has brief biographies of Voroshilov, Mikoyan, Suslov, Molotov, Kaganovich and Malenkov as typical servants of Stalin who survived. These essays reveal indirectly how little is known about Soviet politics and leaders. See (46).

66 Rzheshevsky, Oleg (1984) *World War II: Myths and Realities*, translated from the Russian by Sergei Chulski. Moscow: Progress

Westerners interested in the way Soviet historians described their history before Gorbachev, and to some degree even now, should read this volume because of its incredible distortions.

Some Memoirs and Analyses

67 Sakharov, Andrei (1990) *Memoirs*, translated by R. Lourie. New York: Knopf; London: Hutchinson

The autobiography by the great Soviet physicist who became a leading fighter for human rights, a peaceful Soviet foreign policy, and negotiated settlements with the West is an essential book for those interested in the past fifty years of Soviet life. Sakharov's death in 1990 deprived the democratic movement in the Soviet Union of its most impressive and effective leader.

68 Kagarlitsky, Boris (1988) *The Thinking Reed: Intellectuals and the Soviet State from 1917 to the Present*, translated by B. Pearce. London; New Jersey: Verso

A fascinating analysis of Soviet intellectual life, its failure and betrayal, by a young and courageous radical Soviet intellectual.

69 Bonner, Elena (1986) *Alone Together*, translated by A. Cook. New York: Knopf; London: Collins Harvill

The brief memoirs of his wife, Elena Bonner, supplement Sakharov's *Memoirs* (67).

70. Yanov, Alexander (1984) *The Drama of the Soviet 1960s: A Lost Reform,* translated by Stephen P. Dunn. Berkeley, CA: University of California International Studies

    Yanov, who left the Soviet Union and became an American professor of political science in Brooklyn College, looks back at the failure to achieve reform in the 1960s. Yanov has long feared the return to rule of the radical Russian nationalist right.

71. Orlova, Raisa (1983) *Memoirs.* New York: Random House

    An example of the many intellectuals finally convinced of the mistakes of past beliefs. The re-awakening cannot be other than painful.

72. Tumarkin, Nina (1983) *Lenin Lives! The Lenin Cult in Soviet Russia.* Cambridge, MA: Harvard University Press

    An excellent analysis of the Lenin cult in Soviet Russia that has survived even attacks by some Soviet reformers, who describe him as the forerunner of Stalin and founder of the Soviet totalitarian system. Whether or not this legend retains its power is one of the critical keys for observers to watch. Tumarkin is an associate professor of history at Harvard.

73. Kaminskaya, Dina (1982) *Final Judgment: My Life as a Soviet Defense Attorney,* translated by M. Glenny. New York: Simon and Schuster

    Interesting insight into the Soviet legal system.

74. Micunovic, Veljko (1980) *Moscow Diary,* translated by David Floyd with an introduction by George Kennan. London: Chatto and Windus

    Published originally in Zagreb in 1977, this remains one of the most valuable sources on the years after Stalin's death.

The Gorbachev Years

75. Laqueur, Walter (1990) *The Glasnost Revelations.* New York: Scribner's

    This fascinating assessment of how much new information glasnost has provided concludes the West has not learned much not already known, but that its knowledge painfully acquired from sifting the limited sources available earlier has been confirmed. Laqueur is a learned and prolific scholar of the Soviet Union and one of the shrewdest observers concerning its policies. He is a senior fellow at the Center for Strategic and International Studies and a professor of politics at Georgetown University, after earlier careers in Israel and England with Leo Labedz.

76. Nove, Alec (1989) *Glasnost in Action: Cultural Renaissance in Russia.* Boston: Unwin Hyman

    This is one of the most thorough and keenest analyses of the Gorbachev years, particularly because it examines so many aspects of Soviet life, including historical scholarship.

77. Daniels, Robert V. (1988) *Is Russia Reformable? Change and Resistance From Stalin to Gorbachev.* Boulder, CO: Westview Press

    This volume is of exceptional merit for one on contemporary affairs, in part because Daniels places Gorbachev's efforts in historical perspective. A leading specialist of the Revolution, Daniels is sceptical concerning the likelihood of a significant change, largely because he considers Russia's long history reflects a political culture of despotism which reform efforts in the nineteenth century and revolution in the twentieth century have both failed to weaken. Daniels is an emeritus professor of history at the University of Vermont.

78 Lewin, Moshe (1988) *The Gorbachev Phenomenon: A Historical Interpretation.* Berkeley, CA: University of California Press; London: Radius

A valuable study, by an American professor of history at the University of Pennsylvania, who was once a Soviet scholar. Lewin, a specialist on the Revolution and the years between 1917 and 1939, like Daniels, puts Gorbachev's efforts into historical perspective.

79 Oberg, James E. (1988) *Uncovering Soviet Disasters: Exploring the Limits of Glasnost.* New York: Random House

Oberg, an aerospace engineer in the space shuttle programme in the Manned Control section of NASA in Houston, in this volume has compiled the information released since 1986 concerning Soviet disasters in the military forces, science, nuclear programmes, the space programme, and Chernobyl.

80 Zinoviev, Alexander (1988) *Gorbachevizm.* New York: Liberty Pub. House

An interesting treatment of the early stages of the influence of Gorbachev.

81 van Goudoever, Albert P. (1986) *The Limits of DeStalinization in the Soviet Union: Political Rehabilitations in the Soviet Union since Stalin,* translated by Frans Hijkoop. New York: St. Martin's Press; London: Croom Helm

This study by a Dutch historian, translated into English, uses the historical approach to place the rehabilitations under Gorbachev in the perspective of other attempts since Stalin. It is thorough and systematic, providing statistical and quantitative statistics as well as individual case studies, and showing that much remains to be done.

CHAPTER THREE

Society and Culture

Dr Terry Cox
University of Strathclyde

Perestroika and the Study of Soviet Society

Social change takes longer than political or legal reforms and the changes in Soviet society over the last few years have not been as dramatic as those in public policy and political institutions. Nevertheless, changes in social life and social structure have been a very important aspect of the perestroika reforms. Social changes can be seen both as a factor underlying the reforms, and as a result or aim of them. From the beginning, perestroika was understood by the Gorbachev leadership as a programme made necessary by a growing crisis in Soviet society, and its aim was seen as the creation of new social institutions capable of regulating the interests of different social groups and enabling people to change established patterns of behaviour and use their initiative in socially useful ways.

The literature on Soviet society and culture has reflected the social changes associated with perestroika in different ways. Through the work of a number of pro-reform Soviet sociologists, it has provided an inspiration and a resource for the reform process itself. At the same time, in the work of both Soviet and Western scholars, it has provided description and analysis of the social changes that contributed to perestroika, and more recently, of the social effects of the reforms.

Soviet Sociology and Perestroika

A significant influence on the formulation of the ideas of perestroika was provided by sociologists and other social analysts in the Soviet Union, and much of their work is now becoming available in English translation. Their work is important, not only in providing insights to some of the thinking behind perestroika, but also for the light they shed on the character of Soviet society. Although they operated under strict political constraint, by the late 1960s and early 1970s Soviet sociologists had become an important source of information about Soviet society. Within the confines of the official Soviet view of the nature of social change in Soviet society, the sociologists produced increasingly detailed data, especially on questions of social inequality, social mobility, work organisation and lifestyles. By the early 1980s, while still working within the same official definitions, the research had become more sophisticated, producing information on a wider range of occupational groups and inequalities between them, and beginning to explore the idea that the inequalities underlay divisions of political and social interest. Some of the best Soviet work of this kind was translated and collected in a volume edited by Murray Yanowitch (4).

On the basis of the advances achieved by the early 1980s, Soviet sociologists were able to develop an increasingly incisive critique of their society which fed directly into political debates on perestroika. The leading figure here was Tat'yana Zaslavskaya. Using data from sociological surveys as support, she emerged as a leading proponent of the view that Soviet society in the 1980s was facing a crisis characterised by stagnation in production, the increasing alienation of the population, a lack of commitment to social goals, the stifling of innovation and critical debate, and a growth in corruption and cynicism. In general, the solution advocated was to put more stress on the 'human factor' in the management of the economy and society, by means of the various policies that now go under the headings of glasnost and perestroika. More specifically, Zaslavskaya and other sociologists turned to more detailed discussions of social policy in their work, examining questions of unearned income, poverty and social justice. Samples of their work have been translated in two anthologies edited by Yanowitch (2, 3). Most recently Zaslavskaya has written a book aimed at readers in the West, outlining her views on social policy and the politics of social reform in the Soviet Union (1). Further examples of the best of current Soviet sociology in translation can also be found in the journal *Soviet Sociology* (5).

The increased range and sophistication of Soviet sociology in recent years have provided an important resource for Western studies of Soviet society. Although it was becoming possible at the end of the 1980s for Western sociologists to carry out empirical research in the Soviet Union, such possibilities are too recent to have found much expression in published works. Before the development of Soviet empirical research, Western studies had to rely on press reports and official statistics from within the Soviet Union, supplemented by surveys of the opinions and recollections of emigrés living in the West. By the 1980s however, a growing number of Western writers were able to draw on Soviet studies as a substantial source both for the preparation of general works and textbooks on Soviet society, and for more specialist monographs on particular subjects.

Introductory and General Books on Soviet Society

There is now a wide range of books on Soviet society in general, or covering a selection of different aspects of it. Some have been written primarily
as introductions or student texts, while others consist of collections of articles or conference papers on different aspects of Soviet society. A selection is included in the bibliography below. The first major textbook on
Soviet society was *Politics and Society in the USSR*, written by David
Lane in the 1970s. By 1985, in updating his earlier text, the growth of information had enabled him to split it into two volumes. Discussion of different aspects of Soviet society was now expanded to take up the major
part of one of the volumes (22). Lane's text was soon joined by others, including one by Basile Kerblay (24), which was updated and translated
from the original French, and a collection edited by Jerry Pankhurst and
Michael Sacks entitled *Contemporary Soviet Society*. More recently Lane,
and Sacks and Pankhurst, have produced new texts which both update
their earlier volumes, and also go beyond them in scope.

In *Understanding Soviet Society* (15) Sacks and Pankhurst have at-
tempted to put together chapters that both cover the main empirical areas
of the study of Soviet society, and do so in such a way that they contribute
to wider debates in the comparative sociology of industrial societies. To
attempt this by means of an edited volume of articles from contributors
who were not working closely together as a team was a very ambitious
project, and some chapters do not sustain the theme as well as others.
However, the editors' intention surely points the way to an important future direction for sociological studies of the Soviet Union, especially if the
old stark differences in ideology and social organisation between East and
West continue to be eroded.

Although *Understanding Soviet Society* was published after Gorbachev had come to power, it came too early to deal with the question of
perestroika and its social impact. By contrast Lane's latest version of his
textbook, *Soviet Society Under Perestroika* (7), deals explicitly with such
issues and uses them as the organising theme of his volume. While updating his account of the main features of the social structure, Lane also discusses the political and economic reforms associated with perestroika,
their social origins, and their likely effects on Soviet society. His general
conclusion is that the reforms of perestroika are the latest stage in a longer
process of gradual democratisation and reform beginning under the
leadership of Khrushchev.

Theoretical Approaches

As well as offering good general discussion of aspects of social structure
and social change in the Soviet Union, the above-mentioned texts have,

with varying degrees of explicitness, made important contributions to the-oretical debates on the social character of Soviet society and other so-cieties organised on a similar basis. Until the beginning of the 1970s, the debate had been dominated by the theory of totalitarian society. This put forward the idea of an 'atomised' mass society, where group solidarity, community spirit and the articulation of alternative interests had been stifled by an all-powerful elite. Although less popular now than in the past, this view still has many adherents. For example, emigré writers such as Zinoviev (28, 30) and Heller (75) support variants of the totalitarian thesis, while Hosking (6) discusses the possibility that Soviet society may only now be emerging from totalitarianism as a result of perestroika.

The growth in information about the complexity of Soviet society, the extent of inequalities and differentiation within it, and the variety of its culture and values, prompted many sociologists to join writers from other disciplines who were questioning the accuracy of the hitherto predomi-nant totalitarian view of Soviet society. This alternative view is sometimes known as the 'developmental' approach. It suggested that as Soviet society became more industrialised and modernised, its social structure became based on increasing social differentiation, leading in turn to changes in culture and family patterns more similar to those of other industrial so-cieties, and to the emergence of new social group loyalties with their own specific interests and values. Empirical data on some of these changes is provided by Ryan and Prentice (34), while Jones and Grupp (33) have at-tempted to trace the impact of modernisation on changes in social values and fertility.

A more comprehensive example of the modernisation approach can be found in the work of David Lane (7, 22). In his view, the main factors underlying the development of Soviet society are aspects of its economic modernisation. A recurrent theme in his work is to stress that, although Soviet society differs from Western societies in the nature of its ruling ide-ology and political and economic organisation, it has also developed many characteristics, ranging from the division of labour to trends in fam-ily life, which are more similar to those of other industrial societies.

A similar approach is taken by Moshe Lewin (32). In developing an explanation of the rise of Gorbachev, Lewin traces the roots of perestroika to long term social changes that produced an increasingly complex social differentiation of Soviet society. Lewin, however, puts more stress on ur-banisation as the key process bringing about social change. From a pre-dominantly rural society, the Soviet Union rapidly became a complex urban society consisting of a wide range of different social groups and, in particular, an increasingly influential intelligentsia. The basis was created for the emergence of a civil society at the same time as the intelligentsia's influence grew within the Party, thus creating the social conditions for Gorbachev and a reformist programme by the mid-1980s.

A different view again is taken by a third set of writers who argue that both the above-mentioned views fail to take account of the extent to which Soviet Union is distinct from Western industrial societies. Totalitarian theory, it is argued, implies Western societies are the norm for modern industrial societies and therefore Soviet society is somehow a deviant case. The developmental approach on the other hand argues that, as a consequence of industrialisation, Soviet society has developed more features in common with Western societies and, according to some writers, is gradually becoming more like Western societies.

By contrast, the third view argues that Soviet society (along with those of Eastern Europe and China) should be treated as a distinct type in its own right. Even if particular institutions or social trends are similar to some found in Western societies, their significance can only be understood by studying them in the context of their own society. While this approach is less well established than the other two, it has attracted a growing number of supporters. In particular, significant work has been done by some Hungarian sociologists such as Feher et al. (31), as well as by some Marxist scholars in the West. These writers reject Soviet official claims to have built a socialist society, but nevertheless argue that Soviet society represents a distinct type, different from capitalism, which must be understood in terms of its own laws and tendencies. Examples here include Furedi (27), and the analysis developed by the journal *Critique*.

While the growth in the range of good introductory and general books has been invaluable in the teaching of courses about Soviet society, the various contributions to the theoretical debate have helped to structure discussion about the nature of Soviet society. In turn, they both rely on the expansion of specialist research on particular aspects of Soviet society that has appeared in recent years. Also drawing on the increased range and sophistication of data produced within the Soviet Union, the specialist Western studies have been able to bring a more open-ended questioning approach to their subject than has been possible for Soviet sociologists until very recently. Their results are reflected both in essays on particular subjects in the edited collections listed in the bibliography, and in a growing number of specialist monographs.

Social Differentiation

Of particular importance has been a wide range of studies of various aspects of the social differentiation and group structure of Soviet society. Works in this category have combined Soviet data with conceptual approaches developed in Western sociology to examine various aspects of inequalities between groups, their status position in Soviet society, power relations, economic relations, and the different interests and political and cultural outlooks of the various groups.

Within the general category of differentiation, many studies have been concerned with social stratification in terms of income, status or influence. Most of the general studies and collections in the bibliography have sections or chapters on this theme. It has also formed the specific focus of a number of studies. Comparisons between inequality in the USA and the Soviet Union form the subject of work by Barrington Moore (35). Focusing more specifically on the significance of stratification in Soviet society, Lane (38) and Littlejohn (29), each arguing in very different ways, conclude that although such inequalities are a distinctive feature of Soviet society, they do not form the basis of clear social divisions that would lead to class or other conflicts. However, a different conclusion has been drawn by some other writers.

Starting at the top in terms of power, influence and economic strength, a number of studies have identified a ruling elite and other elite groups associated with them. While there is no consensus in the literature, either on a precise definition or on the boundaries of a ruling elite, interesting contributions have been made to the debate by Matthews (39), Voslensky (37), and in some of the essays in volume two of the collection edited by Shtromas and Kaplan (11). These writers have suggested that a clear division exists in terms of power, privilege, or economic strength between the elite and other groups in society. Marxist writers such as Furedi (27), on the other hand, have been critical of the need for such precise empirical delineation of elite membership, and have focused more on the social relations of the elite with other sections of society, and on their roles and function in the organisation of production. Their interpretations are disputed by Lane (7), who has preferred to talk in terms of several interacting elites reflecting different social and economic interests. Some writers, for example Rywkin (10), accept the existence of a ruling elite, but also identify the intelligentsia as a rising middle class who are closing the gap between themselves and the elite.

Examining the other end of the stratification scale, Matthews (89) has made an important contribution in attempting to interpret available Soviet data in order to identify the extent and nature of poverty in Soviet society. Further aspects of this topic are also discussed by Porket in the volume edited by Potichnyj (14). However, surprisingly little attention has been paid in recent years to the question of whether the persistence, or even growth of inequality and poverty will lead to increased class consciousness and working-class militancy. The main, detailed sociological, discussion arguing tentatively in favour of this conclusion has been provided by Connor in essays in his own collection of articles (12), and in his contribution to the volume edited by Sacks and Pankhurst (15). No doubt, in view of the wave of militancy among miners and other workers at the end of the 1980s, more sociological studies of this question will appear during the 1990s.

A similar situation prevails in studies of ethnic relations and the question of ethnic conflicts. Until recently the majority of Western publications in this area tended to reflect the concern of Soviet researchers for the collection of ethnographic material. A number of detailed surveys have been published providing details of the languages, material culture, religious beliefs and ways of life of the large number of Soviet ethnic minorities (48, 50, 53, 54). However, a smaller number of studies developed a more analytical sociological approach. They have provided a wealth of detailed discussion of the extent and significance of differences and inequalities between ethnic groups but, reflecting the predominant view held until the end of the 1980s, tended to the conclusion that the differences were unlikely to be a cause of ethnic conflict. Nevertheless, it is interesting to note the different reasoning by which they reached their conclusions.

On the one hand Lane (22) put stress on the role of economic and social development in creating a modern urbanised society where differences between Soviet nationalities were being gradually eroded. Some evidence of such a trend was found in improved standards of living and educational levels among the formerly less developed peoples and regions of the Soviet Union. However, he also expressed doubts that such trends would lead to a complete eradication of the significance of ethnic differences. Policy on political appointments, and cultural policies supporting the preservation of ethnic languages and cultures, had in some ways reinforced ethnic identities and interests.

Other writers put greater stress on the likely persistence of ethnic differences. Karklins (51), using surveys of emigrés and Soviet sociological data, supported the idea that Soviet policies reinforced ethnic identities, and provided a detailed account of regional differences in the degree to which resentments between ethnic groups have arisen. Motyl (49) went further in arguing that the Soviet state was always predominantly a Russian state, whose policies have been geared to maintaining a political and ideological hegemony in order to stifle any potential developments towards national autonomy among Soviet ethnic groups.

Despite differences in approach to the question, until the very end of the 1980s the predominant view was that Soviet society was successfully containing, if not eroding, potential conflicts between ethnic interests. Only the most recent publications contain any revision of this view. In his most recent book, Lane (7) now concludes that 'national consciousness has proved to be stronger than class allegiance' (p.200). His explanation however is still in terms of the effects of modernisation and economic change. Rather than eroding differences, modernisation reinforced the aspirations of 'previously backward peoples', while the uncertainties of the recent reforms have accentuated peoples' concerns with ethnic identity. On the other hand Motyl, in his contribution to Bialer's edited collection (8), develops his own previous approach and explains recent ethnic conflicts as the result of the failure of central state control, involving the realignment of local elites with their own nationalities.

While class and ethnic differentiation have been undergoing radical, and as yet, unpredictable changes, the effects of the reforms have been less drastic on differentiation by gender. Glasnost has led to changes in predominant images of women in the Soviet media, and perestroika has prompted debates on the desirability of encouraging women out of the full-time workforce, but as yet there seems to have been little change in the position of women in the family or in the public sphere. As a result, the sociological literature on women in Soviet society has been concerned less with re-evaluation and more with consolidation on the basis of past research.

Building on the foundation of Western feminist sociological research of the 1970s, and in particular on the work of Lapidus (46), work in the 1980s has further explored barriers to women's equal participation at work, in politics and in access to social services, and has further discussed the conceptualisation of the 'woman problem' in Soviet ideology (40, 42). Furthermore the scope of research has been broadened by the important work of Bridger (41) on the place of women in rural development. Soviet thinking on women in society has been made more accessible by the publication of volumes of translations of Soviet sociological work (45), of the writings of Soviet feminists (43), and of interviews with Russian women (44). Finally, a continuing gap in the literature should be mentioned. As yet there seems to have been no sociological study of gender issues in relation to Soviet men.

One of the liveliest growth areas in the recent study of Soviet society has been in relation to Soviet youth and youth culture. Perhaps this should not be surprising in view of the contribution of Soviet young people to the cultural and political changes of perestroika. While various problems of youth in Soviet society and politics have been discussed by Wilson and Bachkatov (59), aspects of youth culture and youth groups have received more specific attention from the contributors to Riordan's edited volume (57). Two important aspects of Soviet youth culture have received particular attention from recent studies. First, Artem Troitsky (58) has provided a lively, informed account of the development of Soviet rock music. Soviet rock played a significant role in promoting alternative values and outlooks to the official ones before perestroika, and is now expanding into a new, legalised role. Secondly, the subcultures of Moscow youth gangs has been studied through an examination of their graffiti in a pioneering study by John Bushnell (56).

Culture, Popular Attitudes and the Media

As well as Soviet youth, other sections of society were also able to benefit from glasnost and the general relaxation of controls over their everyday lives in the late 1980s. However, as with youth culture, changes in culture and private life have been taking place gradually since the 1960s. Some of these developments have been traced in articles in the collections edited by Brine (26), and Thompson and Sheldon (16) and, drawing extensively on recent Soviet sociology, in Shlapentokh's important recent study of Soviet public and private life (69). Another aspect of the interrelation of formal and informal spheres was explored in Christel Lane's pioneering study of ritual and symbolism in the lives of Soviet citizens (72). Lane's study also contributes to the understanding of political power by exploring the ways in which people participate in activities which sustain social control and elite interests in society.

As informal aspects of life in Soviet society have been accorded a higher profile, questions of popular attitudes, public opinion and how they are influenced have acquired a more central focus in sociological studies. While Zaslavskaya and other Soviet sociologists have been promoting an expanded and more sophisticated system of public opinion polling in the Soviet Union, some Western writers have turned their attention to the main processes and institutions through which public opinion is influenced. A pioneer in this field was Mickiewicz. After carrying out work in the early 1980s on public reception of the media and attitudes to it (78), she has more recently produced the first major study of Soviet television, analysing it as a medium of power and influence, but also stressing the complexity of its relation to the public and, thus, the 'split signals' it conveys (74).

Meanwhile, the relation between offical ideology and public opinion has been the subject of research by Shlapentokh (77), exploring the complex ways in which ideology can act both as a practical medium of communication and as a means of restricting knowledge in the interests of the powerful. A further important contribution has been made by Wedgwood Benn (73) in his examination of Soviet thinking about propaganda as a means of more overt persuasion of the public by those in power. In arguing that the effectiveness of Soviet propaganda has been limited by the lack of attention paid by the Soviet authorities to their audience and its reception of propaganda, Benn's work challenges conventional views about the character of elite influence over the Soviet public. Taken as a whole, the recent work in the areas of ideology, public attitudes and means of persuasion raises important questions about the way in which power and domination in Soviet society has been understood. It is to be hoped that they will inspire further research into the complex relations of power, ideology and political change in Soviet society.

Social Policy

Another 'growth area' in the study of Soviet society has been in the area of social problems and social policy, and given the development of Soviet interest in this area, as sociologists enter debates about the social consequences of the development of a market economy, interest seems likely to remain high. In the West during the 1980s, major studies have been published on poverty, its extent and character, by Mervyn Matthews (89); on the quality of life edited by Herlemann (86); and on problems of the disabled edited by McCagg and Siegelbaum (82). Lane has written one book and edited another on questions of labour, employment and Soviet policy towards them, while Ryan has produced a study of the Soviet health service (83). Problems of urban development and housing provision have been studied by Andrusz (79), Morton (80) and Bater (81). There have also been several works on aspects of educational policy and provision (see section on Education in the bibliography). Comparative issues have been explored in relation to social and economic rights in Eastern Europe (85), welfare policy and provision between the USA and the USSR (84), and generally between the Soviet Union and the West (90).

Finally, it should be noted that there are many aspects of Soviet society and culture that have received very little attention. Two in particular deserve mention here. First, there is little recent work on the sociology of the urban family. Two studies on aspects of marriage were published at the beginning of the 1980s (61, 62), there have been a few articles on urban families, for example in (80) and (16) and in several of the studies of Soviet women (see section on Women in Soviet Society), and there have been studies of rural families in Dragadze (60), and in chapters of Humphrey (55) and Bridger (41). However, a detailed up-to-date monograph on the urban family would be a useful addition to the literature. Secondly, apart from studies dealing with corruption (70, 71), there has been little recent research on the sociology of deviance in Soviet society. In view of all the changes in Soviet social and cultural life in recent years, current studies of these areas would be particularly valuable.

Overall, the literature on Soviet social and cultural issues is large, and has been growing. Its expansion has been the result of two main factors. First, the policy of glasnost in the Soviet Union has allowed much more information about Soviet society to become available through the Soviet media, and from sociological research. Secondly, there has been a notable revival of interest (and a slight improvement in research funding) in the West. If the growth of research on Soviet society is to be sustained, much will depend on whether these recent trends continue.

Bibliography

Soviet Sociologists and Perestroika

1   Zaslavskaya, T. (1990) *The Second Socialist Revolution: An Alternative Soviet Strategy.* London: I.B. Tauris

A wide-ranging discussion by the Soviet Union's leading sociologist, examining the social causes of the crisis of Soviet society in the early 1980s, the character of its social problems and her proposals for policies to deal with them.

2   Yanowitch, M. (1989) Editor. *New Directions in Soviet Social Thought.* New York: M.E. Sharpe

A selection of translations of work by Soviet sociologists who have contributed to the new thinking of recent years by examining the character of the social problems faced by the Soviet Union and discussing the reforms aimed at their solution. Topics dealt with include problems of industrial management, democratisation, social justice, property relations and questions of social psychology.

3   Yanowitch, M. (1989) Editor. *A Voice of Reform: Essays by Tat'yana Zaslavskaya.* New York: M.E. Sharpe

A selection of translated articles reflecting the range of Zaslavskaya's work. Among the themes discussed are the sociology of economic organisations, group interests in Soviet society, the sociology of work, and problems in achieving social justice.

4   Yanowitch, M. (1986) *The Social Structure of the USSR.* New York: M.E. Sharpe

A selections of translations by Soviet sociologists representing their work of the early 1980s. The main focus of the book is on questions of inequalities between social groups, social status and social mobility.

5   *Soviet Sociology.* New York: M.E. Sharpe

A bi-monthly journal of translations of Soviet sociological publications.

Introductory and General Books

6   Hosking, G. (1990) *The Awakening of the Soviet Union.* London: Heinemann

A 'contemporary history' of social developments under Gorbachev. Hosking portrays the Soviet Union as a totalitarian society in which independent social forces have begun to emerge. He focuses on the challenge to the old order posed by the emergence of unofficial political groups, and the resurgence of national and religious feelings. A lively and readable account.

7   Lane, D. (1990) *Soviet Society Under Perestroika.* Winchester, MA: Unwin Hyman

Lane offers an account of the main political and economic changes associated with perestroika along with an updated discussion of selected social institutions of Soviet society. Along with family, ethnic relations and stratification, there are also discussions of processes of social control through education, the mass media, and the organisation of welfare. Lane attempts to situate perestroika within longer term processes of social development since the death of Stalin.

8   Bialer, S. (1989) Editor. *Politics, Society and Nationality in Gorbachev's Russia.* Boulder, CO: Westview Press

A well-integrated set of essays on Soviet politics and society including useful discussions of the development of civil society and the emergence of ethnic problems up to mid-1988.

9   Hill, R. (1989) *The Soviet Union: Politics, Economy and Society.* London: Pinter

A general introduction to the Soviet Union, including one chapter on society, dealing mainly with questions of the group structure of society, stratification, education and the nationalities.

10   Rywkin, M. (1989) *Soviet Society Today.* New York: M.E. Sharpe

A very readable basic introduction to Soviet society with imaginative use of short excerpts from Soviet sources for illustration. The book covers a wide range of issues from the formal political system and social stratification to standards of living, lifestyles and culture.

11   Shtromas, A. and Kaplan, M. (1989) Editors. *The Soviet Union and the Challenge of the Future.* New York: Paragon House

A four-volume series of collected articles by leading Western experts, mainly written in the mid-1980s. The first three volumes contain articles relevant to the themes of Soviet society and culture, especially the second half of volume two which provides extensive discussions of the nature of the elite in Soviet society, and questions of deviance and dissent.

12   Connor, W. (1988) *Socialism's Dilemmas: State and Society in the Soviet Bloc.* New York: Columbia University Press

A collection which brings together several of Connor's essays from the 1970s and 1980s on Soviet politics and society, including his studies of dissent, changes in the Soviet working class, and Soviet social policy.

13   Cracraft, J. (1988) Editor. *The Soviet Union Today*, 2nd edn. Chicago: University of Chicago Press

A very useful introduction to a broad range of topics including Soviet society and culture. In the section on Soviet society there are chapters on class, ethnic relations, religion, women in society, law and social problems.

14   Potichnyj, P.J. (1988) Editor. *The Soviet Union: Party and Society.* Cambridge: Cambridge University Press

A collection of conference papers from the Third World Congress for Soviet and East European Studies in 1985. Along with papers on various aspects of politics, this volume includes discussions of society and social policy, social stratification, ethnic relations, poverty, abortion, and the operation of the social security system.

15   Sacks, M.P. and Pankhurst, J.G. (1988) Editors. *Understanding Soviet Society.* Winchester, MA: Allen and Unwin

A very useful student reader containing sociological discussion of a range of issues including social stratification, the relation between the Communist Party and wider society, aspects of everyday life and social problems. Originally intended as an updated version of the editors' earlier volume, *Contemporary Soviet Society* (1980), the final result went well beyond its predecessor in the range of topics covered, and in its attempt to integrate discussion of Soviet society into wider issues of comparative sociology.

16   Thompson, T.L. and Sheldon, R. (1988) Editors. *Soviet Society and Culture: Essays in Honour of Vera S. Dunham.* Boulder, CO: Westview Press

A collection of essays covering economic, social, ideological and literary themes reflecting the varied aspects of Dunham's career. The section on social themes includes essays on family, ethnicity, culture and social attitudes.

17 Friedberg, M. and Isham, H. (1987) Editors. *Soviet Society Under Gorbachev: Current Trends and the Prospects for Reform.* New York: M.E. Sharpe

A useful collection of essays providing commentary on social and political themes immediately prior to the main reforms of perestroika, including a chapter on the family, a topic relatively poorly represented in recent literature.

18 Medish, V. (1987) *The Soviet Union.* Englewood Cliffs, NJ: Prentice-Hall

A useful basic introduction to the Soviet Union covering a wide range of topics including social issues such as ethnic groups, social stratification, the education system, the mass media and social problems.

19 Millar, J.R. (1987) Editor. *Politics, Work and Daily Life in the USSR.* Cambridge: Cambridge University Press

Based on interview surveys of recent Soviet emigrants to the USA, this collection of articles discusses a wide range of aspects of social life in the Soviet Union, including political beliefs, demographic trends, attitudes to work, income, social status and ethnic relations. Although a sample of emigrés is not necessarily representative of the wider Soviet population, the book contains many insights on Soviet society, and covers some issues not usually covered in Soviet sociological surveys.

20 Veen, H. (1987) *From Brezhnev to Gorbachev: Domestic Affairs and Soviet Foreign Policy.* Leamington Spa: Berg

A wide-ranging collection of articles. The 'society' section covers questions of nationality, religion, the position of intellectuals in society, and ideology.

21 Jones, E. (1985) *Red Army and Society: A Sociology of the Soviet Military.* London: Allen and Unwin

This innovative study examines Soviet policy in relation to the military, army careers, the roles of officers, the military as an agent of socialisation, and the social and ethnic background of soldiers.

22 Lane, D. (1985) *Soviet Economy and Society.* Oxford: Blackwell

In its clarity and thoroughness, this was the best textbook on Soviet society before perestroika. It usefully linked social structure to economic organisation, and provided detailed discussion of a range of social institutions, including stratification, the family, ethnic relations, religion and education. Lane argued that Soviet society was based mainly on a consensus of values, while inequalities persisted as features of the typical division of labour and family relations of an industrial society.

23 Sonnenfeldt, H. (1985) Editor. *Soviet Politics in the 1980s.* Boulder, CO: Westview Press

A collection of articles on Soviet political trends in the early 1980s that also includes discussions of social issues such as demography, labour supply, alcohol abuse and the quality of life.

24 Kerblay, B. (1983) *Modern Soviet Society.* London: Methuen

A comprehensive textbook covering various aspects of Soviet society and culture in the context of the physical environment and population trends. There are chapters on urban and rural society, family, education, work, social class and national cultures.

25 Zaslavsky, V. (1982) *The Neo-Stalinist State: Class, Ethnicity and Consensus in Soviet Society.* New York: M.E. Sharpe

The author explores the processes through which Soviet society generates a certain degree of stability and consensus. He develops this theme by means of detailed discussions of political socialisation processes, patterns of inequality and social mobility, and ethnicity.

26 Brine, J. (1980) *Home, School and Leisure in the Soviet Union.* London: Allen and Unwin

A collection of articles on themes including housing, the position of women in society, socialisation, education, sport and leisure.

Theories

27 Furedi, F. (1986) *The Soviet Union Demystified.* London: Junius

Drawing on critical strands of Western Marxist theory, Furedi develops a critique of Soviet society arguing that, while not genuinely socialist, it has to be understood as a distinctive type of society, governed by its own social laws.

28 Zinoviev, A. (1985) *Homo Sovieticus.* London: Gollancz

An extended essay on the human condition in the Soviet Union from an exiled Soviet citizen. Zinoviev discusses the general characteristics as the product of Soviet political and social conditions. In general *homo sovieticus* is presented as conformist, amoral, and prone to 'doublethink'.

29 Littlejohn, G. (1984) *A Sociology of the Soviet Union.* London: Macmillan

By means of a critique of concepts drawn from classical Marxist and Weberian theories, Littlejohn attempts to develop definitions of 'class' and 'relations of production' appropriate to the conditions of Soviet society. He argues that, under the influence of the particular form of economy, state, welfare system, and consumption relations that have developed in the Soviet Union, class relations are very weakly defined.

30 Zinoviev, A. (1984) *The Reality of Communism.* London: Gollancz

A powerful essay combining a sustained critique of communism as a closed system, which is self-sustaining and impervious to change, with a descriptive account of the main features of Soviet society. The author was, for many years, a philosopher in the Soviet Union until he was expelled for his critical views in 1978.

31 Feher, F., Heller, A. and Markus, G. (1983) *Dictatorship Over Needs.* Oxford: Blackwell

An original and stimulating attempt to theorise the social character of Soviet-type societies in general by three Hungarian writers who were exiled to the West. In place of classical Marxist concepts of 'class' and 'relations of production', they offer an explanation of the dynamics, and the causes of the crisis of such societies in terms of the state's 'dictatorship' in imposing its own definition of the needs of its citizens.

Social Change

32 Lewin, M. (1988) *The Gorbachev Phenomenon.* London: Radius

Lewin traces the roots of the Gorbachev reforms back to underlying changes in the Soviet social structure that were taking place beneath the seemingly static political structure since the 1930s. The focus is on urbanisation, changes in the employment structure, and the growth of the intelligentsia and their role in creating a new civil society.

33 Jones, E. and Grupp, F.W. (1987) *Modernisation, Value Change and Fertility in the Soviet Union.* Cambridge: Cambridge University Press

Drawing on Soviet statistical and sociological data, this study attempts to test a series of hypotheses about the relation between modernisation, changes in social values, and fertility, and then to assess the impact of Soviet public policy on the changing relation between these variables.

34 Ryan, M. and Prentice, R. (1987) *Social Trends in the Soviet Union From 1950.* London: Macmillan

A collection of statistical tables drawn from Soviet official and academic sources with accompanying commentary from the authors. The information covers a range of demographic aspects, including population change, urbanisation, migration, child-bearing, marriage and family composition, ethnic composition, and two chapters on aspects of social service provision, covering education and health.

Inequality and Social Class

35 Moore, J. Barrington (1987) *Authority and Inequality Under Capitalism and Socialism: USA, USSR and China.* Oxford: Oxford University Press

A discourse on the problems of creating an egalitarian society based on comparisons of the extent and nature of inequalities between the study's selected societies.

36 Zemtsov, I. (1985) *The Private Life of the Soviet Elite.* New York: Crane Russak

A former Soviet sociologist examines the recruitment and socialisation of elite members, their standards and style of life, privileges, and involvement with crime and corruption.

37 Voslensky, M. (1984) *Nomenklatura: The Soviet Ruling Class.* New York: Doubleday

A study of the power and privileges of the ruling group in Soviet society, interpreted here as those holding top posts for which they have to be approved by special vetting procedures within the Communist Party.

38 Lane, D. (1982) *The End of Social Inequality? Class, Status and Power Under State Socialism.* London: Allen and Unwin

Like its predecessor study, *The End of Inequality?* (1971), this work makes thorough use of Soviet sociological research on various aspects of stratification in Soviet society, and integrates their findings into a discussion of different theoretical approaches. Lane argues that while social inequalities do not give rise to conflict relations between classes in Soviet society, inequality is nevertheless a necessary and permanent feature.

39 Matthews, M. (1978) *Privilege in the Soviet Union: A Study of Elite Life-Style Under Communism.* London: Allen and Unwin

A model study, now dated in its empirical detail, but still useful for the questions asked and approaches adopted. Despite the impossibility of precise measurement, the author establishes the evidence for 'institutionalised elitism' and the existence of a clear gap between elite privileges and the living conditions of the rest of the population.

Women in Soviet Society

40 Green, C. (1989) Editor. *Soviet Women.* Ontario: York University

A collection of articles offering a comprehensive and up-to-date coverage of different aspects of the position of women in Soviet society, including work, social conditions and political organisation.

41 Bridger, S. (1987) *Women in the Soviet Countryside: Women's Roles in Rural Development in the Soviet Union.* Cambridge: Cambridge University Press

This work examines women's experience of rural development in Soviet society, examining changes in their roles and statuses since the Revolution, and assessing the inequalities and problems they have faced in recent years. Separate chapters focus on employment, the family and rural culture.

42 Holland, B. (1985) *Soviet Sisterhood: British Feminists on Women in the USSR.* London: Fourth Estate

This collection of essays examines a wide range of issues concerning the position of women in Soviet society and the nature of gender-based inequalities. Topics include the position of rural women, Soviet women's magazines, problems of child-bearing and maternity care, and the relation between Soviet ideology and the actual situation of Soviet women.

43 Mamonova, T. (1984) Editor. *Women and Russia.* Oxford: Blackwell

A collection of essays by Soviet feminists covering a wide range of aspects of Soviet life and women's experiences of it, including work, family, relations with the state, deviance and socialisation.

44 Hansson, C. and Liden, K. (1983) *Moscow Women.* New York: Random House

A collection of interviews with Moscow women from different walks of life, combining to produce a revealing picture of Soviet society and attitudes to women.

45 Lapidus, G. (1982) Editor. *Women, Work and Family in the Soviet Union.* New York: M.E. Sharpe

A collection of translated articles by Soviet sociologists on women in Soviet society, with particular focus on work and family relations.

46 Lapidus, G. (1978) *Women in Soviet Society.* Berkeley, CA: University of California Press

Although now a little dated, this is still one of the best sociological studies of the position of women in Soviet society. It provides a detailed examination of the position of women in employment, education, politics and the family, and an analysis of the changes in women's social position as a consequence of Soviet ideology and policy.

Nationality and Ethnic Groups

47 Nahaylo, B. and Swoboda, V. (1990) *Soviet Disunion: A History of the Nationalities Problem in the USSR.* London: Hamish Hamilton

The first major work on the nationalities issue to appear since the emergence of nationalist independence movements at the end of the 1980s, this work offers a historical perspective on the development of the Soviet nationalities problem.

48 Kozlov, V. (1988) *The Peoples of the Soviet Union.* London: Hutchinson

A translation into English of a key text by a leading Soviet ethnographer, this work reviews historical, geographical, demographic and ethnographic aspects of the relative position of ethnic groups in Soviet society.

49 Motyl, A. (1987) *Will the Non-Russians Rebel?* Ithaca, NY: Cornell University Press

Focusing on the case of the Ukrainians, whom he sees as the nation most able successfully to rebel, the author examines both factors favouring the emergence of an autonomous national movement and those inhibiting it. He concludes that the Soviet state is likely to be too strong for any rebellion to be successful.

50 Benningsen, A. and Wimbush, S.E. (1986) *Muslims of the Soviet Empire: A Guide.* Bloomington, IN: Indiana University Press

The authors provide a detailed regional survey of Muslims in different parts of the Soviet Union with discussion of the various sects, religious institutions, demographic trends, and questions of ethnic and religious identity within the Soviet Muslim community.

51 Karklins, R. (1986) *Ethnic Relations in the USSR: The Perspective From Below.* London: Allen and Unwin

Drawing on Soviet sociological studies and her own interview survey of emigrés from the Soviet Union, the author examines popular attitudes and behaviour relating to ethnic questions. Going beyond questions of nationality politics this study focuses more on ethnicity in particular institutional settings such as marriage, schools and workplaces.

52 Connor, W. (1984) *The National Question in Marxist-Leninist Theory and Practice.* Princeton, NJ: Princeton University Press

A comparative study of various Communist Party-led societies including the Soviet Union, and examining the impact of ideologies and policies on national and ethnic issues.

53 Wixman, R. (1984) *The Peoples of the USSR: An Ethnographic Handbook.* New York: M.E. Sharpe

A comprehensive reference book providing details of the language, population, religion, and location of ethnic groups in Soviet society.

54 Akiner, S. (1983) *Islamic Peoples of the Soviet Union.* London: Kegan Paul International

A region by region survey of the wide range of Muslim ethnic groups in Soviet society, giving details of population, location, culture, language, and religion.

55 Humphrey, C. (1983) *Karl Marx Collective: Economy, Society and Religion in a Siberian Collective Farm.* Cambridge: Cambridge University Press

By means of her in-depth study of collective farms in the Buryat area of Siberia, based in part on her own field work, the author analyses a range of issues including the economic organisation and practices of collective farms, and questions of the ethnicity, family life and religion of the Buryat people.

Young People and Youth Culture

56 Bushnell, J. (1990) *Moscow Graffiti: Language and Subculture.* Winchester, MA: Unwin Hyman

A unique and fascinating account of the subcultures of various youth groups in Moscow, approached through a study of the graffiti they have produced on the walls of city buildings since the end of the 1970s.

57 Riordan, J. (1989) Editor. *Soviet Youth Culture.* London: Macmillan

After a useful first chapter which traces the historical background and current issues, the following articles in this collection provide detail on different aspects of Soviet youth culture. Topics include the role of the official youth movement, political socialisation, rural youth, rock music fans and teenage gangs.

58 Troitsky, A. (1988) *Back in the USSR: The True Story of Rock in Russia.* London: Faber

A lively account of the development of Soviet rock music from underground to mainstream youth culture. The book gives a good impression not only of developments in the music, but also of its relation with the political system and wider society.

59 Wilson, A. and Bachkatov, N. (1988) *Living With Glasnost: Youth and Society in a Changing Russia.* Harmondsworth: Penguin

In providing a readable account of the culture, lifestyle, attitudes and problems of Soviet youth, this study also succeeds in giving a clear impression of the problems faced by Soviet society more generally in undergoing reform.

Family, Kinship and Marriage

60   Dragadze, T. (1988) *Rural Families in Soviet Georgia: A Case Study in Ratcha Province*. London: Routledge

Based on her own field work the author examines the interrelations of kinship, culture and politics in rural Georgia.

61   Rueschmeyer, M. (1981) *Professional Work and Marriage: An East-West Comparison*. London: Macmillan

An comparative examination of the problems in combining marriage and a professional career in the USA, former East Germany and the Soviet Union.

62   Fisher, W. (1980) *The Soviet Marriage Market: Mate-Selection in Russia and the USSR*. New York: Praeger

Drawing on Soviet sociological studies, the author examines factors affecting trends in marriage, including age at marriage and choice of partner. Although surveys show there is general support for the idea that love should determine choice of marriage partners, the main finding is that economic factors strongly affect actual choices.

Education

63   Riordan, J. (1988) Editor. *Soviet Education: The Gifted and the Handicapped*. London: Routledge

This collection contains essays on the provision of different kinds of special education, on the one hand for academically gifted pupils and those with special sporting abilities, and on the other hand for deaf, blind, and other disabled pupils and those with learning difficulties.

64   Avis, G. (1987) Editor. *Soviet Higher and Vocational Education from Khrushchev to Gorbachev*. Bradford: Bradford Univeristy

A loosely connected set of essays on aspects of Soviet post-school education, political education, students' career aspirations, industry-education links and vocational training.

65   Dunstan, J. (1987) Editor. *Soviet Education Under Scrutiny*. Glasgow: Jordanhill College Publications

A collection of conference papers on different aspects of education including Soviet education theory, the school curriculum, and student lifestyles.

66   Tomiak, J. (1983) *Soviet Education in the 1980s*. London: Croom Helm

Includes essays on environmental, political, physical and vocational education, ethnicity and education, primary schooling, and access to higher education.

67   Matthews, M. (1982) *Education in the Soviet Union: Policies and Institutions Since Stalin*. London: Allen and Unwin

An historical overview of changes in Soviet education, with specific chapters on selected parts of the schools system, higher education, students and their problems, and support services for the education system.

Lifestyles, Culture and Deviance

68   Matthews, M. (1990) Editor. *Party, State, and Citizen in the Soviet Union: A Collection of Documents*. New York: M.E. Sharpe

This edited collection offers translations of key official documents setting out regulations governing everyday life and citizens' relations to the state.

69 Shlapentokh, V. (1989) *Public and Private Life of the Soviet People: Changing Values in Post-Stalin Russia*. Oxford: Oxford University Press

Making use of sociological surveys and illustrations from Soviet popular culture, the author traces the decline of the influence of official collectivist ideology and the growing importance of private life and values, distinct from the public sphere in Soviet society.

70 Clarke, M. (1983) Editor. *Corruption: Consequences and Control*. London: Pinter

An international comparative approach including four essays on Soviet themes, including the reporting of corruption, social attitudes to it, and its place in Georgian popular culture.

71 Simis, K. (1982) *Secrets of a Corrupt Society*. London: Dent

Insights into privileges, crime and corruption in Soviet society by a former Soviet lawyer, drawing on personal observations and Soviet written sources.

72 Lane, C. (1981) *The Rites of Rulers: Ritual in Industrial Society*. Cambridge: Cambridge University Press

This work examines the significance of ritual and symbolism in various aspects of the lives of Soviet citizens, such as in stages of the family life cycle, starting work, and joining the Communist Party. Ritual is seen as an important means of structuring power relations between the elite and the rest of society.

Public Opinion and the Media

73 Wedgwood Benn, D. (1989) *Persuasion and Soviet Politics*. Oxford: Blackwell

This work breaks new ground in examining Soviet writing and thinking about propaganda and the influencing of public opinion. The author points to the concentration in Soviet thinking on the organisation of propaganda at the expense of consideration of its reception and effectiveness.

74 Mickiewicz, E. (1988) *Split Signals: Television and Politics in the Soviet Union*. Oxford: Oxford University Press

Based on interviews and detailed monitoring of Soviet television programmes, this study explores both the influence of television on the public, and the use of it by those in power. The author argues that, because television's message is more complex than older forms of persuading the public, its growth has had significant repercussions for the conduct of Soviet politics.

75 Heller, M. (1988) *Cogs in the Soviet Wheel: The Formation of Soviet Man*. London: Collins

A powerful critique from an exiled Soviet writer, portraying the Soviet Union as a totalitarian society. The main theme of the book is an analysis of the processes of social control by which people are turned into 'cogs' in the wheel of society.

76 Roxburgh, A. (1987) *Pravda: Inside the Soviet News Machine*. London: Gollancz

An account of the paper's history, its organisation, and its place within the Soviet media, along with a selection of articles and letters to the editor reflecting a wide range of political and social themes.

77 Shlapentokh, V. (1986) *Soviet Public Opinion and Ideology: Mythology and Pragmatism in Interaction*. New York: Praeger

Drawing on Soviet sociological research, the author argues that Soviet ideology has both a pragmatic aspect that allows the elite to come to a realistic understanding of the world, and a mythological aspect by means of which the system is justified to the public.

78   Mickiewicz, E. (1981) *Media and the Russian Public.* New York: Praeger

The author makes good use of Soviet audience and readership surveys to examine such questions as the exposure of people in Russia to the media, and factors influencing their attitudes to it. Different chapters discuss television, newspapers, film and theatre, and specific audience groups such as rural dwellers and Party members.

Housing and Urban Development

79   Andrusz, G. (1984) *Housing and Urban Development in the USSR.* London: Macmillan

A very thorough discussion of urban development policies and the growth of different forms of housing tenure in the Soviet Union, combined with analysis of current problems in access to and the distribution of housing, spatial, technical and economic aspects of current policy.

80   Morton, H. and Stuart, R. (1984) Editors. *The Contemporary Soviet City.* London: Macmillan

An integrated set of essays examining the political, economic and social organisation of Soviet city life, with a focus on social problems and the provision of urban services.

81   Bater, J. (1980) *The Soviet City.* London: Edward Arnold

The author examines Soviet theory of urban development and assesses it in relation to actual conditions in Soviet cities, discussing the spatial organisation of cities, the politics of urban development, and the problems and patterns of life of Soviet city dwellers.

Social Problems and Policy

82   McCagg, W. and Siegelbaum, L. (1989) Editors. *The Disabled in the Soviet Union.* Pittsburgh, PA: University of Pittsburgh Press

A pioneering collection of articles on a very under-researched topic, this book combines discussion of the history of problems of the disabled and policy towards them up to the mid-1980s.

83   Ryan, M. (1989) *Doctors and the State in the Soviet Union.* London: Macmillan

This work examines changes in the organisation, standards, and principles of health care in the Soviet Union, covering its history, but focusing on current problems and attempts to restructure the health service.

84   Lapidus, G. and Swanson, G. (1988) Editors. *State and Welfare USA/USSR: Contemporary Policy and Practice.* Berkeley, CA: University of California Press

An edited collection of conference papers on comparisons between Soviet and American social welfare systems. Along with contributions on comparative and American themes, the collection includes discussion of the following aspects of welfare in the Soviet Union: access to higher education, the health service, pensions and social security for the elderly, and the access of citizens to welfare administrations.

85   Urban, G. R. (1988) Editor. *Social and Economic Rights in the Soviet Bloc.* Oxford: Transaction Books

This collection draws mainly on articles first appearing in the reports of Radio Liberty and Radio Free Europe. Along with some other extracts, including speeches of Soviet leaders, they provide a vivid snapshot of the situation concerning the rights of Soviet citizens, for example in relation to health care, housing, work, and political rights in the Soviet Union, and more widely in Eastern Europe.

86 Herlemann, H. (1987) Editor. *The Quality of Life in the Soviet Union*. Boulder, CO: Westview Press

The collected proceedings of a US/German conference which attempted to go beyond purely quantitative assessments of living standards and to examine the quality of life in Soviet society. The contributions range from discussions of how to assess quality of life, to specific explorations of various aspects of the question including consumer goods and services, medical care, education, housing, working conditions and rural life.

87 Lane, D. (1987) *Soviet Labour and the Ethic of Communism: Full Employment and the Labour Process in the USSR*. Brighton: Wheatsheaf

By means of an examination of the labour process and the nature of employment provision in Soviet society, the author sets out to investigate whether unemployment is a central feature of all industrial societies, and concludes that while there were strong institutional and group pressures favouring full employment, this may be changing as a result of current policies.

88 Lane, D. (1986) Editor. *Labour and Employment in the USSR*. Brighton: Harvester

This edited collection brings together the work of a variety of writers on different aspects of employment in the USSR. Topics include a discussion of the ideology of full employment, the history and economics of Soviet employment policy, and a variety of social issues and problems associated with the particular character of employment in Soviet conditions. A final section discusses Soviet employment law.

89 Matthews, M. (1986) *Poverty in the Soviet Union*. Cambridge: Cambridge University Press

An impressive analysis of the wide range of factors that affect Soviet standards of living and poverty in a society where money income, taken by itself, is usually an inadequate guide. Through a reinterpretation of Soviet data, Matthews attempts to measure the extent of poverty in Soviet society and provides an analysis of the social composition of the Soviet poor.

90 George, V. and Manning, N. (1980) *Socialism, Social Welfare and the Soviet Union*. London: Routledge

In the context of a discussion of the relation between Marxist ideas about welfare and the development of Soviet social policy, the authors offer a review of provision in the areas of social security, education, health and housing. They conclude that, in a number of ways, Soviet social services compare favourably with those in the West.

Personal Accounts of Soviet Social Life

91 Richards, S. (1990) *Epics of Everyday Life*. London: Viking

Through an account of her visits to the Soviet Union between 1988 and 1990, and the people she met there, Richards provides a vivid and perceptive account of social life and problems under perestroika.

92 Walker, M. (1986) *The Waking Giant: The Soviet Union Under Gorbachev*. London: Martin Joseph

This very readable account by the former '*Guardian*' correspondent in Moscow offers many insights into the changing social and political scene in the early years of Gorbachev's reforms.

93 Willis, D. (1985) *Klass: How Russians Really Live*. New York: St. Martin's Press

An extended essay on the theme of class and inequality and their pervasive effects on the ways of life of Soviet citizens. The author draws on his personal experiences and observations while working as a foreign correspondent in the Soviet Union.

CHAPTER FOUR

Government and Politics

Dr Stephen White
University of Glasgow

The literature on Soviet government and politics is as old as the Soviet political system itself, and the changes it has undergone have been hardly less remarkable. The earliest studies that still repay attention are probably those of Sidney and Beatrice Webb, whose *Soviet Communism: A New Civilisation?* (31) includes a solid if naïve treatment of the institutions of early Soviet government, and Julian Towster, whose *Political Power in the USSR 1917-1947* (84) still retains its value as an account of the operation of those institutions in the early post-war period. There were comparable studies of the formal aspects of Soviet government in several more general works of the inter-war period; and there were of course some accounts of a rather different character such as Samuel Harper's *Civic Training in Soviet Russia* (119), a work that brought together extensive firsthand experience and an interest in political attitudes and values that was remarkably in advance of its time. With some notable exceptions of this kind, however, the earliest studies of the Soviet political system shared a number of serious shortcomings: they concentrated almost exclusively upon the Soviet state rather than the Communist Party, they took official sources very largely at face value, and they were overwhelmingly concerned with formal structures rather than broader patterns of attitudes and behaviour.

The Totalitarian Orthodoxy

The modern period in the study of Soviet politics may be said to begin in the 1950s with the publication of the first edition of Carl Friedrich and Zbigniew Brzezinski's *Totalitarian Dictatorship and Autocracy* (27). Study of the Soviet Union, as of many other political systems, was powerfully influenced at this time by the experience of Nazi Germany: its ideology, its personalist leadership, and its apparent ability to mobilise an entire population through the use of modern methods of communication. Equally, the reproduction of a Soviet-type political system throughout Eastern Europe, and later in China, appeared to suggest that this was a distinct type of system with a distinctive set of identifying attributes. Writing in their first edition, Friedrich and Brzezinski argued that totalitarianism was a 'novel form of government' which was in turn a logical extension of some of the traits of modern industrial society. Friedrich had originally drafted a study along these lines in the late 1930s; but now, with the experience of Nazi Germany and Fascist Italy, he and his co-author were able to advance a series of more general propositions about a type of political system that had reached an advanced stage of development in these countries as well as in Soviet Russia.

The term 'totalitarian' had entered scholarly discourse (or at any rate the English language) as early as the 1920s, when it began to be used to describe a political system of the inclusive, corporativist kind that was already being constructed in Mussolini's Italy. As developed by Friedrich and Brzezinski in the 1950s and 1960s, however, the term became all but the only legitimate means of identifying a Soviet-type system. As compared with earlier work, totalitarian approaches did at least extend the scope of analysis beyond the formal institutions of state to education, the economy and social life, and they took account of the omnipresence of coercion and terror. For Friedrich and Brzezinski, indeed, terror was the single most important feature of a totalitarian political system, and the means by which it could most readily be distinguished from autocracy.

All totalitarian dictatorships, Friedrich and Brzezinski argued, shared a 'syndrome' of six essential and related features. The first was an official ideology, binding upon all members of the society. The second was a single mass party typically led by one man. The third was a system of terroristic police control; and fourth, fifth and sixth came near-complete state monopolies of the means of effective armed combat, mass communications, and economic management. Friedrich, writing later, added territorial expansion and administrative control of the courts. These features were held to constitute an identifiable cluster of characteristics, separating out the Soviet Union and its counterparts in Eastern Europe from the liberal democracies. Friedrich and Brzezinski were of course aware of the changes that were taking place in the Soviet Union in the 1950s and 1960s. They insisted, however, that the 20th Party Congress of 1956 had produced no 'fundamental change' in the Soviet political system and Friedrich, who revised the text for its second edition in 1965, continued to argue that the Soviet Union at that time manifested 'all the essential features' of the totalitarian model.

As late as the 1970s it was still being argued, for instance by Odom (114), that political systems of the Soviet type were better understood in totalitarian than in any other terms. Surprisingly, perhaps, totalitarianism became accepted usage in the USSR itself in the late 1980s, usually as a means of referring to the political system of the years before perestroika (and sometimes even after it). During the 1960s, however, reflecting the Khrushchevian thaw and parallel changes in Eastern Europe, totalitarian approaches came under increasingly severe attack. It was pointed out, for instance, that many of Friedrich and Brzezinski's six or eight points applied to other states as well, particularly in the developing world. Central control and direction of the economy, for instance, was a familiar feature in many of the countries of the post-colonial world, and so too was a single-party system. Government control over the means of effective armed combat, indeed, was a characteristic of virtually all states. Conversely, many of Friedrich and Brzezinski's list of characteristics seemed difficult to apply to the countries of post-Stalinist communism, not at least without a great deal of qualification. Friedrich and Brzezinski had spoken, for instance, of a 'massive and arbitrary' system of terror of a kind that no longer obtained in the Soviet Union and most of the countries in Eastern Europe; and they had suggested that control of the ruling party would at least 'normally' be in the hands of a single ruler, which was difficult to reconcile with the development of more oligarchical forms of party management.

For social scientists who were beginning to take their disciplinary specialisations more seriously in the 1960s there was a further shortcoming to the totalitarian model: it was 'static', in that it tended to give too little attention to development and change beyond a rather loosely conceptualised process of 'maturation'. This shortcoming was particularly important to scholars who were part of the 'behavioural revolution' in comparative politics and who were therefore concerned with more general relationships between socio-economic change and the polity. An influential statement of these very different concerns was Chalmers Johnson's collection *Change in Communist Systems* (23); there were also two readers that provided a focus for this change of emphasis, Frederick Fleron's (24) and Roger Kanet's *The Behavioral Revolution and Communist Studies* (22). Work of this kind was strongly influenced by 'modernisation' and related theories that were being applied at the same time to countries in the developing world. Like them, it was argued, Soviet-type systems would have to accommodate the pluralising pressures of social and economic change and would eventually have to develop the competitive, bargaining kind of political system that corresponded to their economic maturity.

From Totalitarianism to Modernisation

Modernisation theories took as their point of departure the work of the American sociologist Talcott Parsons and his work on 'evolutionary universals' ('Evolutionary Universals in Society', *American Sociological Review*, 1964). As a society emerged from the primitive level, Parsons argued, it would tend to evolve a system of social stratification based upon functional differentiation and achievement rather than kinship and ascription. A specialist political function would emerge which was independent of religious authority for its legitimation. An administrative bureaucracy and a market system would come into existence, and a secular and impersonal legal system which was a prerequisite for the remaining evolutionary universal, the 'democratic association with elective leadership and fully enfranchised membership'. Parsons argued more specifically that what he called 'communist totalitarian' states would prove incapable of competing with liberal-democratic regimes in the long run, and that they would be compelled to make adjustments in the direction of electoral democracy and a plural party system if they were not to regress into less advanced forms of social organisation. This, Parsons concluded, could only mean that 'eventually the single monolithic party must relinquish its monopoly of such organisation'.

The theory of political modernisation in relation to the Soviet Union and its associated states was developed more fully by a number of other writers, many of whom explicitly acknowledged their debt to Parsons. Like Parsons, modernisation theorists assumed that communist systems – variously conceptualised as 'mobilising' or 'modernising regimes' – would manifest the same linkages between socio-economic change and the polity as did political systems elsewhere. Robert Dahl summed up these linkages in his *Polyarchy* (Yale University Press, 1971) as follows: a high socio-economic level and competitive politics were associated; not only competitive politics but political pluralism were significantly associated with high levels of socio-economic development; and the higher the socio-economic level the more competitive the political system, and vice versa. Because of its inherent requirements, Dahl suggested, an advanced economy and its supporting social structures automatically distributed political skills and resources to a wide variety of individuals, groups and organisations. The monopoly of political power enjoyed by the Soviet and other communist leaderships, Dahl concluded, was therefore likely to be undermined by the processes of social and economic development that they themselves had sponsored. The change from Stalinist hegemony to the post-Stalin system was a 'profound step towards liberalisation'; further moves in this direction were inescapable as a centrally dominated political system became increasingly difficult to reconcile with the pluralistic pressures of a modern economy and society.

Most writers in the political modernisation school pointed out that there need be no one-to-one correspondence between socio-economic and political change; external influences and cultural traditions could modify the relationship substantially. The central thesis, that the USSR must eventually acquire the 'modern' political system that corresponded to its economic maturity, nonetheless found support across a very wide spectrum. Roy Medvedev (20), for instance, spoke of some kind of democratisation of the USSR as an 'inevitable tendency'. Michel Tatu (69) argued that a move towards a more liberal parliamentary regime 'cannot fail to occur' because it corresponded to the 'overall evolution of Soviet society'. Gabriel Almond, in perhaps the most far-reaching of such prognostications, spoke of the 'pluralistic pressures of a modern economy and society' and of a 'secular trend in the direction of decentralisation and pluralism'. Already Soviet successes in science, education, economic productivity and national security had produced some decentralisation of the political process. 'I fail to see how these decentralising, pluralistic tendencies can be reversed, or how their spread can be prevented', Almond concluded in his *Political Development* (Little, Brown, 1970).

Empirical investigations, in fact, found little direct association between industrial development and individual 'modernity' (see the account in White, (17)). Some studies, in fact, found that differences in values might actually increase, rather than diminish, with higher levels of industrialism. Nations, it was found, 'need not be universalistic to develop a modern industrial economy, and they do not necessarily become more universalistic in the process of becoming industrialised'. Studies of communist political systems more particularly found no clear evidence of increasingly competitive and bargaining politics as economic development advanced. Indeed it seemed clear more generally that competitive politics and socio-economic 'modernity' might be at best indirectly, rather than directly, related. Several of the East European states, up to the late 1980s, showed little sign of pluralism despite their relatively advanced levels of development; while the United States, in the nineteenth century, and India, in the twentieth, showed that a relatively low level of economic development could nonetheless be associated with an open and competitive political system. The underlying dichotomy between 'modernity' and 'tradition' itself came increasingly to be seen as a simplistic and overstated one.

Back to the State

With the benefit of hindsight, and particularly after the overthrow of a series of communist governments in Eastern Europe in 1989, some kind of association between political change and (for example) higher levels of urbanisation and education became somewhat more plausible. The developments of 1989, however, were more directly a response to the failure of communist economies to deliver the kind of performance that had come to be expected of them, and developments took different forms in the East European countries as they were influenced by cultural and historical factors that were indigenous to each of them. An emphasis upon 'political modernisation' or 'convergence', in the late 1960s, certainly seemed premature as Khrushchevite reform hardened into Brezhnevite immobilism and, as reformers in Eastern Europe were crushed by force of arms and then placed within the ambit of the 'Brezhnev doctrine', it began to appear misconceived as well. An emphasis on process and change still seemed appropriate; but there was less certainty, after the 1960s, that economic development of itself must necessarily lead in a single, liberal-democratic direction.

The reassertion of state power that had been apparent in the crushing of reform and dissent in Eastern Europe and in the USSR itself in fact led many scholars in the 1970s and 1980s to return to the study of the state itself, and particularly to its full-time central apparatus. Those who took this approach argued in terms of 'bureaucratic politics'; their central concern was the central party-state apparatus and the struggles for influence that took place within its ambit. The system as a whole was conceived as a 'mono-hierarchical' one, with the top leadership standing in relation to other political actors much as the board of a large Western corporation stood in relation to their management and staff. Alfred Meyer, in one of the most influential early statements of this approach, suggested that the Soviet political system was best conceived as a 'giant bureaucracy, something like a modern corporation extended over the entire society' (30, 28). Writers like T.H. Rigby focused upon the 'crypto-politics' that took place within a system of this kind, with ministries and other institutions lobbying for investment funds in a manner not very different from large-scale governments and public corporations in the West (116, 1). Jerry F. Hough and Darrell Hammer (67, 68) were prepared to use terms such as 'bureaucratic' or 'institutional pluralism' to describe these relationships. By the late 1970s writers such as Valerie Bunce (15) were arguing for a 'corporatist' approach to the same phenomena.

An emphasis upon the central bureaucracy was also a characteristic of critical Marxist approaches, which became more influential during the 1960s. Work of this kind took its inspiration from Leon Trotsky, particularly from his book *The Revolution Betrayed* (32). In this work Trotsky argued that the USSR was still a socialist society because it was one in which the means of production had been taken into public ownership. The productive resources of the society, however, were not being used for the benefit of all its members because the bureaucracy, the 'sole privileged and commanding stratum in Soviet society', had taken control over the state machinery and was beginning to use that control to further its own selfish interests. The means of production belonged to the state; the state, however, 'belonged' to the bureaucracy, who had 'expropriated the proletariat politically'. If the bureaucracy succeeded in making their position a more permanent and legally-based one, particularly through the creation of special forms of private property, the gains of the October Revolution would eventually be liquidated. The Revolution, however, had been betrayed but not yet overthrown, and it could still be redeemed by a 'supplementary revolution' in which the working class seized political power back from the bureaucracy.

Approaches of this kind, which concentrate more upon social relations than political forms, are exemplified in several studies of the late 1980s. Ernest Mandel's *Beyond Perestroika* (4), for instance, applied an orthodox Trotskyist analysis to Soviet foreign and domestic policy; Furedi (9), in a work that stood outside the mainstream tradition, sought to demonstrate the 'laws of motion' of a social formation of the Soviet type. Several journals, particularly *Critique* (Glasgow) and *Labour Focus on Eastern Europe* (London), reflected similar concerns; so too did the writings of the Moscow-based scholar and political activist Boris Kagarlitsky (3,5,46). There were still considerable problems in employing Marxist terminology to a society of the Soviet type: it was often difficult to define the 'bureaucracy' precisely, and it was far from clear how it reproduced itself in the absence of the kind of guaranteed social position provided by private property. Nor were material inequalities, in themselves, evidence of exploitation in a Marxist sense. For some writers in this tradition, indeed, Soviet-type societies were best conceptualised in their own, quite specific terms. In such a 'dictatorship over needs', political power conferred economic advantage, not vice versa, and it was forms of political control rather than economic ownership that must accordingly be central to any adequate analysis (13).

The Study of Soviet Politics in the 1980s and 1990s

The academic literature on Soviet politics of the late 1980s had a number of distinctive strengths. There were studies of the longer-term processes of change that gave meaning to the Soviet experience: Robert Tucker pioneered such a 'political cultural' approach (8). White (17) is still the fullest available study on the USSR specifically; and Brown (10) provides the best critical discussion. Cohen (11) offers an insightful discussion of the Soviet political experience as a whole; Medvedev (61), Schmidt-Hauer (62), Hough (56), Eklof (52), Sakwa (49) and White (50) provide detailed accounts of Gorbachev's own career and of his general secretaryship to date. Changes in official Soviet doctrine are considered in Scanlan (43), White and Pravda (37) and Woodby and Evans (34). The wider question of the relationship between Gorbachev's reforms and the socialist project is the subject of Kagarlitsky (3), Mandel (4) and Davies (33). The changes that took place in the Soviet state system in the late 1980s are the subject of Urban's *More Power to the Soviets* (72).

Political participation, particularly through the local Soviets, is the theme of Friedgut (111) and of Hahn (102). Centre-local relations, making use in many cases of budgetary data, are the subject of Bahry (75), Bunce

(107) and Ross (76). The CPSU itself is considered in Hill and Frank (87) and its Rules and Programme more specifically in Gill (86) and White (85). Several studies of the late 1980s have considered political communication and the media, among them Wedgwood Benn (96), Mickiewicz (104) and Remington (36). Shlapentokh (100) considers the wider question of changing patterns of values over the post-Stalin period. Studies of policy-making are considered elsewhere in this volume, according to their context; but Skilling and Griffiths' (115) seminal contribution to the question of group influence on policy should be noted, together with Lowenhardt's (109) review of the evidence, and Solomon's (82) discussion of the process of law reform. The legal system itself is fully and authoritatively covered in Butler's *Soviet Law* (73); an institution of particular importance in this connection, the KGB, is the subject of Knight (74). Yeltsin (95), however misleading, provides the first extended study of Soviet decision-making at the highest levels written by one of its participants; it enjoyed a ready sale in the USSR as well as outside it.

Entering the 1990s, it appeared likely that this diversity of approaches would continue; equally, that the impact of the Gorbachev reforms would allow the study of Soviet politics to move much closer to mainstream disciplinary concerns. One reason was that a whole range of new sources became available in the late 1980s. There was much more information about the Communist Party itself, for instance, in the new Central Committee journal *Izvestiia Tsentral'nogo Komiteta KPSS*, including data on the operation of the Politburo and Secretariat, membership statistics, analyses of the flow of communications to the Party from all parts of the country, and archival publications such as Khrushchev's secret speech (delivered in 1956 but not officially published in the USSR until 1989). A much wider range of local papers became available for foreign purchase, including (as from the beginning of 1990) more than 200 regional-level publications. A substantial unofficial press developed, although it was still difficult to gain access to it in the West. And archival access became much easier, for Western as well as for Soviet investigators; by the beginning of the 1990s even access to party archives had become possible in some circumstances.

Together with a wider range of sources, a broader range of investigative techniques became available. Survey research, for instance, developed considerably in the USSR itself in the late 1980s with the establishment of the All-Union Institute for the Study of Public Opinion, and by the late 1980s Western scholars were able to conduct their own inquiries of this kind or (more commonly) take part in the planning and execution of joint Soviet-Western investigations. Electoral studies, for so long a staple of political science in the West, began to have some meaning with the liberalisation of the election laws in late 1988, and the emergence of (by 1990) about 20 nationally organised political parties and about 100 more in the republics. Biographical work, and in particular the preparation and analysis of large-scale data sets, became more feasible with the publication of full records of Central Committee members including (for the first time) the family circumstances of the political leadership. It became easier to conduct interviews in the USSR itself, even of members or former members of the Politburo. Legislative analysis of a kind familiar to students of the US Congress became possible with the introduction of roll-call voting in the Congress of People's Deputies and the new-style Supreme Soviet. The work of representative institutions, even of the Central Committee, could be followed on television and radio, and full protocols were made available. Public information of many other kinds improved considerably, enriching the potential for policy analysis on a single-nation or comparative basis.

What appeared unlikely to prosper, in the 1990s and thereafter, was work of the Kremlinological character that had flourished in earlier decades. There were many ways in which Soviet politics, in effect, became less Soviet as a result of perestroika. Studies of ideology and policy-making, for instance, required at least some reconsideration at a time when orthodox Marxist teachings were being increasingly obscured by 'all-human values'. The CPSU remained a Leninist party in its inspiration, but the operational principles of Leninism – such as democratic centralism – were reinterpreted and substantially modified (following the unsuccessful coup of August 1991 the Party was itself suspended and its future in any form became uncertain). State institutions began to assert their independent authority (in some cases, they declared in favour of full independence); and bodies like the trade unions lost their status as 'transmission belts' – indeed, by the end of the 1980s, strikes had become widespread and an unofficial labour movement was well-established. The mass media, supported by a new press law of 1990, were affected by commercial and other pressures at least as much as by party control, and even the churches began to rediscover their traditional role as articulators of eternal values. In fact, by the early 1990s, the greatest difficulty in the study of Soviet politics was hardly one of sources, methods or access: it was simply that the pace of change was so rapid and its scope so far-reaching that almost all the work that was being produced was overtaken by events before it had appeared.

The list that follows reflects both the achievements and the shortcomings of the study of Soviet politics up to the end of 1990. Necessarily a personal choice and one that is limited in scope, it does, I hope, nonetheless incorporate a wide range of what would be agreed to have been the most important and enduring contributions to the subject up to that date. It is limited almost entirely to books, and to material in the English language; this material is then arranged, as in almost all the other chapters of this Guide, by sub-topic, by year of publication, and then alphabetically within the same year. The following sub-headings have been employed:

Approaches and Interpretations (a relatively large section); Ideology; From Stalin to Gorbachev (another large section, including some recent texts); State and Law; The Communist Party; and The Political Process. The serious student of Soviet politics will obviously find it necessary to consult a wide range of journal literature in addition to the sources suggested in this list. Those that were publishing relevant articles in the 1980s and 1990s include *Soviet Studies*, the *Journal of Communist Studies*, *Soviet Union*, *Problems of Communism* and *Studies in Comparative Communism*; developments in the USSR itself could be followed through the *Current Digest of the Soviet Press* and Radio Liberty's *Report on the USSR*.

Bibliography

Approaches and Interpretations

1   Rigby, T.H. (1990) *The Changing Soviet System: Mono-Organizational Socialism from its Origins to Gorbachev's Restructuring*. Aldershot, Hants: Edward Elgar

Reflections, for the most part previously published, on the 'origins, nature and evolution of the Soviet socio-political order'.

2   Gerner, Kristian and Hedlund, Stefan (1989) *Ideology and Rationality in the Soviet Model: A Legacy for Gorbachev*. London: Routledge

This study 'casts doubt on the likelihood of new policies defeating decades of Bolshevik and social indoctrination'.

3   Kagarlitsky, Boris (1989) *Dialectic of Change*. London: Verso

A study, from the perspective of a democratic socialist, of the 'interplay between reform and revolution in Western and Eastern Europe in the twentieth century'.

4   Mandel, Ernest (1989) *Beyond Perestroika: The Future of Gorbachev's USSR*. London: Verso

A Trotskyist analysis of Gorbachev's foreign and domestic policies.

5   Kagarlitsky, Boris (1988) *The Thinking Reed: Intellectuals and the Soviet State*. London: Verso

A 'panoramic account of political culture in the Soviet Union by one of the leading voices of unofficial radical socialism'.

6   Lewin, Moshe (1988) *The Gorbachev Phenomenon*. Berkeley, CA: University of California Press

A sociological treatment of the emergence of the reform movement.

7   Churchward, Lloyd G. (1987) *Soviet Socialism: Social and Political Essays*. London: Routledge

A collection of interconnected papers on social structure, Stalinism and democracy.

8   Tucker, Robert C. (1987) *Political Culture and Leadership in Soviet Russia: from Lenin to Gorbachev*. Brighton: Harvester

Seven essays on political culture, Stalinism and 'Gorbachev's fight for Soviet reform'.

9   Furedi, Frank (1986) *The Soviet Union Demystified: A Materialist Analysis*. London: Junius

An attempt to examine the 'movement of Soviet society from a Marxist point of view'.

10 Brown, Archie (1985) Editor. *Political Culture and Communist Studies.* London: Macmillan

A series of studies dealing with the Soviet Union, Czechoslovakia and more general issues of analysis.

11 Cohen, Stephen F. (1985) *Rethinking the Soviet Experience.* New York: Oxford University Press

Reflective essays on (among others) the 'Stalin question since Stalin' and the 'friends and foes of reform' by liberal American Sovietologist.

12 Harding, Neil (1984) Editor. *The State in Socialist Society.* London: Macmillan

A helpful collection of essays on Soviet state theory and practice, with some account of experience in other communist-ruled systems.

13 Feher, Ferenc, Heller, Agnes and Markus, Gyorgy (1983) *Dictatorship over Needs: An Analysis of Soviet Societies.* Oxford: Blackwell

A post-Marxist analysis of the social nature of the USSR and comparable societies.

14 Solomon, Susan G. (1983) Editor. *Pluralism in the Soviet Union.* London: Macmillan

A series of essays, mostly of a conceptual character, by friends and colleagues of H. Gordon Skilling; especially useful for its discussion of 'corporatism'.

15 Bunce, Valerie and Echols, John M. (1980) Soviet politics in the Brezhnev era: 'Pluralism' or 'Corporatism'? In Donald R. Kelley, Editor, *Soviet Politics in the Brezhnev Era.* New York: Praeger

An attempt to apply corporatist theory to Soviet politics.

16 Hill, Ronald J. (1980) *Soviet Politics, Political Science and Reform.* Oxford: Martin Robertson

An analysis of the discussions on political reform that took place in the Brezhnev era, many of which have come to fruition in more recent times.

17 White, Stephen (1979) *Political Culture and Soviet Politics.* London: Macmillan

The fullest available study of its kind, based upon Soviet sociological and other sources.

18 Brzezinski, Zbigniew K. and Huntington, Samuel N. (1977) *Political Power USA/USSR.* Harmondsworth: Penguin

Originally published in 1964, this remains a provocative exercise in comparative politics.

19 Hough, Jerry F. (1977) *The Soviet Union and Social Science Theory.* Cambridge, MA: Harvard University Press

A collection of reprinted essays on the 'reconceptualisation of the Soviet system' and its 'implications for social science theory'.

20 Medvedev, Roy (1975) *On Socialist Democracy.* London: Macmillan

A reformist treatise of the Brezhnev period by the political commentator and historian of Stalinism.

21 Brown, A.H. (1974) *Soviet Politics and Political Science.* London: Macmillan

A thoughtful and still useful discussion of the applicability of political science concepts to the Soviet system.

22 Kanet, Roger (1971) Editor. *The Behavioral Revolution and Communist Studies.* New York: Free Press

A collection of some of the earlier attempts to apply modern social science techniques to Soviet-type systems; invites comparison with Fleron (24).

23 Johnson, Chalmers (1970) Editor. *Change in Communist Systems.* Stanford, CA: Stanford University Press

An influential collection of studies devoted to the 'change to change' in the analysis of Soviet-type systems.

24 Fleron, Frederick (1969) Editor. *Communist Studies and the Social Sciences.* Chicago: Rand McNallly

A collection of some of the earliest attempts to apply social science methodology to Soviet-type systems.

25 Arendt, Hannah (1967) *The Origins of Totalitarianism*, 3rd edn. London: Allen and Unwin

An influential study, first published in 1951. The third edition notes that the Soviet Union can 'no longer be called totalitarian in the strict sense of the term'.

26 Deutscher, Isaac (1967) *The Unfinished Revolution: Russia 1917-1967.* London: Oxford University Press

Originally a series of lectures, this remains a compelling analysis of the Soviet system by the Polish-born biographer of Trotsky.

27 Friedrich, Carl J. and Brzezinski, Zbigniew K. (1965) *Totalitarian Dictatorship and Autocracy*, 2nd edn. Cambridge, MA: Harvard University Press

The classic study of its subject; first published in 1956.

28 Meyer, Alfred G. (1965) *The Soviet Political System: An Interpretation.* New York: Random House

An extended account of the Soviet system as a 'bureaucracy writ large'.

29 Moore, Barrington Jr. (1965) *Soviet Politics: The Dilemma of Power.* New York: Harper

First published in 1950, this remains a provocative study of the 'role of ideas in social change'.

30 Meyer, Alfred G. (1961) USSR incorporated. *Slavic Review*, vol. 20, no. 3, October, 369-76.

An early version of Meyer's thesis that the Soviet system is best conceived as a large-scale modern bureaucracy.

31 Webb, Sidney and Beatrice (1944) *Soviet Communism: A New Civilisation?* 3rd edn. London: Longman

The authors intended to provide an 'objective view of the whole social order of the USSR as it exists today'; still of some value on social arrangements in the 1930s. First published in 1935; 2nd edn. 1937.

32 Trotsky, Leon (1937) *The Revolution Betrayed.* London: Faber and Faber

The classic study of Stalinism conceived as a bureaucratic counter-revolution.

Ideology and Theology

33 Davies, R.W. (1990) Gorbachev's socialism in historical perspective. *New Left Review*, no. 179, January-February, 5-27.

An analysis of Gorbachev's reforms in the context of socialist theory.

34 Woodby, Sylvia and Evans, Alfred B. (1990) Editors. *Restructuring Soviet Ideology: Gorbachev's New Thinking.* Boulder, CO: Westview Press

A survey of current developments in Soviet official thinking, with some emphasis on foreign relations.

35   Bloomfield, Jon (1989) Editor. *The Soviet Revolution: Gorbachev and the Remaking of Socialism*. London: Lawrence and Wishart

A collection of articles by academics and activists from a broadly sympathetic perspective.

36   Remington, Thomas F. (1988) *The Truth of Authority: Ideology and Communication in the Soviet Union*. Pittsburgh, PA: University of Pittsburgh Press

A study of the management of political communications in the USSR, concentrating upon oral political propaganda and the mass media.

37   White, Stephen and Pravda, Alex (1988) Editors. *Ideology and Soviet Politics*. London: Macmillan

A collection of papers focusing on doctrinal change in general and more policy-specific terms.

38   Gorbachev, Mikhail S. (1987a) *Perestroika: New Thinking for Our Country and the World*. London: Collins

The Soviet leader's celebrated bestseller and the fullest available exposition of his own views about the process of reform he has initiated.

39   Gorbachev, Mikhail S. (1987b) *Selected Speeches and Articles*, 2nd expanded edition. Moscow: Progress

The fullest available collection in authoritative Soviet translation; covers the period April 1985 to October 1987.

40   Gorbachev, Mikhail S. (1987c) *Socialism, Peace and Democracy. Speeches, Writings and Reports*. London; Atlantic Highlands, NJ: Zwan

Speeches and other statements, often in excerpted form, covering the period from 1984 to 1987.

41   Gorbachev, Mikhail S. (1987d) *Speeches and Writings, Volume 2*. Oxford: Pergamon

Covers the period from June 1986 to May 1987; for Volume 1 see Gorbachev (42)

42   Gorbachev, Mikhail S. (1986) *Speeches and Writings*. Oxford: Pergamon

This is in effect volume 1 of a two-volume set, covering the period from 1984 to the 27th Party Congress; for Volume 2, see Gorbachev (41) above.

43   Scanlan, James P. (1985) *Marxism in the USSR: A Critical Survey of Current Soviet Thought*. Ithaca, NY: Cornell University Press

A philosopher's account of official Soviet thought in the pre-perestroika period.

44   Moore, Barrington Jr. (1965) *Soviet Politics: The Dilemma of Power*. New York: Harper

First published in 1950, this remains a provocative study of the 'role of ideas in social change'.

From Stalin To Gorbachov

45   Hosking, Geoffrey (1990) *The Awakening of the Soviet Union*. London: Heinemann

A well-judged overview of the Soviet Union at the end of the 1980s, based on the 1988 BBC Reith Lectures.

46   Kagarlitsky, Boris (1990) *The Year the Walls Came Down. 1989: A Soviet Chronicle*. London: Verso

Part diary, part analysis, this is an unusual study of the electoral and other changes that took place in the USSR in 1989 by a democratic socialist who is also a prominent member of the Moscow Popular Front.

47 Lane, David (1990) *Soviet Society under Perestroika*. London: Unwin Hyman

A sociological treatment of a changing Soviet Union with some discussion of political processes.

48 McCauley, Martin (1990) Editor. *Gorbachev and Perestroika*. London: Macmillan

A series of essays on political and other developments.

49 Sakwa, Richard (1990) *Gorbachev and his Reforms 1985-1990*. Hemel Hempstead: Philip Allan

A substantial and detailed discussion of the Gorbachev reforms.

50 White, Stephen (1990) *Gorbachev in Power*. Cambridge: Cambridge University Press

A detailed and comprehensive analysis of the first five years of the Gorbachev general secretaryship.

51 White, Stephen, Pravda, Alec and Gitelman, Zvi (1990) Editors. *Developments in Soviet Politics*. London: Macmillan

An up-to-date survey covering political institutions, policy formation and critical perspectives.

52 Eklof, Ben (1989) *Soviet Briefing: Gorbachev and the Reform Period*. Boulder, CO: Westview Press

An overview of the Gorbachev reforms.

53 Joyce, Walter, Ticktin, Hillel and White, Stephen (1989) Editors. *Gorbachev and Gorbachevism*. London: Cass

Originally a special issue of the *Journal of Communist Studies*, this collection deals with developments in cultural life, the economy, government and foreign relations with particular emphasis upon the period from January 1987 to the 19th Party Conference of 1988.

54 Sakwa, Richard (1989) *Soviet Politics: An Introduction*. London: Routledge

A comprehensive, historically oriented text.

55 Doder, Dusko (1988) *Shadows and Whispers. Power Politics Inside the Kremlin from Brezhnev to Gorbachev*. Baltimore, MD: Penguin

An informed study of Kremlin politics by a *Washington Post* journalist. First published in 1986 (New York: Random House), this edition contains additional material.

56 Hough, Jerry F. (1988) *Russia and the West: Gorbachev and the Politics of Reform*. New York: Simon and Schuster

An overview of political change in the Gorbachev era and its implications for the West.

57 McCauley, Martin (1987) Editor. *The Soviet Union under Gorbachev*. London: Macmillan

A collection of essays on political and other developments.

58 Bialer, Seweryn (1986) *The Soviet Paradox: External Expansion, Internal Decline*. London: Tauris

Reflections on the Soviet Union in the early Gorbachev period by a well-connected American scholar.

59 Colton, Timothy (1986) *The Dilemma of Reform in the Soviet Union*, revised edn. New York: Council on Foreign Relations

A slim but elegant review based upon the deliberations of a high-level research seminar; originally published in 1984.

60   Current Digest of the Soviet Press (1986) *Current Soviet Policies IX: The Documentary Record of the 27th Congress of the CPSU.* Columbus, OH: CDSP

A full though incomplete record of the proceedings, conveniently indexed. *Current Soviet Policies* was first published in 1953, with the records of the 19th Party Congress; volume X on the 19th Party Conference appeared in 1988, and a volume on the 28th Congress is in preparation.

61   Medvedev, Zhores (1986) *Gorbachev.* Oxford: Blackwell

The best biographical study, covering both the general secretary's early years and the beginning of his period of rule. Revised paperback editions appeared in 1987 and 1988.

62   Schmidt-Hauer, Christian (1986) *Gorbachev: The Path to Power.* London: Tauris

One of the first biographies of the new general secretary by a West German journalist; gives some attention also to Raisa Gorbachev and her academic training.

63   Medvedev, Zhores (1983) *Andropov.* Oxford: Blackwell

The best study of its kind; the paperback edition (1984) contains additional material.

64   Breslauer, George (1982) *Khrushchev and Brezhnev as Leaders: Building Authority in Soviet Politics.* London: Allen and Unwin

A political analysis of successive general secretaryships.

65   Brown, Archie and Kaser, Michael (1982) Editors. *Soviet Policy for the 1980s.* London: Macmillan

A series of chapters on economic and social policy, with contributions on the CPSU and leadership succession.

66   Bialer, Seweryn (1980) *Stalin's Successors.* New York: Cambridge University Press

A study of 'leadership, stability and change in the Soviet Union' by a senior American scholar.

67   Hough, Jerry F. and Fainsod, Merle (1979) *How the Soviet Union is Governed.* Cambridge, MA: Harvard University Press

A massive and somewhat controversial study of the political process in the later Brezhnev years, with a substantial historical introduction.

68   Hammer, Darrell P. (1974) *USSR: The Politics of Oligarchy.* Hinsdale, OH: Dryden Press

A solid text; a third edition appeared in 1990 (Boulder, CO: Westview Press).

69   Tatu, Michel (1969) *Power in the Kremlin.* London: Collins

A Kremlinological analysis of the early and middle 1960s by the well-informed *Le Monde* journalist.

70   Linden, Carl (1966) *Khrushchev and the Soviet Leadership 1957-1964.* Baltimore, MD: Johns Hopkins University Press

Still a useful study; a new edition (1990) contains an epilogue on Gorbachev.

71   Conquest, Robert (1961) *Power and Policy in the USSR.* New York: Macmillan

An analysis of changing patterns of Kremlin politics.

State and Law

72   Urban, Michael E. (1990) *More Power to the Soviets.* Aldershot, Hants: Edward Elgar

A study of the reform of Soviet state institutions in the late 1980s.

73   Butler, William E. (1988) *Soviet Law,* 2nd edn. London: Butterworths

A comprehensive and authoritative text.

74   Knight, Amy (1988) *The KGB: Police and Politics in the Soviet Union.* Boston: Unwin Hyman

The fullest available study of its subject; the paperback edition (1990) contains a new epilogue.

75   Bahry, Donna (1987) *Outside Moscow: Power, Politics and Budgetary Policy in the Soviet Republics.* New York: Columbia University Press

A close study of the fiscal relationship between the central government and the republics.

76   Ross, Cameron (1987) *Local Government in the Soviet Union.* London: Croom Helm

A solid study, with some emphasis on budgetary matters.

77   van Goudoever, Albert P. (1986) *The Limits of DeStalinization in the Soviet Union.* London: Croom Helm

A detailed study of political rehabilitations from the immediate post-Stalin period to about 1980.

78   Lampert, Nicholas (1985) *Whistleblowing in the Soviet Union: Complaints and Abuses under State Socialism.* London: Macmillan

A study of 'feedback' from below in the period before perestroika; draws on legal, economic and sociological as well as political material.

79   Jacobs, Everett (1983) Editor. *Soviet Local Politics and Government.* London: Allen and Unwin

A useful collection of conference papers on this relatively under-studied subject.

80   Unger, Aryeh L. (1981) *Constitutional Development in the USSR.* London: Methuen

Contains editions of all Soviet constitutions up to that of 1977 together with extensive introduction and commentary. The most useful of several volumes of this kind.

81   Feldbrugge, F.J.M. (1979) Editor. *The Constitutions of the USSR and the Union Republics.* Alphen aan den Rijn: Sijthoff and Noordhoff

A scholarly edition of the 1977 Soviet Constitution and of the constitutions adopted in 1978 by the fifteen republics.

82   Solomon, Peter H. (1978) *Soviet Criminologists and Criminal Policy: Specialists in Policy Making.* London: Macmillan

A model analysis of specialist influence on policy formation based on interviews and other sources as well as printed materials.

83   Vanneman, Peter (1977) *The Supreme Soviet: Politics and the Legislative Process in the Soviet Political System.* Durham, NC: Duke University Press

A substantial study of the USSR Supreme Soviet during its unreformed state; a new edition is in preparation.

84   Towster, Julian (1948) *Political Power in the USSR 1917-1947.* New York: Oxford University Press

A thorough study, still valuable for its account of legal theory and state institutions.

The Communist Party

85   White, Stephen (1989) *Soviet Communism: Programme and Rules.* London: Routledge

Official translations of the 1986 Party Programme and Rules with extensive introduction.

86   Gill, Graeme (1988) *The Rules of the Communist Party of the Soviet Union*. London: Macmillan

The texts of all editions of the CPSU Rules from 1898 to 1986 with extensive introduction and commentary.

87   Hill, Ronald J. and Frank, Peter (1986) *The Soviet Communist Party*, 3rd edn. Boston: Unwin Hyman

The most satisfactory general study of the CPSU, covering the period up to the 27th Party Congress.

88   Harasymiw, Bohdan (1984) *Political Elite Recruitment in the Soviet Union*. London: Macmillan

A detailed and often statistical study of the recruitment of CPSU members and activists over the post-Stalin period.

89   Lowenhardt, John (1982) *The Soviet Politburo*. Edinburgh: Canongate

A careful study by a Dutch scholar.

90   Schapiro, Leonard B. (1970) *The Communist Party of the Soviet Union*, 2nd edn. London: Eyre and Spottiswoode

Still the most satisfactory history of the Soviet Union's ruling party, although its coverage extends no further than the end of the Khrushchev years.

91   Hough, Jerry F. (1969) *The Soviet Prefects: The Local Party Organs in Industrial Decision-Making*. Cambridge, MA: Harvard University Press

Still a valuable analysis of party-industrial relations.

92   Rigby, T. H. (1968) *Communist Party Membership in the Soviet Union 1917-1967*. Princeton, NJ: Princeton University Press

A landmark study of the evolution of party membership in general and in terms of age, gender and other variables.

93   Avtorkhanov, Abdurakhman (1966) *The Communist Party Apparatus*. Cleveland; New York: World Publishing Company

A detailed study by an emigré scholar of the structure and operation of the Soviet 'partocracy'.

94   Armstrong, John A. (1961) *The Politics of Totalitarianism: The Communist Party of the Soviet Union from 1934 to the Present*. New York: Random House

A detailed and still valuable historical study.

The Political Process

95   Yeltsin, Boris (1990) *Against the Grain*. London: Cape

A smoothly written political memoir by the former Politburo member and Russian republican president.

96   Wedgwood Benn, David (1989) *Persuasion and Soviet Politics*. Oxford: Blackwell

The 'first full-length account of the historical background to Soviet thinking about propaganda'.

97   Brown, Archie (1989) Editor. *Political Leadership in the Soviet Union*. London: Macmillan

A variety of essays dealing with leadership change from an historical as well as contemporary perspective.

98 Nove, Alec (1989) *Glasnost in Action*. Boston: Unwin Hyman

A study of the 'cultural renaissance in Russia', dealing with literary, historical and other themes in the Soviet press and journals.

99 Rigby, T.H. (1989) *Political Elites in the USSR: Central Leaders and Local Cadres from Lenin to Gorbachev*. Aldershot, Hants: Edward Elgar

A collection of essays, most of which are reprinted, on leadership change and centre-local relations.

100 Shlapentokh, Vladimir (1989) *Public and Private Lives of the Soviet People: Changing Values in Post-Stalin Russia*. New York: Oxford University Press

An insightful study by an emigré sociologist.

101 Urban, Michael E. (1989) *An Algebra of Soviet Power: Elite Circulation in the Belorussian Republic, 1966-1986*. Cambridge: Cambridge University Press

An examination of the Belorussian 'nomenklatura' which makes a more general contribution to the study of political elite formation.

102 Hahn, Jeffrey (1988) *Soviet Grassroots: Citizen Participation in Local Soviet Government*. Princeton, NJ: Princeton University Press

A thoughtful study of popular involvement in Soviet local government which stresses the potential for the development of a participant culture.

103 Lane, David (1988) Editor. *Elites and Political Power in the USSR*. Aldershot, Hants: Edward Elgar

A collection of general and more specific studies.

104 Mickiewicz, Ellen (1988) *Split Signals: Television and Politics in the Soviet Union*. New York: Oxford University Press

An important study of change in the Soviet broadcast media.

105 Millar, James R. (1987) Editor. *Politics, Work and Daily Life in the USSR: A Survey of Former Citizens*. New York: Cambridge University Press

The 'first comprehensive survey of life in the USSR since the Harvard Project over 33 years ago', designed to illuminate the operation of the Soviet system as it is actually experienced by its citizens. The main outcome of the Soviet Interview Project, which was based on 'thousands' of interviews with former Soviet citizens now resident in the United States.

106 Voslensky, Michael (1984) *Nomenklatura: Anatomy of the Soviet Ruling Class*. London: Bodley Head

A solid, sometimes sensational account of administered privilege and the Soviet leadership by a recent emigré.

107 Bunce, Valerie (1981) *Do New Leaders Make a Difference? Executive Succession and Public Policy under Capitalism and Socialism*. Princeton, NJ: Princeton University Press

A study of the impact of changing leaderships upon budgetary allocations in the USSR and elsewhere.

108 Gustafson, Thane (1981) *Reform in Soviet Politics: Lessons of Recent Policies on Land and Water*. Cambridge: Cambridge University Press

Considers the ability of the 'third generation' of Soviet leaders to resolve policy dilemmas, with particular reference to the modernisation of agriculture.

109 Lowenhardt, John (1981) *Decision Making in Soviet Politics*. London: Macmillan

Reviews a series of case studies and then considers at greater length the reorganisation of the Academy of Sciences in 1954-61 in terms of group influence.

110 Hough, Jerry F. (1980) *The Soviet Leadership in Transition*. Washington, DC: Brookings Institution

A study of political change up to the Brezhnev era with particular reference to the changing composition of political elites.

111 Friedgut, Theodore H. (1979) *Political Participation in the USSR*. Princeton, NJ: Princeton University Press

Largely a study of citizens and local Soviets, this is still a valuable account of participation in the Brezhnev years.

112 Tarschys, Daniel (1979) *The Soviet Political Agenda: Problems and Priorities 1950-1970*. London: Macmillan

A study of changing priorities based upon a quantitative analysis of *Pravda* editorials.

113 Hill, Ronald J. (1977) *Soviet Political Elites: The Case of Tiraspol*. Oxford: Martin Robertson

A 'local politics' study based in Moldavia.

114 Odom, William (1976) A dissenting view on the group approach to Soviet politics. *World Politics*, vol. 28 no. 4, July, 542-67.

Argues for the continuing utility of the totalitarian model.

115 Skilling, H. Gordon and Griffiths, Franklyn (1971) Editors. *Interest Groups in Soviet Politics*. Princeton, NJ: Princeton University Press

Still an important source for the study of group influence in Soviet politics, embracing theoretical issues as well as a series of more specific case studies.

116 Rigby, T.H. (1964) Crypto-politics, *Survey*, no. 50, January, 183-94.

An early consideration of the nature of politics in a 'mono-organisational society'.

117 Inkeles, Alex and Bauer, Raymond A. (1959) *The Soviet Citizen*. Cambridge, MA: Harvard University Press

An analysis of daily life in the Soviet Union based on interviews with about three thousand former citizens; the main published outcome of the 'Harvard Project'.

118 Fainsod, Merle (1958) *Smolensk under Soviet Rule*. Cambridge, MA: Harvard University Press

A detailed study of inter-war politics in this Soviet city based upon its captured archives.

119 Harper, Samuel (1929) *Civic Training in Soviet Russia*. Chicago: University of Chicago Press

A study of the formation of a Soviet citizenry based on firsthand observation.

CHAPTER FIVE

International Relations

Dr Margot Light
London School of Economics

Soviet relations with other countries have had important implications for international security ever since the formation of the first socialist state. Not surprisingly, therefore, the study of Soviet foreign policy has always been a major concern of scholars, journalists and government officials in various countries and there is a voluminous literature on the subject. Since much of it has been written by area specialists and by practitioners rather than by academics within the discipline of international relations, in the past there have sometimes been noticeable differences between the way the study of international relations was developing on the one hand, and much of the work that was published about Soviet foreign policy on the other, particularly in respect of methodology. For example, foreign policy analysis became a significant branch of international relations some thirty years ago. But it is only relatively recently that this approach has been applied to the study of Soviet foreign policy.

The aim of foreign policy analysis was straightforward: to improve the understanding of, and the ability to predict, the foreign policy of states in general, or of particular types of state. It tended to concentrate on studying decision-making in the context of foreign policy, focusing on the domestic sources of foreign policy, or on domestic political processes. In doing so it drew attention to the importance of perceptions and the effects of strongly held belief systems on perceptions and, therefore, on foreign policy decisions. It also demonstrated that the traditional approach to the study of foreign policy often fell short of reality. In other words, the implicitly assumed or explicitly espoused 'rational-actor' model that underlay many traditional accounts of foreign policy was based on the premise that governments are united and purposive, that they possess full information and that they can, therefore, calculate and implement foreign policy actions which they have chosen in order to maximise the power and security of the state. But many of the case studies undertaken by foreign policy analysts indicated that this was not an accurate reflection of the way in which governments worked.

Foreign policy analysts began to examine what the effects were of group decision-making, particularly in crisis situations, to utilise what had been discovered in other social sciences about how bureaucracies operate and to apply the findings of organisational theory to the study of foreign policy. Their critics often objected that the shift in focus to the domestic political process had been made at the expense of examining policy outcomes or effects. Analysts, they pointed out, were neglecting foreign policy itself and they often ignored the international environment in which foreign policy occurred. Many of these criticisms were justified but whatever its shortcomings, foreign policy analysis encouraged a more rigorous and systematic ordering of data and the application of an explicit methodology. It also made it impossible to neglect domestic and perceptual influences on foreign policy.

For many years there were few studies of Soviet foreign policy that incorporated these developments. In a 1981 paper, Light (3) argued that one of the causes was lack of data about Soviet decision-making processes. Ideological factors also militated against attempts to incorporate the Soviet Union in studies that aimed to reach general conclusions. While Soviet studies had burgeoned in the atmosphere of the Cold War, the aim was to know the enemy and that implied stressing the unique features of the Soviet system, rather than looking for or examining elements that were common to many types of political system. There was a third reason why the study of Soviet foreign policy diverged from foreign policy analysis. Since those who wrote about Soviet foreign policy tended to be area specialists, they were sceptical about the methodological developments in foreign policy analysis. According to Snyder (1), they believed that methodology was irrelevant to the study of the Soviet Union. Their argument was strengthened by the fact that much of the theoretical work in foreign policy analysis had been based on empirical evidence gathered by examining American foreign policy. In any case, the pressure (on American specialists in particular) to produce policy-relevant work, often at short notice, was not conducive to the painstaking application of complex methodologies. Snyder (2) argued that methodological rigour was, in fact, more likely to result in policy-relevant findings.

Although many Soviet foreign policy scholars decried the term 'theory', disapproved of the use of models and concentrated almost exclusively on outputs rather than the policy process, their own work was based implicitly on an unmistakeable rational-actor model. They viewed the Soviet Union as a unitary actor, attributed an extraordinary high degree of rationality to it, and they rarely related Soviet foreign policy to events in the external environment or regarded it as response rather than initiative. This does not mean that all the published work based on an implicit or explicit rational-actor model was valueless. On the contrary, a number of important books were written within the traditional framework. Moreover, the views expressed in many of them either reflected those of Western government decision-makers or affected their perceptions. After all, American presidents often chose their national security advisers from among their authors. Zbigniew Brzezinski, whose impeccably scholarly account of the establishment of Soviet power in Eastern Europe (68) remains a seminal study, and Richard Pipes, an historian by profession who turned to international relations and became an ardent advocate of confrontation with the Soviet Union (57), are two of the many examples of American academics who became eminent members of the government administration. Others combined professional diplomacy with scholarship. George Kennan, who both invented the policy of containment and then became a vocal critic of how it was practised (55), is perhaps the most famous. Raymond Garthoff, whose perspicacious and detailed analysis of détente (50) was published in 1985, was a prominent member of the American team that negotiated the first SALT agreement and continued to serve as a diplomat until he joined the Brookings Institution in 1980. In Britain senior diplomats sometimes turned to scholarship when they retired. Robin Edmonds, for example, updated his 1975 account of Soviet foreign policy to include the events of Brezhnev's declining years in his analysis of the paradox of superpower (14), while Sir Curtis Keeble edited a volume devoted to the domestic context of Soviet foreign policy (34).

As a matter of course, all past and present government officials in the West disassociate the personal interpretations they offer in books and articles from those of the governments they serve. But their advice to their governments must surely be coloured by their views. This in itself makes their work important. But apart from their influence on government thinking, sound analyses, whether or not they are based on a traditional rational-actor model, clearly have intrinsic merit.

Prominent Soviet diplomats and officials also sometimes write (or lend their names to) books about foreign policy. They never make the same disclaimer that Western diplomats make but even if they did, they would hardly carry conviction. Until glasnost began, there was little difference between the views of Soviet scholars and those of policy makers. The many editions of the two-volume work edited by Gromyko and Ponomarev (20), for example, can be considered the authorised, official, chronological account of Soviet foreign policy before the 'new political thinking' began to affect Soviet scholars.

During the 1980s the gap between foreign policy analysis and the Western study of Soviet foreign policy seemed to become narrower. For one thing, the aspirations of foreign policy analysts became more modest. But specialists in Soviet foreign policy also changed. Even those who had been most opposed to 'theory' began to display greater methodological rigour. Moreover, some of their assumptions had been tempered by the détente of the 1970s. And more scholars began to be interested in Soviet perceptions and the domestic and international contexts in which Soviet foreign policy was made. Even after the Soviet invasion of Afghanistan, when East-West relations deteriorated to a distinct chill, ideology affected Western studies less pervasively than it had during the first Cold War. There were, of course, intensely critical studies of Soviet foreign relations. Staar, for example, demonstrated his hostility to all Soviet activity abroad (10) by maintaining that those who were less implacably opposed to the Soviet Union acted, wittingly or not, as 'informal agents' for the Soviet government. Generally, however, scholars began to realise that the Soviet Union was, as Dibb expressed it (6), an incomplete superpower, since its power was flawed and one-dimensional.

Soviet theories about the wider world changed radically after Gorbachev came to power in 1985. In the Soviet Union the new world view was called 'the new political thinking'. Foreign policy changes followed quite quickly. Curiously, however, it took some time for these developments to be reflected in Western literature. After all, it was not only Soviet policy that had changed at the end of the previous decade: the first Reagan administration and the first Thatcher government both took far more hardline positions towards the Soviet Union than their predecessors. Although Mrs Thatcher claimed to admire Gorbachev, neither American nor British policy changed immediately when he came to power. The delay was caused in part by the suspicion that words would not be followed by significant deeds. But it probably also resulted from the conviction that it was precisely Western toughness that had forced Gorbachev to modify his policy. A firm stance might produce further change. At first, therefore, there were few concrete results that could be reflected in the literature.

Paradoxically, however, when Soviet policy began to shift in 1987 it was the unprecedented speed at which change occurred that made it impossible for it to be reflected in the literature. The unavoidable (but perhaps reducible) lag between completion of manuscript and publication of book or article had two results: many of the works published in the last years of the decade were out of date by the time they reached bookshops and library shelves, and many scholars turned to daily newspapers and weekly news magazines in an attempt to capture change before their analyses could be rendered futile (or foolish) by the impact of subsequent events.

Despite these problems, however, and the fact that Soviet policy was clearly still in tremendous flux at the end of the decade, the literature on the international relations of the Soviet Union published in the 1980s is characterised by its great volume, its varied subject matter and its good quality. For the sake of convenience and to provide a means of steering around this vast field, in the remaining discussion the literature will be divided into topics. Readers should be warned, however, that there are inevitable overlaps between categories. Moreover, some books discussed and listed under one heading also deal with other topics. Historical studies have been placed in the general and historical section if they deal with the history of Soviet foreign policy in general, but those that treat particular issues or particular regions have been listed in the appropriate section.

General and Historical Topics

Access to Soviet archives has been improving since glasnost began and, with it, the re-assessment of Soviet history. Some important official disclosures have resulted, but so far they have usually concerned events about which Western scholars (and, at least in private, many of their Soviet colleagues) had few doubts. The existence of secret protocols attached to the Nazi-Soviet Pact dividing Poland and recognising that the Baltic states were in the Soviet sphere of interest is one example. Soviet responsibility for the massacre in Katyn forest of Polish officers is another. But scholars still experience difficulty with archives relating to Soviet foreign policy and it is too soon for much new material to be reflected in the literature. Nevertheless, some interesting historical works have been published in the last decade. Jonathan Haslam's two-volume study (13, 15), for example, together with E.H. Carr's two volumes on the Comintern (12, 18) provide a detailed examination of Soviet inter-state and inter-party relations during the 1930s.

A number of general studies of Soviet foreign policy have been published in the last few years which treat the subject more or less historically. Nogee and Donaldson (7) have updated their useful textbook on Soviet policy since 1945. Rubinstein's rival textbook on post-Second World War policy (21) has not been updated but it is worth reading, particularly since it contains a chapter on Soviet policy in the United Nations, a topic that is rarely treated in the literature on Soviet foreign policy. Some general studies cover limited periods of time. Ulam (17), Edmonds (14) and Steele (11), for example, confined themselves mainly to détente, while Luttwak (16) and Staar (10) concentrated on Soviet foreign policy after détente broke down. The question of Soviet power has exercised many scholars and most Western policy makers over the last decade. The former were interested not only because of the build-up in Soviet military strength, but also because of the curious mismatch between increasing military power and obviously declining economic indices. The monograph by Dibb (6) and the essays edited by Menon and Nelson (5) investigate the constraints on Soviet power.

Collections of essays all too often lack a convincing theme to tie the contributions together. And even when there is a clear theme, they can sometimes be confusing, particularly when editors do not explain why various contributors reach contradictory explanations or conclusions. But confusions and inconsistencies can be valuable: they may illustrate a variety of methodological approaches, or the divergent views expressed may demonstrate that there is more than one possible interpretation of events. At the beginning of the decade Hoffmann and Fleron published a new edition of their landmark book of readings (22), intended precisely to offer students a variety of views. A few years later Hoffmann teamed up with Laird to produce a new collection of reprinted articles (9) almost exhaustive in its coverage of processes, instruments and regions.

Soviet Theory of International Relations

The perennial debate about whether Soviet foreign policy is motivated by ideology or by national interest has been replaced in recent years by the awareness that the two are far from mutually exclusive. And to scholars who believed that understanding Soviet perceptions facilitates the analysis of policy, the relationship between perceptions, the belief systems of policy makers, and the policies they advocated seemed important and so too did the content of Soviet ideology. Western specialists were also concerned to compare what was said by Soviet theorists and politicians with what was done in terms of concrete policy, and conversely, to investigate whether doctrine changed to reflect policy. The result was that Western academics began to pay more attention to what Soviet theorists and policy makers wrote about the ideology underlying their policy.

The credit for establishing that there was a coherent Soviet theory of international relations, and relating it to Western theories, belongs to Kubalkova and Cruickshank (30). Mitchell analysed doctrinal revisions under Brezhnev (29) and seemed to claim a one-to-one correspondence between doctrine and future policy, which made him fear that the doctrine of limited sovereignty would, in the long run, be universally applicable. Lynch (25), Light (24) and Jones (23) were more interested in how Soviet doctrine had changed over time or in response to events. Other academics concentrated on specific aspects of theory. Lider (28) and Shenfield (26), for example, examined the concepts of 'correlation of forces' and peace and security, while Hough (27) and Valkenier (83) looked at Soviet analyses of the Third World. Most of the books that were published after 1987 included sections on the new political thinking but Kubalkova and Cruickshank (100) devoted an entire book to it, showing how it relates to Marxism-Leninism.

Foreign Policy Making and Domestic Factors

The influence of foreign policy analysis is most evident in studies of foreign policy that are devoted to various aspects of the decision-making process. Although many of the books discussed in the general and historical section contain chapters devoted to domestic inputs, a number of works have been published in the last decade that concentrate on the domestic context in which foreign policy matters are decided. Bialer edited an interesting collection of essays on this theme (38), and a later British collection was edited by Keeble (34). Although both collections contain interesting chapters about various domestic factors and institutions that influence and are concerned with decision-making, the interrelationship between domestic factors and foreign policy is not really explored in either. Valenta and Potter devoted their interesting collection (36) to the more specific question of decision-making for national security, looking particularly at the role of the military.

Crisis decision-making has always preoccupied foreign policy analysts and a number of interesting case studies have been published. Karen Dawisha's carefully documented study of the decision to intervene in Czechoslovakia in 1968 (33) has contributed both to the general literature on crisis decision-making, and to a deeper understanding of decision-making in the Soviet Union.

A fair idea about Soviet perceptions of various countries and areas can be obtained by examining published sources. Soviet views of Latin America were analysed by Prizel (31), who suggested that Soviet Latin Americanists are more influential in Soviet policy than most other area specialists. In examining Soviet theories about Third World economic and political development, Hough (27) and Valkenier (83) offered a spectrum of specialist perceptions. Malcolm looked at the work and influence of North Americanists (35) and later at new views about Western Europe (101), while Lenczowski used the press for more popular images of the United States (37). There is very little material specifically on Soviet-Japanese relations, and Robertson's portrayal of the Soviet image of Japan (32) was a welcome first step in filling this gap.

East-West Relations

Given the bipolarity of the international system and the centrality of superpower relations in determining its security, it is perhaps not surprising that a large part of the literature published in the last decade about Soviet foreign policy has been devoted to East-West relations or, more particularly, to Soviet-American relations. White's diplomatic history of the origins of those relations (52) demonstrates how much misunderstanding there has always been in East-West relations. Garthoff used recently declassified information and new Soviet revelations to add a fascinating book to the extensive literature on the Cuban missile crisis (41).

Since 1947 Western policy has been based, by and large, on various interpretations of the strategy of containment. However, few books on Soviet policy towards the West are explicit about the strategy to which the Soviet leadership has been responding. It is very useful, therefore, to look at one or more of the excellent analyses of containment that have been published in recent years by, for example, Gaddis (54) or Deibel and Gaddis (47). And since Kennan was not only the author of containment but also one of its major critics, his essays, primarily concerned with Soviet-American relations, are interesting (55).

Every decade seems to produce new studies of the Cold War. In recent years authors have begun to look beyond particular causal events and to ask more general questions about Cold Wars. In a recently published book, Kaldor (39) challenged conventional wisdom by suggesting that the Cold War was primarily a way of managing conflicts within the two blocs. Halliday, on the other hand, in relation particularly to the second Cold War, believed that it was a conflict of ideologies (53, 42).

The second Cold War prompted a number of studies about the period of détente that preceded it and the reasons why it gave way so soon to confrontation. Bowker and Williams (45) explained the failure of détente through the differing expectations each side had about what it could achieve. Pipes, by contrast, was unequivocal in condemning America's détente policy and took it for granted that the Soviet leadership was pursuing nefarious aims (57). The most comprehensive book about Soviet-American détente and its aftermath, filled with historical detail and acute insight, was written by Garthoff (50).

Interesting studies have been made of various areas of Soviet-American cooperation and the fate of the agreements when détente ended. George, Farley and Dallin compiled an excellent analysis of security agreements (46), Jamgotch and colleagues examined six areas of collaboration at the level of 'low politics' (51), while Caldwell and Diebold concentrated on East-West trade (56). During the first Cold War West European policy towards the Soviet Union was virtually indistinguishable from American policy. During the second Cold War, however, the distinctions were quite marked. The contributors to the volume edited by Ullman and Zucconi (48), many of them European, considered the transatlantic tensions that developed.

The change from confrontation to co-operation after Gorbachev came to power prompted a spate of new studies about East-West relations. The contributors to Kaldor, Holden and Falk (43) included both official East European and Soviet writers, and activists in the new social movements in those countries. The Laird and Clark collection (40) contains some useful analyses of Soviet policy towards individual West European countries, while Bialer and Mandelbaum (44) were primarily concerned with the implications of perestroika for American policy.

Soviet Relations with Socialist Countries

The long-standing Sino-Soviet conflict seemed, until recently, to be the most intractable problem in relations between socialist states. Those who have already forgotten the early rounds in the conflict will find the factual résumé from Keesings Contemporary Archives sources (63), and Jacobsen's analysis of Sino-Soviet relations after the death of Mao (66) very useful. But both books were published well before the substantial improvement that took place in Sino-Soviet relations at the end of the 1980s. Although the changes in Sino-Soviet relations were momentous, they paled into insignificance compared to the transformations that occurred in Soviet relations with the East European socialist states.

The events of 1989 and 1990 were so little anticipated by Western specialists of Soviet foreign policy that none of the books written about Soviet-East European relations during the 1980s predicted them. Even those that were published well after Soviet perestroika had begun to spread to some East European countries, assumed that the Soviet leadership would not tolerate the loss of the leading role of the communist and workers' parties in Eastern Europe. Complete defection from the bloc seemed inconceivable.

Yet, with the benefit of hindsight it seems that the conclusions reached by many scholars writing about Eastern Europe in the 1980s indicated that conditions were ripe for dramatic change. Hutchings (62) found that Soviet efforts to consolidate the bloc after 1968 had failed. The contributors to the volume edited by Terry concluded that there were a number of outstanding problems in bilateral relations within the bloc (65). In a perspicacious study of Central European political culture, Gerner (64) suggested that Poland, Czechoslovakia and Hungary would never be stable Soviet allies because their ruling regimes had failed to establish 'auxiliary legitimation'. Stern analysed why and how international communism had gradually declined (60). In a retrospective study of 40 years of communism in the area, Brown (61) found that economic decline was almost as serious in Eastern Europe as in the Soviet Union. Systemic change was long overdue. By the time the studies examining the implications of reform and change in Eastern Europe were published by Gati (59) and Dawisha (58), it was clear that the bloc could not hold. Why did local communists and Moscow find it impossible to manage the change in Eastern Europe and retain their influence?

Some answers are suggested by an earlier study of Soviet policy in Eastern Europe. Jones argued that Soviet influence in Eastern Europe depended crucially on control from Moscow of key appointments (67).

Once reform began in Eastern Europe, however, there could be no question of Soviet interference in appointments. In many countries reform communists were rapidly replaced by non-communists. The chain of command between the CPSU and East European governments had been broken. In the past when that chain was threatened, for example in Hungary in 1956 and in Czechoslovakia in 1968, military force had been used to re-establish it. But military intervention was not an option that could be used to control events in Eastern Europe in 1989 unless Gorbachev was prepared to lose his new détente with the West and his domestic reform programme. There was, therefore, no means by which the speed or the direction of change could be controlled.

Soviet-Third World Relations

There has been almost as much literature on Soviet relations with the Third World in the last decade as there have been books on East-West relations. In fact, many authors have tied the two subjects together. In the United States, in particular, there has been a tendency to see Soviet-Third World relations as a function of superpower relations and to count each Soviet 'gain' as an American 'loss'.

There is no doubt that Soviet policy in the Third World in the 1970s contributed significantly to the decline of détente. It is a curious fact, however, that although the new, active Soviet policy in this region caused great alarm and despondency in the West, and made Soviet policy makers claim that the 'correlation of forces' had changed in favour of socialism, many analysts who examined Soviet Third World policy in the 1980s concluded that Soviet policy had been less than successful. Moreover, the Soviet Union tended to exploit opportunities rather than to create them, as the contributors to Campbell and MacFarlane (69) demonstrated. Menon's monograph (80) and the volume edited by Kolodziej and Kanet (75) indicated what the limits were to Soviet power projection in the Third World. Despite the limits and the new policy adopted after 1985, both Rubinstein (76) and Korbonski and Fukuyama (78) were sceptical that there had been a long-term, substantive change in what Rubinstein calls Moscow's 'new imperial policy'.

The real limit to Soviet influence in the Third World was economic. Soviet-Third World relations soon turned into an 'economic bind', as the subtitle to Valkenier's early study of the problem (83) put it. The lack of complementarity between the Soviet economy and the economies of friendly Third World countries was amply illustrated by the scholars who contributed to the collection by Cassen (81), and by Miller (71). And this is why military instruments of foreign policy began to predominate. Duner (77), Menon (80), Hosmer and Wolfe (82) and Katz (85) all examined aspects of Soviet military policy in the Third World, while the essays in Saikal and Maley (72) are devoted to the aftermath of military intervention in Afghanistan.

Although a profit and loss reckoning of Soviet-Third World relations would probably conclude that Soviet gains were far less impressive than was generally believed at the beginning of the 1980s, diplomatic links were established with a great number of non-aligned countries. Allison's meticulous study (73) examined the development of Soviet policy towards non-aligned states in general, while Soviet relations with India were the subject of both Duncan's short study (70) and of Mehrotra's analysis of Soviet aid and trade policy (93). A number of interesting studies were published about Soviet policy in various Third World regions or towards individual countries. Prizel (31) and Miller (71) both examined Latin America, for example, while Shearman concentrated on Cuba (79). Heldman (86) focused on relations with Africa under Khrushchev. And while Freedman studied Soviet policy in the whole Middle East region (84), Soviet-Syrian relations were the subject of Karsh's monograph (74).

Defence Issues

The chapter on the Armed Forces deals with military matters, but it is clear that defence issues are important in foreign policy and a few books about security policy are included in this chapter as well. We have seen in the previous section how predominant military instruments became in Soviet policy in the Third World. Kaplan et al (92) provide an exhaustive analysis of the use made by the Soviet Union of military diplomacy. Changes in the Warsaw Pact can reflect developments in strategy but they also reflect changes in the political relations between the Soviet Union and the countries of Eastern Europe. Students of Soviet foreign policy would, therefore, find the volume edited by Holloway and Sharp (91) useful. Nelson's 1986 study (90) and Holden's book, published in 1989 (89), updated developments in the Pact, though both appeared too early to be able to consider its demise.

Perestroika brought about a reconceptualisation of the nature of security in the Soviet Union. The contributors to Hudson (88) examined why and how this happened and suggest what the agents of change were. MccGwire (87) argued that domestic economic reform required a new détente with the West which, in turn, entailed a change in the Marxist-Leninist theory of international relations and scaling down the Soviet armed forces. In this study he set the arguments of his previous book, published in 1987, (*Military Objectives in Soviet Foreign Policy*. Washington, DC: Brookings Institution) in the wider context of foreign policy and extended them to cover developments up to the end of the decade.

Foreign Economic Policy

Given how important economic relations have been with the Third World, within the Soviet bloc and in East-West relations, where it can be argued that the need to import technology and improve trade relations both stimulated détente and, as Hough argued (95), was a major factor in the new political thinking, there are surprisingly few books devoted to Soviet foreign economic policy. Over the years the Soviet leadership has used economic instruments of foreign policy both as a carrot (economic and military aid both fall into this category) and as a stick, by applying economic sanctions, for example against Yugoslavia, Albania and China. But the Soviet Union has more frequently been the recipient of economic sanctions, and Hanson (94) considered how effective Western economic statecraft has been. He concluded that in general carrots work better than sticks. Parrott and his colleagues (98), investigating American trade and technology transfer to the Soviet Union, came to the same conclusion.

The Soviet Union might import technology from the West, but it also exports it to the Third World. Mehrotra (93) examined Soviet trade and technology transfer to India which, he concluded, is beneficial to India's balance of payment problems. But he foresaw, as did all the authors mentioned in the Third World section who examine economic relations, that complementarity will increasingly be a problem.

There have been two predominant fears in the West about economic relations with the Soviet Union. The first relates to the uses to which imported technology might be put and the unilateral benefits that the Soviet Union might gain from trade. The second fear centres on Soviet energy exports and the possibility of Western dependence and a resultant potential for economic pressure. Stern (97) argued that exports fulfil Soviet domestic economic needs and it is unlikely that oil or gas will be used for strategic purposes against the West. In any case, as Sokoloff demonstrated (96), there is far more Soviet economic dependence on the West than vice versa.

The 'New Political Thinking' and Gorbachev's Foreign Policy

There has been a great deal of interesting Soviet writing on the new political thinking, but most of it has appeared in periodicals or in the press. The joint venture American-Russian selection of articles initially published in *Mirovaia Ekonomika i Mezhdunarodnye Otnosheniia*, edited by Hirsch (99), is particularly welcome and goes a small way towards making the new political thinking accessible to people who do not read Russian.

Much of the Western literature on this subject has also appeared in journals and newspapers, or as individual chapters in books devoted to perestroika. Kubalkova and Cruickshank (100) investigated the sources of new political thinking and related it to Marxism-Leninism and traditional Soviet thinking. Malcolm (101) examined one particular aspect, the range of Soviet attitudes to Western Europe. But perhaps the best place to start thinking about new thinking is by reading Gorbachev himself. His bestseller, *Perestroika* (102), now in its second edition, was written well before the optimism about the future of the Soviet Union had begun to fade.

Some of the books that consider Gorbachev's policy rather than the ideas behind it have already been discussed in the relevant sections. Hough (103), who dated the change in foreign policy to the summer of 1987, offered an interesting historical account of how the reform became possible and what it was intended to achieve. But here too a great deal has been published in journals and newspapers, both Soviet and Western, and most of the books on the subject have been unable to keep up with the pace of events.

Any survey must, for practical reasons, be selective. It will also perforce be subjective. It will be clear, however, that there is a great deal of recent literature on the Soviet Union and the wider world and that there is no shortage of variety of views, approaches or topics. In the bibliography that follows the same divisions have been used as in the text, but one section has been added so that the few sources on methodology referred to at the beginning of the chapter can be listed.

Bibliography

Methodological Problems in the Study of Soviet Foreign Policy

1   Snyder, J. (1988) Science and Sovietology: bridging the methods gap in Soviet foreign policy studies. *World Politics*, XL, 2, 169-193.

   This article combines a lucid description of traditional and positivist methods with a demonstration of how they can be blended to enrich research into Soviet foreign policy.

2   Snyder, J. (1984-5) Richness, rigor and relevance in the study of Soviet foreign policy. *International Security*, 9, 3, 89-108.

   Snyder argues that richness of area specialisation, rigorous basic research and relevant policy applications can be attained by using comparative case studies of Soviet foreign policy behaviour.

3   Light, M. (1981) Approaches to the study of Soviet foreign policy. *Review of International Studies*, 7, 3, 127-43.

   An examination of why the methodology of foreign policy analysis has been used so little in the study of Soviet foreign policy and a review of some of the works that do attempt to employ Western models.

General and Historical Questions

4   Gromyko, A.A. (1989) *Memories*. New York: Doubleday

Gromyko's memoirs, originally written in 1988, reveal very little about Soviet foreign policy decision-making. In 1989 he added some new material and an additional chapter for the American edition. Although thin in revelations, the rarity of memoirs by a Soviet official of his stature make it worth reading.

5   Menon, R. and Nelson, D. (1989) Editors. *Limits to Soviet Power*. Lexington, MA: Lexington Books

An examination of what the internal and external constraints are on Soviet power and an assessment of their significance. The introductory and concluding chapters consider how power is assessed in international relations and what the paradoxes are of Soviet power.

6   Dibb, P. (1988) *The Soviet Union: The Incomplete Superpower*, 2nd edn. London: Macmillan for the International Institute of Strategic Studies

Dibb concludes that domestic economic problems, the prospect of rebellion in Eastern Europe, global over-commitment and a deteriorating strategic situation contributed to the decline in Soviet power in the 1980s.

7   Nogee, J. L. and Donaldson, R. H. (1988) *Soviet Foreign Policy since World War II*, 3rd edn. Oxford: Pergamon

A valuable textbook with chapters on Soviet international relations theory and the policy-making process as well as a chronological analysis of Soviet foreign policy after 1945. The third edition includes a chapter on Gorbachev's policy.

8   Rowen, H. S. and Wolf, C. Jr. (1988) Editors. *The Future of the Soviet Empire*. London: Macmillan for the Institute of Contemporary Studies

These essays cover the 'inner' empire as well as the 'outer' empire in Eastern Europe and the Third World. Two unusual and interesting chapters analyse the effects of Soviet demography and poverty in the CMEA countries on the future of the empire.

9   Laird, R.F. and Hoffmann, E.P. (1986) Editors. *Soviet Foreign Policy in a Changing World*. New York: Aldine de Gruyter

This huge collection of reprinted essays includes contributions from academics, present and past American officials and government advisers. They examine general issues, Soviet policy towards various regions, Soviet military power, policy-making and implementation.

10   Staar, R.F. (1985) *USSR Foreign Policies after Detente*. Stanford, CA: Hoover Institution Press

Staar argues that despite shifts in rhetoric, Soviet policy was still essentially messianic in 1985. He deals with perceptions, policy formulation and implementation and the instruments of Soviet foreign policy before turning to Soviet relations with various regions of the world.

11   Steele, J. (1985) *The Limits of Soviet Power*. Harmondsworth: Penguin

Steele's examination of Soviet thinking and intentions, as well as of the historical record, suggested declining power and influence by the 1980s which belied the impression created by a crude counting of Soviet capabilities.

12   Carr, E.H. (1984) *The Comintern and the Spanish Civil War*. London: Macmillan

In this short, posthumous volume Carr demonstrated that Stalin's attitude to the republican forces in Spain was dictated by national and not revolutionary interest.

13 Haslam, J. (1984) *The Soviet Union and the Struggle for Collective Security in Europe, 1933-1939*. London: Macmillan

The second of a two-volume study of Soviet foreign policy in the 1930s, this is an analysis of the pro-Western Litvinov era which was characterised by persistent efforts to negotiate a security agreement against Nazi Germany.

14 Edmonds, R. (1983) *Soviet Foreign Policy: The Brezhnev Years*. Oxford: Oxford University Press

The first half of this book was published in 1975 under the subtitle 'the paradox of superpower'. It examines how the Soviet Union acquired a global role but, at the same time, became the prisoner of the accompanying responsibilities and its own military power.

15 Haslam, J. (1983) *Soviet Foreign Policy, 1930-1933: The Impact of the Depression*. London: Macmillan

Haslam analyses how preoccupation with industrialisation caused a cautious and conservative foreign policy and led to the mistaken judgement that international events were moving to the advantage of the Soviet Union.

16 Luttwak, E.N. (1983) *The Grand Strategy of the Soviet Union*. London: Weidenfeld and Nicolson

Luttwak maintains that the intervention in Afghanistan represents a new phase of imperial strategy. He argues that the Soviet Union has sufficient military power to expand but that a firm Western response will deter further expansion.

17 Ulam, A.B. (1983) *Dangerous Relations: The Soviet Union in World Politics 1970-1982*. Oxford: Oxford University Press

Taking up the story where his *Expansion and Coexistence: Soviet Foreign Policy 1917-73* (2nd edn. New York: Praeger, 1974) left off, Ulam examines the vicissitudes of détente, focusing on the dilemma of nuclear weapons.

18 Carr, E.H. (1982) *The Twilight of Comintern, 1930-1935*. London: Macmillan

This, the last work Carr published before he died, covers the history of the Comintern in the years before it adopted the popular front policy.

19 Kanet, R.E. (1982) Editor. *Soviet Foreign Policy in the 1980's*. New York: Praeger

This collection of essays looking back at the 1970s and forward to the 1980s includes a section devoted to domestic factors affecting Soviet foreign policy and contains a prescient chapter on the impact of domestic nationalism on foreign policy.

20 Gromyko, A.A. and Ponomarev, B.N. (1981) Editors. *Istoriia Vneshnei Politiki SSSR*. 2 vols. Moscow: Nauka

This two-volume, multi-authored, often tendentious account of the history of Soviet foreign policy has been reissued in several updated versions. Gromyko and Ponomarev, probably only nominal editors, endow it with official sanction.

21 Rubinstein, A.Z. (1981) *Soviet Foreign Policy Since World War II: Imperial and Global*. Cambridge, MA: Winthrop

A useful textbook, with useful suggestions for further reading. Rubinstein examines the instruments of foreign policy and also includes a chapter on Soviet policy in the United Nations.

22 Hoffmann, E.P. & Fleron, F.J. Jnr (1980) Editors. *The Conduct of Soviet Foreign Policy*, 2nd edn. New York: Aldine

Initially published in 1971, this was a landmark collection of articles because it paid attention to methodological problems and included alternative interpretations to encourage discussion. The internal and external factors that shape Soviet foreign policy are examined.

Soviet International Relations Theory

23   Jones, R.A. (1990) *The Soviet Concept of Limited Sovereignty from Lenin to Gorbachev: The Brezhnev Doctrine*. London: Macmillan

Despite its title Jones deals with more than just the concept of limited sovereignty. He also offers a typology comparing old and new thinking.

24   Light, M. (1988) *The Soviet Theory of International Relations*. Brighton: Wheatsheaf

An analysis of the changes in the content of Soviet international theory from classical Marxism-Leninism to the present day and the role played by Soviet theory. Light concludes that although it does not influence policy directly, theory has a powerful indirect impact on perceptions.

25   Lynch, A. (1988) *The Soviet Study of International Relations*. Cambridge: Cambridge University Press

Lynch examines the debates in Soviet international relations literature. He finds that recent Soviet theory diverges in many ways from its Leninist origins and that it shares some aspects of Western theory.

26   Shenfield, S. (1987) *The Nuclear Predicament: Explorations in Soviet Ideology*. London: Routledge & Kegan Paul for the Royal Institute of International Affairs. (Chatham House Papers, 37)

Shenfield traces the origins of the debate that led to the new political thinking about peace and security and argues that the most substantial contribution was made by those who supported increasing interdependence as the basis of international security and cooperation.

27   Hough, J. (1986) *The Struggle for the Third World: Soviet Debates and American Options*. Washington, DC: Brookings Institution

Hough argues that Soviet policy in the Third World was far less successful than is commonly believed. An important reason was the inadequacy of the Soviet economic system as a model for industrial growth.

28   Lider, J. (1986) *Correlation of Forces: An Analysis of Marxist-Leninist Concepts*. Aldershot: Gower

Lider compares the concepts of 'correlation of forces' and balance of power. He concludes that there is no suitable methodology to measure either the correlation of military forces or the broader idea of correlation in an objective way.

29   Mitchell, R.J. (1982) *Ideology of a Superpower: Contemporary Soviet Doctrine on International Relations*. Stanford, CA: Hoover Institution Press

Mitchell identifies and evaluates the most important components of doctrinal revision under Brezhnev. Positing a close connection between doctrine and policy, he comes to gloomy conclusions about future Soviet policy.

30   Kubalkova, V. and Cruickshank, A.A. (1980) *Marxism-Leninism and Theory of International Relations*. London: Routledge and Kegan Paul

The authors argue that Marxism-Leninism is a coherent theory of international relations. They reconstruct the theory and compare it to Western theories.

Foreign Policy Making and Domestic Factors

31 Prizel, I. (1990) *Latin America through Soviet Eyes: The Evolution of Soviet Perceptions during the Brezhnev Era 1964-1982.* Cambridge: Cambridge University Press

In this carefully documented monograph Prizel analyses the published views of Soviet Latin Americanists to chart changing perceptions about Latin America's domestic politics, its role in the international system and its relations with the Soviet Union.

32 Robertson, M. (1988) *Soviet Policy towards Japan.* Cambridge: Cambridge University Press

Given its potential importance, surprisingly little has been written about Soviet-Japanese relations. Much of this book is devoted to what image the Soviet Union has of Japan, but the author also looks at economic relations.

33 Dawisha, K. (1985) *The Kremlin and the Prague Spring.* London & Berkeley, CA: University of California Press

A study of the motivations behind the decision to intervene in Czechoslovakia in 1968 which illuminates Soviet decision-making processes and contributes to the theoretical literature on crisis decision-making.

34 Keeble, C. (1985) Editor. *The Soviet State: The Domestic Roots of Soviet Foreign Policy.* Aldershot: Gower for the Royal Institute of International Affairs

The individual chapters of this examination of the domestic factors that affect foreign policy are interesting, but little attention is given to the interrelationship between domestic and foreign policy.

35 Malcolm, N. (1984) *Soviet Political Scientists and American Politics.* London: Macmillan

Malcolm investigates the development of American Studies in the Soviet Union and demonstrates that in 1984, well before the new political thinking, divergent views were common.

36 Valenta, J. and Potter, W.C. (1984) Editors. *Soviet Decisionmaking for National Security.* London: Allen and Unwin

An interesting collection of essays combining sections on how to conceptualise Soviet decision-making and what role the military plays in the process, with three case studies. Two concluding chapters draw methodological conclusions and make suggestions for future research.

37 Lenczowski, J. (1982) *Soviet Perceptions of US Foreign Policy: A Study of Ideology, Power and Consensus.* Ithaca, NY; London: Cornell University Press

Lenczowski uses press articles to reconstruct Soviet views of the shifting balance of power in the world and of the domestic and foreign issues facing American policy makers. He finds less divergence in current views than Malcolm does.

38 Bialer, S. (1981) Editor. *The Domestic Context of Soviet Foreign Policy.* London: Croom Helm; Boulder, CO: Westview Press

An early investigation into the interrelationship between Soviet domestic and foreign policy. There are two overview chapters but neither really uses the other contributions to draw conclusions.

East-West Relations

39   Kaldor, M. (1990) *The Imaginary War: Understanding the East-West Conflict.* Oxford: Blackwell

The imaginary war is the Cold War and Kaldor maintains that it concealed, and was the means of managing, parallel but separate conflicts within the two blocs. This new study of East-West relations challenges conventional explanations.

40   Laird R.F. and Clark, S.L. (1990) Editors. *The USSR and the Western Alliance.* London: Unwin Hyman

The parts are better than the sum of this collection. Most of the contributors consider the changes that have occurred in Soviet policy little more than cosmetic but there are useful contributions on Soviet relations with individual West European countries.

41   Garthoff, R. (1989) *Reflections on the Cuban Missile Crisis,* revised edn. Washington, DC: Brookings Institution

Garthoff revised the 1987 version to include newly declassified American information and fresh Soviet and Cuban revelations. He pays particular attention to Soviet perceptions and the interaction of American and Soviet perceptions and actions before, during and after the crisis.

42   Halliday, F. (1989) *Cold War, Third World: An Essay on Soviet-American Relations.* London: Century Hutchinson

Both superpowers used Third World conflicts as weapons in their confrontation. Halliday considers the policies and ideologies each produced to conduct their rivalry and predicts that cooperation between the two will not end all Third World conflicts.

43   Kaldor, M., Holden, G. and Falk, R. (1989) Editors. *The New Detente: Rethinking East-West Relations.* London: Verso

The diverse contributors to this volume included East European official reformers and activists in the new social movements. They consider the future of Europe and the relationship between state and society, exploring different conceptions of détente.

44   Bialer, S. and Mandelbaum, M. (1988) Editors. *Gorbachev's Russia and American Foreign Policy.* Boulder, CO: Westview for East-West Forum

Cautious optimism that the reform will succeed characterises the tone of this collection of essays which examines perestroika within the Soviet Union and the implications for American foreign policy.

45   Bowker, M. and Williams, P. (1988) *Superpower Detente: A Reappraisal.* London: Sage for the Royal Institute of International Affairs

Organised thematically, this study examines the differing expectations the two superpowers had of détente and charts its rise and decline.

46   George, A.L., Farley, P.J., Dallin, A. (1988) Editors. *US-Soviet Security Cooperation: Achievements, Failures, Lessons.* New York: Oxford University Press

Twenty-two cases studies of Soviet-American efforts to develop and implement agreements to improve their own and international security are followed by six essays considering the implications and problems of security cooperation.

47   Deibel, T.L. and Gaddis, J.L. (1987) Editors. *Containing the Soviet Union: A Critique of US Policy.* London: Pergamon-Brassey

Valuable insights can be gained from this examination of the policy to which the Soviet leadership was responding after 1947. These essays focus on how containment has changed over time in response to changes in the international system.

48 Ullman, R.H. and Zucconi, M. (1987) Editors. *Western Europe and the Crisis in US-Soviet Relations.* New York; London: Praeger

The European focus and individual contributions by European scholars are valuable in this examination of transatlantic tensions that arose over American policy towards the Soviet Union and Eastern Europe during the Second Cold War.

49 Vine, R.D. (1987) Editor. *Soviet-East European Relations as a Problem for the West.* London: Croom Helm

An analysis of Western policy objectives and policies towards Eastern Europe and the Soviet Union in the light of the changes that were occurring there.

50 Garthoff, R. (1985) *Detente & Confrontation: Soviet-American Relations From Nixon to Reagan.* Washington, DC: Brookings Institution

A comprehensive historical account of Soviet-American relations during and after détente by an active participant in the events. Garthoff demonstrates that Soviet policy is often reactive, and pays particular attention to the perceptions of both countries.

51 Jamgotch, N.Jr. (1985) Editor. *Sectors of Mutual Benefit in US-Soviet Relations.* Durham, NC: Duke University Press

Based on functionalist theory, this is an investigation of the fate of the many cooperative agreements signed between the Soviet Union and the United State at the height of détente. It finds that agreements within the category of 'low politics' tended to fall victim to hostility at the level of 'high politics' when détente ended.

52 White, S. (1985) *The Origins of Detente: The Genoa Conference and Soviet-Western Relations, 1921-1922.* Cambridge: Cambridge University Press

White's diplomatic history of the Genoa Conference shows how easily détente could have begun in 1922 and why it did not.

53 Halliday, F. (1983) *The Making of the Second Cold War.* London: Verso

An analysis of what constitutes a Cold War and what the differences were between the first and second Cold Wars forms the framework for Halliday's examination of why détente came to an end.

54 Gaddis, J.L. (1982) *Strategies of Containment: A Critical Reappraisal of Post-War American National Security Policy.* Oxford: Oxford University Press

This analysis of containment, based on Alexander George's theory of an 'operational code', is a useful aid to understanding the policy to which the Soviet Union was responding.

55 Kennan, G.F. (1982) *Nuclear Delusion: Soviet-American Relations in the Atomic Age.* New York: Pantheon

A collection of essays written over a thirty-year period by the man who invented containment, but believed that it had been misunderstood and misapplied, concentrating particularly on Soviet-American relations and the effects of nuclear weapons.

56 Caldwell, L.T. and Diebold, W. Jr. (1981) *Soviet-American Relations in the 1980s: Super-Power Politics and East-West Trade.* New York: McGraw-Hill

The authors come to the conclusion that the Soviet Union will inevitably come to play a greater role in the world economy and that this will probably make them abide by its rules.

57 Pipes, R. (1981) *US-Soviet Relations in the Era of Detente.* Boulder, CO: Westview Press

Reprinted essays which marked Pipes' shift from history to international relations and his subsequent appointment as a national security adviser to Reagan.

Soviet Relations with Socialist Countries

58   Dawisha, K. (1990) *Eastern Europe, Gorbachev and Reform: The Great Challenge*, 2nd edn. Cambridge: Cambridge University Press

A cogent assessment of the historical roots and contemporary state of Soviet-East European relations looking at those relations from both the Soviet and the East European points of view. The revised second edition includes events up to spring 1990.

59   Gati, C. (1990) *The Bloc that Failed: Soviet-East European Relations in Transition.* London: Tauris

Gati reviews Soviet policy towards Eastern Europe from Stalin to Chernenko and then examines the early reform era in the Soviet Union and its effect on Eastern Europe, before turning to the revolutions of 1988 and 1989.

60   Stern, G. (1990) *The Rise and Decline of International Communism.* Aldershot: Edward Elgar

Stern analyses the philosophical and political background to the idea of an international communist movement before tracing its establishment via the Comintern, its transferral to a state system in 1945 and its decline.

61   Brown, J.F. (1988) *Eastern Europe and Communist Rule.* Durham, NC; London: Duke University Press

Brown's inclusion of Yugoslavia and Albania in this retrospective look at forty years of communist history is valuable. He concluded, well before the revolutions of 1989, that there was a profound need for systemic change in the region.

62   Hutchings, R.L. (1987) *Soviet-East European Relations: Consolidation and Conflict*, 2nd edn. Madison, WI: University of Wisconsin Press

Hutchings deals primarily with the period between 1968 and 1980, tracing the key dimensions of relations within the Soviet bloc. A preface is added to the second edition to cover Gorbachev's relationship with Eastern Europe up to 1987.

63   Day, A.J. (1985) Editor. *China and the Soviet Union, 1949-1984.* Keesings International Studies, compiled by P. Jones and S. Kevill. Harlow: Longman

A brief factual résumé of the Sino-Soviet dispute, updating the account Keesings published in 1970, consisting of statements and actions. Evaluation and analysis are left to the reader.

64   Gerner, K. (1985) *The Soviet Union and Central Europe in the Post-War Era: A Study in Precarious Security.* Aldershot: Gower. (Swedish Studies in International Relations, no. 14)

An unusual investigation into why Poland, Hungary and Czechoslovakia have provided a politically unstable security system for the Soviet Union. Professor Gerner explains it in terms of political culture and the failure to establish 'auxiliary legitimation' in those countries.

65   Terry, S.M. (1984) Editor. *Soviet Policy in Eastern Europe.* New Haven; London: Yale University Press

General issues relating to Soviet policy in Eastern Europe and problems arising from bilateral relations are covered in this collection. Bulgaria and Albania are omitted in favour of examining Soviet-East European relations in the context of East-West relations.

66 Jacobsen, C. (1981) *Sino-Soviet Relations since Mao: The Chairman's Legacy.* New York: Praeger

Jacobsen examines the Sino-Soviet conflict in the context of the balance of power between the two countries. His inclusion of the effects of Japan on Sino-Soviet relations is useful.

67 Jones, C.D. (1981) *Soviet Influence in Eastern Europe: Political Autonomy and the Warsaw Pact.* New York: Praeger

Jones argues that Soviet influence in the Warsaw Pact countries depends on Soviet control, first, of appointments to the leadership in those countries and second, of the military strategies adopted by the armed forces of those countries.

68 Brzezinski, Z.K. (1967) *The Soviet Bloc: Unity and Conflict*, revised edn. Cambridge, MA: Harvard University Press

Originally published in 1960, this study of the establishment of Soviet power in Eastern Europe remains a classic. Brzezinski charts the changes within the Soviet bloc, adding sections on the Sino-Soviet dispute and on the Soviet alliance system in the 1967 edition.

Soviet-Third World Relations

69 Campbell, K.M. and MacFarlane, S.N. (1989) Editors. *Gorbachev's Third World Dilemmas.* London: Routledge

The contributors agree that even under Brezhnev, Soviet policy in the Third World tended towards exploiting opportunities created by regional instability rather than fomenting conflict. They also recognise that there has been a general reduction of Soviet support to Third World clients since Gorbachev came to power.

70 Duncan, P. (1989) *The Soviet Union and India.* London: Routledge for the Royal Institute of International Affairs. (Chatham House Papers)

Focusing on the period 1971-1989, Duncan examines the balance of influence and of costs and benefits in the Indo-Soviet relationship. He finds that both sides benefit from the relationship.

71 Miller, N. (1989) *Soviet Relations with Latin America, 1959-1987.* Cambridge: Cambridge University Press. (Cambridge Soviet Paperbacks)

Miller argues that Soviet policy towards Latin America is determined primarily by political and economic factors which act as constraints, preventing the Soviet Union from attaining the maximal strategic and ideological goals which are usually ascribed to it.

72 Saikal, A. and Maley, W. (1989) Editors. *The Soviet Withdrawal from Afghanistan.* Cambridge: Cambridge University Press

Produced very quickly after Soviet troops left Afghanistan, this collection examines the negotiation of the withdrawal and a variety of issues which arose after it.

73 Allison, R. (1988) *The Soviet Union and the Strategy of Non-Alignment in the Third World.* Cambridge: Cambridge University Press

Allison studies how Soviet thinking and policy towards the non-aligned states has developed, and examines Soviet friendship treaties and the opportunities they offer for selective military access and military co-operation.

74 Karsh, E. (1988) *The Soviet Union and Syria: The Asad Years.* London: Routledge for the Royal Institute of International Affairs. (Chatham House Papers)

Karsh detects two phases in Soviet relations with Syria. In the first, from 1970-1977, Syria had the upper hand, while from 1977-1988 Moscow had the advantage.

75   Kolodziej, E.A. and Kanet, R.E. (1988) Editors. *The Limits to Soviet Power in the Developing World: Thermidor in the Revolutionary Struggle.* London: Macmillan

The contributors assume that Soviet policy is a function of the global competition for influence with the United States. This collection includes twelve regional assessments and four general chapters which connect Soviet policy to the general concerns of international relations.

76   Rubinstein, A. Z. (1988) *Moscow's Third World Strategy.* Princeton, NJ: Princeton University Press

Rubinstein also assumes that Soviet policy in the Third World is a function of Soviet-American relations, and finds no evidence that Gorbachev has ceased to view the Third World as a strategic arena for fostering Soviet goals and diverting American resources and interest.

77   Duner, B. (1987) *The Bear, the Cubs & the Eagle: Soviet Bloc Interventionism in the Third World and the US Response.* Aldershot: Gower

Duner examines the record from 1970 onwards of Soviet, East European and Cuban military activity and looks at American responses to it.

78   Korbonski, A. and Fukuyama, F. (1987) Editors. *The Soviet Union & the Third World: The Last Three Decades.* Ithaca, NY; London: Cornell University Press

The contributors seek to place current relations in the broader context of policy over the last three decades to see if larger historical patterns are at work which might help to predict future Soviet behaviour.

79   Shearman, P. (1987) *The Soviet Union and Cuba.* London: Routledge & Kegan Paul for the Royal Institute of International Affairs

Shearman finds that the costs to the Soviet Union of its relationship with Cuba are significant, while Cuba makes substantial gains.

80   Menon, R. (1986) *Soviet Power and the Third World.* New Haven; London: Yale University Press

Menon investigates the status and significance of Soviet power projection forces and the role and usefulness of arms transfers.

81   Cassen, R. (1985) Editor. *Soviet Interests in the Third World.* London: Sage for the Royal Institute of International Affairs

The contributors depict a beleaguered Soviet Union with an ailing domestic economy and heavy external commitments. They examine Soviet policy towards various regions as well as towards specific countries. One section is devoted to the Soviet economy and the Third World.

82   Hosmer, S.T. and Wolfe, T.W. (1983) *Soviet Policy and Practice toward Third World Conflicts.* Lexington, MA: Lexington/Heath

A study of Soviet intervention in Angola, Ethiopia and Afghanistan, preceded by an analysis of the evolution of Soviet policy since the Second World War.

83   Valkenier, E.K. (1983) *The Soviet Union and the Third World: An Economic Bind.* New York: Praeger

Soviet economic performance and capabilities and the associated Marxist theories had become the Achilles heel of Soviet relations with the Third World by the beginning of the 1980s. Valkenier's analysis of academic and official publications demonstrates that changes in Soviet theory about the Third World predated Gorbachev's accession to power.

84   Freedman, R.O. (1982) *Soviet Policy towards the Middle East since 1970.* New York: Praeger

A narrative account of the complex story of Soviet policy in the Middle East. Freedman takes the story up to Sadat's visit to Jerusalem, which marked the lowest point in Soviet influence on events in that region.

85   Katz, M.N. (1982) *The Third World in Soviet Military Thought.* London: Croom Helm

Katz established how Soviet military views about the Third World changed between 1964 and 1981, paying particular attention to military thinking about Third World conflict. Military views sometimes differed from those of the Communist Party but the Party view always prevailed.

86   Heldman, D. (1981) *The USSR and Africa: Foreign Policy under Khrushchev.* New York: Praeger

Carefully documenting his study by exhaustive empirical analyses, Heldman finds that Soviet policy in North Africa during the Khrushchev era was motivated by strategic concerns and the desire to encourage anti-Western neutrality, and to offer a model of economic development and aid in the struggle against neo-colonialism.

Defence Issues

87   MccGwire, M. (1991) *Perestroika and Soviet National Security.* Washington, DC: Brookings Institution

MccGwire argues that the *sine qua non* for the new détente (required so that domestic reform could take place) was a change in the Marxist-Leninist theory of international relations and the scaling down of Soviet armed forces. He sets Soviet security policy and strategic doctrine in the larger context of foreign policy.

88   Hudson, G.E. (1990) Editor. *Soviet National Security Policy under Perestroika.* Boston: Unwin Hyman. (Mershon Center Series on International Security and Foreign Policy, Volume IV)

The context in which the change in national security policy has occurred and the change agents are examined in these essays, as well as specific aspects of security policy like the concept of reasonable sufficiency, arms control policy and the changes in policy towards Western and Eastern Europe and towards the Third World.

89   Holden, G. (1989) *The Warsaw Pact: Soviet Security and Bloc Politics.* Oxford: Blackwell

Holden combines an examination of the military and political history of the Warsaw Treaty Organization with an analysis of Soviet security and arms control policies in Europe, relating the latter to the external and internal functions of the WTO. The book was published before the dramatic changes of 1989 took place.

90   Nelson, D. (1986) *Alliance Behavior in the Warsaw Pact.* Boulder, CO: Westview Press

Nelson analyses the cohesion and reliability of the Warsaw Pact and the distribution of defence effort within it, and concludes that without coercion the Soviet Union will have little choice other than to accept its continuing evolution.

91   Holloway, D. and Sharp, J. (1984) Editors. *The Warsaw Pact: Alliance in Transition?* London: Macmillan

Developments within the Warsaw Pact in the 1970s are examined to establish whether it has developed into a genuine alliance. The last three chapters turn to the future and predict that economic pressures will provide an impetus for long-term reform.

92 Kaplan, S.S. Tatu, M., Robinson, T.W., Zimmerman, W., Zagoria, D.S., Zagoria, J.D. et al. (1981) *Diplomacy of Power: Soviet Armed Forces as a Political Instrument.* Washington, DC: Brookings Institution

An exhaustive study of the use by the Soviet Union of military diplomacy as an instrument of foreign policy, providing an historical record of military operations and focusing on the political context in which they have been undertaken. The contributors also evaluate how successful the deployment of power has been.

Foreign Economic Policy

93 Mehrotra, S. (1990) *India and the Soviet Union: Trade and Technology Transfer.* Cambridge: Cambridge University Press

Soviet aid to and trade with India since 1970 is examined, including the complex question of technology transfer and its effectiveness. Mehrotra concludes that India benefits through the amelioration of its balance of payments problems. Strategic and political benefits, rather than economic gains, have motivated Soviet leaders. He warns of future problems of complementarity between the two economies.

94 Hanson, P. (1988) *Western Economic Statecraft in East-West Relations: Embargoes, Sanctions, Linkage, Economic Warfare and Detente.* London: Routledge & Kegan Paul for the Royal Institute of International Affairs. (Chatham House Papers, 40)

Western foreign economic policy towards the Soviet Union has produced some serious challenges to Soviet foreign policy since the Second World War. Hanson examines various economic carrots and sticks employed by the West and the Soviet responses, and considers how effective economic instruments have been.

95 Hough, J. (1988) *Opening up the Soviet Economy.* Washington, DC: Brookings Institution

Hough explains why perestroika was necessary in the Soviet Union and explores the foreign policy implications of economic reform.

96 Sokoloff, G. (1987) *The Economy of Detente: The Soviet Union and Western Capital.* Leamington Spa: Berg

Sokoloff examines Soviet purchases of Western equipment from the middle of the 1950s to the middle of the 1970s to investigate Soviet motives for détente. He concludes that even in the 1970s, Soviet economic dependence on the West was obvious.

97 Stern, J. (1987) *Soviet Oil and Gas Exports to the West.* Aldershot: Gower for the Policy Studies Institute and the Royal Institute of International Affairs

A detailed analysis of Soviet energy in the 1980s, and of Soviet gas and oil exports to OECD countries and its commercial behaviour. Stern points out that the Soviet Union is unlikely to use its gas and oil exports for nefarious strategic purposes because it has domestic economic reasons for its export sales.

98 Parrott, B. (1985) Editor. *Trade, Technology, and Soviet-American Relations.* Bloomington, IN: Indiana University Press in association with the Center for Strategic and International Studies, Georgetown University, Washington, DC

The first part of this volume provides a political and economic overview of the Soviet approach to trade and technology transfers. The second part looks at case studies of various branches of the economy, while the third turns the mirror round and looks at the problem from the American angle.

The 'New Political Thinking' in Soviet Foreign Policy

99 Hirsch, S. (1989) Editor. *MEMO: New Soviet Voices on Foreign and Economic Policy.* Washington, DC: Bureau of National Affairs, Inc.

Translations of a selection of Soviet articles published in *Mirovaia Ekonomika i Mezhdunarodnye Otnosheniia* in 1988 and 1989, chosen to illustrate Soviet new thinking. For those who do not read Russian, this books offers an interesting array of views.

100 Kubalkova, V. and Cruickshank, A.A. (1989) *Thinking New about Soviet 'New Thinking'.* Berkeley, CA: University of California Press

The authors argue that 'new thinking' represents a challenge to Western social science and policy-making. They analyse its sources, how it functions as Soviet ideology and whether it is Marxism or Marxism-Leninism.

101 Malcolm, N. (1989) *Soviet Policy Perspectives on Western Europe.* London: Routledge for the Royal Institute of International Affairs. (Chatham House Papers)

An examination of the range of views expressed in the Soviet specialist literature about Western Europe which makes clear the extent to which conventional Soviet attitudes towards the European Community and NATO have been overturned.

102 Gorbachev, M. (1988) *Perestroika,* 2nd edn. London: Fontana Collins

Gorbachev's personal vision of the domestic reconstruction of the Soviet Union and its new role in the international system. The sections on the socialist world and on two German states suggest that the Soviet leadership did not anticipate the events of 1989.

103 Hough, J. (1988) *Russia and the West: Gorbachev and the Politics of Reform.* New York: Simon and Schuster

Hough maintains that Soviet foreign policy changed in the summer of 1987 and that the primary purpose was to encourage foreign investment.

CHAPTER SIX

Armed Forces

Professor John Erickson
University of Edinburgh

Transition and Transformation

During the course of the IV World Congress for Soviet and East European Studies, which convened in Harrogate in July, 1990, one of the sections was devoted to a discussion of the state of professional Soviet 'military studies'. Amidst numerous exchanges, it was suggested that due to the decline in the perception of 'the threat', it was inevitable that there would be a diminution of interest in, let us call them, 'Soviet military studies'. On the surface that would seem to be both an admissible and logical proposition. However, an examination of the published work over the past decade would tend to undermine the legitimacy of such a proposition, for it would seem that there is considerable variation between what might be called 'the threat situation' and the course and content of 'professional Soviet military studies'. Indeed, there is a paradox here: as 'the threat' has begun to recede, or is said to have receded, so the intensity of interest in 'Soviet military affairs' has not only actually increased but also departed in different directions, ranging from the close focus of the transition from Brezhnev to Gorbachev to fundamental examination of the properties of the Soviet military system and, delving even deeper, into the relationship between the *ImperialRussian* and the *Soviet* modes and methods of military organisation.

In the course of the past decade the profile of publication has, of necessity, reflected certain political and operational priorities, part of which has been the personal predilection of authors but also the perception and commitment of particular institutions. At the same time, one of the most important though perhaps less prominent aspects of work in the field of Russian and Soviet military studies has been the 'generational shift', the emergence of a younger generation of scholars, not merely young in years but more particularly not steeped in the idioms, anger and anguishes of the 'Cold War' with all its corrosiveness. Even more important, this rising generation has been able to exploit greater opportunities for travel and exchange in the Soviet Union and to benefit from glasnost, in the sense that original material from the Soviet archives is to hand and can be discussed with Soviet historians. It is to the credit of *cette jeunesse* that they have made bold, original and incisive use of both material and access, which augurs most promisingly for the future.

In essence, both historiographically and politically, the past decade has been one of transition and transformation. As far as I can determine, none of the work undertaken can be seen to have exhausted its potential or its relevance. Whichever way 'reasonable sufficiency' develops and evolves in the Soviet Union, interest in 'doctrine' will be sustained and continuous. Whatever military structure that onset of 'sufficiency' (or its absence) predicates, the investigation of the 'system', including its Imperial antecedents, will be of commanding importance and may well provide the basis for fruitful scholarly interchange and professional discussion. Without acceding wholly to the rubric of 'now thrive the armourers', work on weapons development, on Soviet military technology, on comparative studies of military technology, on the Soviet R&D basis, on Soviet C3 and the Soviet space programme will retain its importance, perhaps less for operational dissection under a 'threat' scenario but rather in terms of arms control, verification systems and pertinent Soviet investigations of 'future war'. This is not to suggest in any way that there is a bent to or desire for war in any Soviet environment, but it is clear that we can learn from Soviet methodology and Soviet insights, again not a few of them derived from the prescience and professionalism of Imperial Russian military thought, an observation confirmed by present Soviet reprinting of a number of Imperial Russian 'classics' and coincidentally a return to the intellectual rigour of Svechin and others, all of Imperial Russian vintage.

In short, in what may well be a true East-West convergence, we are seeing the evolution of a new intellectual amalgam, neither the propagandistic stereotypes of the Cold War and the reprehensible *trahison des clercs* nor a stultified scholarship, but rather fresh intellectual and professional vistas which are emerging from the tense, often tangled discourses, discussions and enquiries of the past decade, whose scholarship may well come to mark a watershed not unlike the first scholarly burgeoning of 'Soviet military studies' in the 1950s and early 1960s. What is certainly marked about the publications of the past decade, be they on Soviet doctrine or strategic thought or the military system at large, is the *quality* of the scholarship, which shows much advance in terms of command of language, coverage of sources, pertinence of analysis and relevance of theme, such as to designate not a few works *locus classicus*. Given then the political circumstances and the possibility of change in the Soviet military system, which in organisational terms may last until the end of the decade, and with respect to military technical advances which will stretch well into the next century, the publications of the past decade must be regarded as 'signposts' or guidelines to the past, present and future. In this respect, they occupy and will continue to occupy a singular place in the entire historiography of 'Soviet military studies', but they do not signify any diminution of interest in, or actual relevance of, Soviet military studies. If anything, this present body of work shows its independence of and detachment from the vagaries, the contrivances, the polemics and the politics of 'the threat'.

Doctrine and Strategy

In the course of his visit to France in 1985, Mikhail Gorbachev startled both the Soviet and non-Soviet world alike with his enunciation of a new principle pertaining to military doctrine, that of 'reasonable sufficiency', *razumnaia dostatochnost*, a concept which proposed the restriction of military potential to the limits of 'reasonable sufficiency' coupled with the notion of implementing 'non-provocative' or 'defensive defence'. The avowedly Delphic terms of this 'new' concept and the confusing tautology of 'defensive defence', coupled with the affirmation of 'war avoidance' or 'war prevention' (*predotvrashchenie voiny*) as a strategic objective, triggered off an increasingly complex debate. This involved not only the Soviet military but also the newly influential civilian analysts, the *institutchiki*, in a debate which became increasingly embittered and marred by rancorous dispute. The struggle over 'doctrine' remains as yet largely unresolved, which requires of Western analysts and historians close attention to the processes and implications of doctrine-formulation in the Soviet Union. This condition ensures the particular relevance of the monograph on doctrine-formulation and dissemination by Harriet and William Scott (32), the collection of papers edited by Gregory Flynn, *Soviet Military Doctrine and Western Policy* (27), and most recently James McConnell's penetrating essay on the 'transformation of Soviet strategy' (26).

While there is much to commend in the Soviet principle of 'war avoidance', this does not of itself solve a number of critical problems, once again illuminating the divisions between the military and civilian analysts. Put briefly 'war avoidance', or 'war prevention' for that matter, can be generally subsumed under the rubric of deterrence (and the maintenance of a credible deterrent, embracing a strategic retaliatory strike capability), but what engages the conflict between the Soviet civilian analysts and the professional military is not so much 'war avoidance' as such, war is neither desired nor entertained, but essentially the business of 'threat assessment' and the relative weight to be accorded to political as opposed to military means in order to guarantee Soviet security.

As for military strategy, one singular addition to the literature in the past decade has been the publication by the National Defense University, Washington, of *The Voroshilov Lectures* (29). This work is valuable not so much for the actual 'operational context', which is essentially dated, but rather for insights into Soviet military methodology and professional approaches. A form of update, if it can be called that, is presented in the translation of Colonel General M.A. Gareev's *M.V. Frunze: Voennyi Teoretik* (30). Two aspects of 'strategy' have received close attention. First and foremost, what form 'future strategy' might assume as the Soviet-American relationship evolves, an aspect investigated in Stephen Cimbala's most recent study *Uncertainty and Control: Future Soviet and American Strategy* (25). The prime preoccupation of Soviet military doctrine, however, one by no means displaced by the emphasis on 'war avoidance', is the projection of 'future war' and the implications for 'military art' which embraces the problems of the actual conduct of operations and the impact of an entirely new range of advanced weapons, not excluding those deployed in or from space. This is a theme developed both politically and technically in the Soviet monograph *Weaponry in Space: The Dilemma of Security* (37), with a counterpoint furnished by Stephen Blank and others in *The Soviet Space Theater of War* (TV), Stratech Studies SS88-, July, 1988, Center for Strategic Technology, Texas A&M University System, College Station, Texas.

While these *exotica* are important and will become increasingly so as space capabilities for offensive and defensive operations are further developed as 'force multipliers', there is much confusion and contumely within Soviet circles over a more overtly terrestrial theme: what precisely is a defensive posture? Or, what is defensivism? This has led not merely to polemics but, at the same time, to quite serious explorations of certain historical models; in particular, Soviet operations in Outer Mongolia on the Khalkhin-Gol in 1939, and the gigantic initial Soviet defensive operations in the Kursk salient in 1943 during the 'Great Patriotic War'. While this may seem to be an almost academic, even pedantic order of discussion, the argument and dissension over 'defensivism' has generated a much wider and more divisive debate over not only what type of armed forces the Soviet Union needs but over the whole nature of the Soviet system, its past, present and future, particularly its future, provoking nothing less than a severe and possibly sustained crisis in Soviet civil-military relations. The tensions of this transition period, for such it is and may well be for some time, are admirably delineated and dissected in a series of papers entitled *Soldiers and the Soviet State: Civil-Military Relations from Brezhnev to Gorbachev* (1).

But there is more to this transition than mere adjustments, most of them verbal, to military doctrine and a shift in the balance between civilian and military assessments of security issues, important though these are and will continue to be. What is pending seems to be a wholesale 'systems shift', involving the political and military structures simultaneously. A process of such an order has to illuminate the importance of *fundamental* investigations of the characteristics of the Soviet military system and its institutions, a commitment which now deeply engages both Soviet and non-Soviet historians. Indeed, 'transition' is perhaps too pallid a term for what is taking place. The fundamental nature of the process is better rendered by 'transformation', the theme of a major work generated by the Twelfth Military History Symposium held at the USAF Academy in 1986. The proceedings have been recently published under the title *Transformation in Russian and Soviet Military History* (3). This is an invaluable and formidably scholarly collection of papers by renowned specialists. The volume is made the more pertinent by the incorporation of material bearing on the Imperial Russian antecedents of the system, material to which Soviet soldiers and others are turning with increasing frequency.

The system and the soldier are under increasing scrutiny. both are under increasing strain, to judge by the tone and content of the Soviet press, with both the military lobby and the anti-military publicists pleading those precedents which best suit their respective cases. As for those self-same precedents, Mark von Hagen's unique and pioneering study of the Red Army as an 'institution of socialisation' and his analysis of the social and political struggles in the Army and over the Army in the 1920s, *Soldiers in the Proletarian Dictatorship: The Red Army and the Soviet Socialist State, 1917-1930*, must act as an indispensable guide to the significance of 'precedents' throughout the coming decade and possibly beyond (2). As for the poor benighted Soviet conscript soldier, or the underpaid, badly housed, overworked and harassed troop officer, or yet again the browbeaten, even physically beaten ethnic recruit, the situation seems not to improve but only to continue to deteriorate, an environment explored in a fine and durable study by Ellen Jones, *Red Army and Society: A Sociology of the Soviet Military* (16). This is a work whose value continues to grow, given present Soviet circumstances and those which might plausibly be projected, particularly inter-ethnic conflict and its effect upon the military system, not to mention overall manpower problems and the demands for a more professionalised military machine based mainly on the volunteer principle or voluntary 'contract service'. Nor does the turmoil end there. The political organs within the military are under heavy fire with not a few calls for the 'depoliticisation' of the Army, an aspect which invests Francesco Benvenuti's study of the early 'politicisation' of the Army, *The Bolsheviks and the Red Army 1918-1922* (6), with a certain contemporary relevance, given among other things recent Soviet interest in the reappraisal, if not the actual rehabilitation of Trotsky.

Operations

The study of military operations, pre-1941, 1941-45 and post-1945, has become yet another intellectual, ideological and political battleground, one where the ammunition is continually supplied by glasnost and reinforcements are furnished by the steady flow of 'revelations'. One example of the relationship between military history, or operational experience, and 'new thinking' in military affairs is the case of operations at Khalkhin-Gol in 1939, cited by some as an example of 'defensivism' coupled with a limited counter-offensive capability, and thus adduced as a viable 'model' upon which to develop both doctrine and force structures. The Khalkhin-Gol operations have been explored in the greatest detail, from both the Soviet and Japanese side, with an astonishing munificence of material in Alvin D. Coox's monumental two-volume study, *Nomonhan: Japan Against Russia, 1939* (45).

While there is much which is fortunate in that 'accidental convergence' of Soviet and Western scholarly interest, there seems to be deliberate convergence in the attention being paid by historians, less to the battlefield performance of the Red Army during the Great Patriotic War and more, a great deal more, to the social impact and the social consequences of that gigantic conflict which did so much to shape the Soviet Union as it is today. Much impassioned Soviet argument centres not so much on the 'victory' as such but on its cost, its excessive cost in human life and national treasure. Part of that theme is developed in the volume of essays edited by Susan J. Linz, *The Impact of World War II on the Soviet Union* (58), a significant complement to which is Mark Harrison's *Soviet Planning in Peace and War 1938-1945* (57). An interesting, even provocative approach to 'performance' in the wider sense of that term is Jonathan R. Adelman's comparative study *Prelude to the Cold War: The Tsarist, Soviet and U.S. Armies in the Two World Wars*, an ambitious but justifiably bold enterprise (5). The horrifyingly inhuman and brutalised face of war on the Eastern Front, still a highly charged and politically controversial topic, has been probed from German Army divisional records by Omer Bartov in *The Eastern Front 1941-45: German Troops and the Barbarisation of Warfare 1985* (56), a theme not enclosed or sealed within the Soviet scene alone but part of a wider, passionately debated controversy and its attendant furious *Historikerstreit* in Germany.

Why? This is a question which reverberates inside and outside the Soviet Union; why the horrendous scale of the 'initial disasters', why did the 'road to Berlin' have to wind its gruesome way through Stalingrad, why did four or more Soviet soldiers have to die for one German soldier fighting in the east, why the calamitous losses in weapons and equipment, why the almost incomprehensible scale of the sacrifices imposed upon and endured by the civilian population, and why the terrible fate of not only Soviet prisoners of war but also those who finally returned from the German camps, much of it as yet undisclosed..? Fresh fuel has been poured on to the fire of controversy with the publication in English of the pseudonymous Viktor Suvorov's *Icebreaker: Who Started the Second World War?* (47) which argues that, in fact, Stalin was preparing offensive war in 1941 designed to facilitate the export of communism and its global emplacement, thus in some respects justifying German pre-emption in June, 1941 and the surprise attack launched by *Barbarossa*. Somewhat earlier Bryan I. Fugate in *OperationBarbarossa* (61) had argued, to the accompaniment of further controversy, that 1941 was not the complete 'shambles' conveniently portrayed by Soviet authors, heaping all conceivable blame on Stalin, but rather a successful exercise in strategic deception, *maskirovka*, whereby carefully masked plans plus deliberate sacrifice of men and material to gain time effectively unhinged German plans. Reference to *maskirovka* draws immediate attention to the contribution of Colonel David M. Glantz of the US Army: *Soviet Military Deception in the Second World War* (49), and to his other volumes in the Cass Series on Soviet Military Theory and Practice covering Soviet operations in 1942-3 and the evolution of Soviet military science.

One most welcome feature is the recourse to contemporary Soviet wartime materials (hitherto largely ignored in spite of their value) exemplified in the publication of two Soviet General Staff operational assessments for 1942 and 1943, *Battle for Moscow* and *Battle for Stalingrad* (50, 51), edited by Michael Parrish and Louis Rotundo respectively. These wartime evaluations of the Red Army's battlefield performance are not all complimentary. Much remains to be done to exploit to the full such wartime materials, which have suffered unjustifiable neglect. The promise of improvement is seen in the massive compilation of data assembled by Robert G. Poirier and Albert Z. Conner in *The Red Army Order of Battle in the Great Patriotic War* (59). In this context of data, or more properly sources, Michael Parrish rendered a considerable service with his bibliography *The U.S.S.R. in World War II: An Annotated Bibliography of Books Published in the Soviet Union, 1945-1975* (66). These two volumes can be usefully supplemented by Gerda Beitter's bibliography of Soviet histories of military formations and units, *Die Rote Armee in 2.Weltkrieg*, Bernard and Graefe Verlag, Koblenz, 1984, listing published Soviet material for fronts, tank armies, mechanised corps, cavalry corps and divisions, engineer and artillery units.

The tussle over doctrine has once more infused fresh life into the argument over Soviet preparedness in 1941 (or the lack of it) and the crucial nature of the 'initial period', a preoccupation now shared by Soviet and Western historians and analysts and likely to last for some time, though the work carried through in the 1980s retains much of its relevance. If we are now speaking of 'lessons', then not everything is subsumed by the

Great Patriotic War. The Soviet military commitment in Afghanistan has not only brought fresh grief to, and further bouts of recrimination in, the Soviet Union but it has inevitably engaged the attention of Western specialists, producing such works as *Afghanistan: The First Five Years of Soviet Occupation* by J. Bruce Amstutz, a massive 545-page volume (69), followed by the end-game, *The Soviet Withdrawal from Afghanistan*, edited by Amin Saikal and William Maley, a set of 10 studies published in 1989.

Much of the work produced in the past decade, both by accident and design, projects itself into the coming decade and even further – the investigation of doctrine, not only in its Soviet context but how it impacts on Western priorities and preferences, the problems of 'transition' turning into 'transformation' with antecedents and analogies reaching back into the Imperial past, the properties of 'the system' and how it has been understood and is now understood by soldiers and civilians alike in the Soviet Union, the 'lessons' of war, whether general, regional or local, and the social consequences of such conflicts. What is especially striking about both Soviet and Western historical writing and analysis is the effect of even limited access to Soviet archives and the imprint of glasnost, facilitating no small degree of personal contact and professional exchange, a trend which began to manifest itself after the middle of the 1980s and which will hopefully persist in one form or another throughout the coming decade.

Arms and Services

But for all the euphoria, the talk of a 'peace dividend' and the promises of 'defensive defence', the Soviet Union remains and is likely to remain the most formidable Eurasian military power, one heavily nuclear-armed, its armed forces reduced in numbers but where 'quantity'is being exchanged for 'quality', and trained for the eventuality of operations on a high-technology battlefield. Well before the advent of Mr Gorbachev, advancing military technology, in particular precision guided weapons using conventional munitions, has obliged the Soviet General Staff to consider *select* defensive operational forms, though not at the cost of relinquishing substantial capabilities for offensive action. Soviet interest in a form of 'defensivism' certainly predates Gorbachev, reaching back at least three decades with the advent of nuclear weapons and the ICBM, thus fusing huge destructive power with long-range deep strike, a 'threat' now revitalised with the appearance of precision guided weapons and advanced conventional munitions which again combine great lethality with extended strike range. Given this set of circumstances, with profound changes in Soviet 'military art' pending, not to mention Soviet military-technical developments in their own right, it is not surprising that much Western analysis has focused on changes in Soviet force structure, operational methods and Soviet military technology.

In this context a curious parallelism has emerged between the work of Soviet and Western analysts, namely a concern with just what is 'the threat'? Such a preoccupation dominated the early years of the 1980s, with multiple examples of 'worst case' analysis on both sides enough to provoke a reaction such as that provided by Tom Gervasi in *The Myth of Soviet Military Supremacy* (12), a serious, well-substantiated work. The battle of the books, or more properly glossy pamphlets or booklets, opened quite early with the publication in September, 1981 of the first edition of the Pentagon's 'glossy', *Soviet Military Power*, presenting details of the Soviet military programme, a little lurid in parts and using 'artist's licence' to depict futuristic weapons systems in glorious technicolour (95). This evoked two responses, one a rather drab Soviet publication *Whence the Threat to Peace* (96) now discontinued, and Tom Gervasi's witty but pointed rejoinder to the Pentagon's 'hype' with his *Soviet Military Power: The Annotated and Corrected Version of the Pentagon's Guide* (12). However, since those early days the Pentagon publication has improved substantially and has dispensed with the poster art, sticking to photographs, pie-charts and histograms.

Important and substantial studies of the military-operational and military-technical aspects of the Soviet war machine were produced during the 1980s, a prime example of which is David Isby's *Weapons and Tactics of the Soviet Army* first published by Jane's in 1981 and revised and reprinted in 1988 (74), detailing the organisation, weapons systems, operational methods and support elements of the Soviet Army. A more general survey of the Soviet system is provided by Christopher Donnelly's *Red Banner: The Soviet Military System in Peace and War* (8), covering such topics as 'the Soviet military mind, the military infrastructure and the Soviet art of war, all subjects presently under review by the Soviet high command. While the proposed agreement on the reduction of conventional forces in Europe envisages the destruction by the Warsaw Pact of some 19,000 tanks (as opposed to 4,000 on the part of NATO), Soviet armoured forces still remain a subject of high interest and great importance: even with an agreement, each alliance will retain 20,000 tanks, 20,000 guns, 30,000 armoured fighting vehicles and 2,000 helicopters. The late and universally respected Richard Simpkin produced in 1984 a highly perceptive study of the 'Soviet mobile force concept' in *Red Armour* (87): for further technical and operational detail of that same force, the volume by Steven J. Zaloga and James W. Loop, *Soviet Tanks and Combat Vehicles 1946 to the Present* (78) is an invaluable source and will continue to be so, for Soviet armoured forces are not about to disappear and are being steadily modernised in relation to growing Soviet interest in a 'land-air battle' concept.

The appearance at Western air displays of advanced, highly manoeuvrable Soviet combat aircraft such as the SU-7, comparable in many respects to Western high-performance fighters, has intensified interest in and observation of the Soviet air force and the Soviet aircraft industry (ironically with the former a potential threat and the latter conceivably a potential partner). The available literature abounds in truly excellent handbooks and photographic collections of particular Soviet aircraft, or types of aircraft, though Soviet air strategy and operations enjoy a somewhat narrower focus as might be expected, but one valuable example is *Aircraft: Strategy and Operations of the Soviet Air Force* by Air-Vice-Marshal R.A. Mason and John W.R. Taylor (82), while that increasingly important and versatile vehicle, the helicopter, is amply catered for in John Everett-Heath's *Soviet Helicopters* in a second edition published by Jane's in 1988 (73).

The size, role and missions of the Soviet Navy is yet another aspect embraced by Soviet 'new thinking' and brought within the context of 'reasonable sufficiency', inducing yet more turmoil within the Soviet military-political scene and causing not a few to predict the virtual demise of the Soviet 'blue water navy'. But the Soviet naval Commander-in-Chief, Admiral Chernavin, is far from disposed to accept only a narrow, constricted defensive mission for the Soviet Navy, arguing that if the naval mission is to defend the Soviet perimeter, then this must perforce mean reaching out into the open sea, extending operations beyond the range of land-based aircraft, hence among other things the importance of the new (and much criticised) *Tbilisi* class aircraft carriers. Indispensable to understanding Soviet naval development, past, present and future are the editions of Norman Polmar's *Guide to the Soviet Navy* (84), while the 'carrier question' and its future, among other major questions, was raised in *The Future of the Soviet Navy: An Assessment to the Year 2000* edited by Bruce W. Watson and Peter M. Dunn (85).

Fascinating and important though actual hardware is, here we come to what might at best be called 'the invisibles' – but no less significant for that, indeed quite the converse. It might said that this command and control technology, space operations, electronic warfare all duly interconnected are the real keys to Soviet strategic and operational developments, hence the continuing relevance of several monographs and collected papers published during the 1980s. In 1982 Brassey's published John Hemsley's *Soviet Troop Control: The Role of Command Technology in the Soviet Military System* (88), an examination of current practice and future concepts in what is generally understood by *upravlenie voiskami*, the search for effectiveness and efficiency and, above all, the ability to cope with decision-making under the most severe time constraints. A broader view of Soviet command and control as applied to all systems was presented in the symposium (including translated Soviet material) edited by Stephen J. Cimbala, *Soviet C3*, with papers which discuss strategic and theatre nuclear warfare, NATO and the Warsaw Pact, war at sea, air warfare, aerospace and space defence and 'war survival' (75).

Deep down and hidden well within the bowels of several layers of official secrecy is the subject of electronic warfare, 'radio-electronic combat' in Soviet usage. Technical manuals and technical journals apart, David G. Chizum produced an extremely useful analysis of Soviet theory and practice in relation to electronic warfare in his *Soviet Radioelectronic Combat*, complete with bibliography and a glossary of select Soviet terms accompanied by transliterations of the Russian originals (86). Leaving apart utopian visions of a nuclear-free world, it may well be that the basic Soviet objective centres on *strategic systems*, on the development and deployment of a deeply echeloned global defensive system, one not only multi-dimensional but also multi-spatial in the connection between space-based and terrestrial assets, with space-based capabilities utilised for both offensive and defensive purposes. In short, here is real 'defence dominance' founded within Soviet territorial confines only but committed to exercising control, offensively and defensively; the 'offence-defence convergence' presently espoused by Soviet military planners over the complex of space, the oceanic perimeter and the electromagnetic spectrum, in which whole context it is relevant to consider the implications of Nicholas L. Johnson's study *Soviet Military Strategy in Space* (33).

Not long ago General Moiseev, now former Chief of the Soviet General Staff, made an announcement of some considerable import, namely that henceforth Soviet defensive operations would be constrained entirely to Soviet territory and to Soviet territory alone. This demonstrably leaves the Warsaw Pact somewhat in limbo, while Marshal Akhromeev has latterly declared that in the current year (1991) the Warsaw Pact will cast off its military functions in favour of a purely political role. Nevertheless changes in both NATO and the Warsaw Pact, even as their roles are modified, emphasise the significance of mobilisation, sustainability and flexibility of forces, hence the relevance of the study edited by Jeffrey Simon, *NATO-Warsaw Pact Force Mobilization* (89) and also his earlier monograph *Warsaw Pact Forces: Problems in Command and Control* (90). While the future of the Warsaw Pact hangs in the balance, the truly massive assembly of data on the Pact's military and political organisation and institutions, compiled and analysed by Professor Teresa Rakowska-Harmstone and others in a three-volume report is in many respects a unique source and available for present and future evaluations of the several East European military establishments as they change and evolve (91).

Perhaps in the final analysis it comes down to personalities, to the human factor, to the men in charge and here one of the most substantial achievements of the 1980s has been the publication of a huge compendium on Soviet military-political personalities, complete with photographs, biographical data, career histories, command appointments and analysis of key policy issues, not the least being the maintenance of public order and internal security in the Soviet Union. This is *Jane's Soviet High Command* edited by Richard Woff, replete with a frequent 'Information Update' furnishing more biographical data (97). A companion publication on the Warsaw Pact is planned, though changing circumstances may yet intrude somewhat abruptly on this intention.

Bibliographical

I have divided the attached bibliography, for which the end-date is September 30, 1990, into five main sections with an addendum or appendix covering sundry directories, yearbooks, one bibliographic entry as such which could not otherwise be emplaced (save to repeat it five times) and relevant papers. Those five sections comprise: Russian and Soviet Military History, Military Organisation and Policy Perspectives; Military Strategy, Doctrine and Tactics; Military Operations, further subdivided into three periods, pre-1941, 1941-1945 and post-1945; Arms and Services, Weapons Systems, Military Technology; the Warsaw Pact.

Each bibliographical entry has a brief annotation and in select instances, few in number, I have cross-referenced a Soviet work or works either as a complement or as an additive. In the case of an English-language version of an original Soviet publication, I have appended the original Soviet title.

Given the aim and circumstances of this compilation, selectivity is not only unavoidable but mandatory. Others may well choose to present a profile after a radically different fashion, omit in one place and add in another, but whatever the nature of the selections it is, I submit, wholly justifiable to register this past decade as one marked by substantial, durable and innovative scholarly achievement and professional perspicacity in the field of Soviet military-political and military-technical studies.

Bibliography

Russian and Soviet Military History, Military Organisation and Policy Perspectives

1   Colton, T.J. and Gustafson, T.(1990) Editors. *Soldiers and the Soviet State: Civil-Military Relations from Brezhnev to Gorbachev.* Princeton, NJ: Princeton University Press

   An examination of the role and influence of the Soviet military addressed in eight essays covering civil-military relations in a the context of political change, the place of the KGB, resource allocation, the defence industry, social change at large and Soviet military involvement overseas.

2   Von Hagen, M.(1990) *Soldiers in the Proletarian Dictatorship: The Red Army and the Soviet Socialist State, 1917-1930.* Ithaca, NY: Cornell University Press

An original and fundamentally important study of the Red Army as an institution of socialisation, the political role of the Red Army, the politics of Trotsky's defeat and the nature of the debates about the form and nature of this armed force developing a political culture best described as 'militarised socialism', in turn one of the sources of Stalinism and the command system of administration associated with Red Army victories in the Civil War.

3   Reddel, C.W. (1990) Editor. *Transformation in Russian and Soviet Military History (Proceedings of the Twelfth Military History Symposium, United States Air Force Academy, October, 1986).* Washington, DC: USAF Academy, USAF

Introduced by John Keep's Memorial Lecture 'Soldiering in Tsarist Russia', this volume is organised into four main sections dealing with the Military Legacy of Imperial Russia, Soviet Military Doctrine, the 'Great Patriotic War' and the emergence of superpower status plus an appendix detailing Soviet bibliographies as research aids, in all ten major research papers with commentaries and panel discussion summaries. An indispensable volume covering both historical experience and current operational issues.

4   Lincoln, Bruce W. (1990/1989) *Red Victory: A History of the Russian Civil War.* New York: Simon and Schuster

The sequel to the first volume *Passage Through Armageddon: The Russians in War and Revolution 1914-1918* (1986, Simon and Schuster). This volume is divided into three main sections following a chronological pattern, 1918, 1919 and 1920, the latter covering the final collapse of the Whites, the Red Army drive on Warsaw and the Kronstadt rising. Illustrated and full annotated, with extensive listing of sources and materials.

5   Adelman, J.R. (1988) *Prelude to the Cold War: The Tsarist, Soviet and U.S. Armies in the Two World Wars.* Boulder, CO; London: Lynne Rienner

A highly original and controversial study of the Imperial Russian, Soviet and American military organisations and military institutions using a comparative approach, analysing these several wartime experiences to illustrate how the Soviet Union and the United States eventually approached 'Cold War' politics.

6   Benvenuti, F. (1988) *The Bolsheviks and the Red Army, 1918-1922.* Cambridge: Cambridge University Press

Published originally in Italy as *I Bolscevichi e l'Armata Rossa 1918-1922* in 1982, this study is concerned principally with the politics of the Red Army during the Civil War, with particular reference to the 'Military Opposition' and Trotsky's policies involving the pursuit of military objectives not always or entirely consonant with Party objectives and ideals. Should be read and consulted in conjunction with Colonel A.G. Kavtaradze's *Voennye Spetsialisty na sluzhbe Respubliki Sovetov 1917-1920gg.* (1988) Moscow: Nauka.

7   Cooper, L. (1988) *The Political Economy of Soviet Military Power.* London: Macmillan

An assessment of the political and economic underpinnings of Soviet military power, with reference to Soviet military thought, economic power and national security, the 'defence burden' and latterly the implications of both glasnost and perestroika after 1985.

8 Donnelly, C. (1988) *Red Banner: The Soviet Military System in Peace and War.* London: Jane's Information Group

A wide-ranging study which surveys the shaping of the Soviet mind including ideology and tradition, the military infrastructure, the place of military doctrine and the Soviet art of war. Fully illustrated, with excellent maps and diagrams.

9 Jacobsen, C.G. (1987) Editor. *The Soviet Defence Enigma: Estimating Costs and Burden.* Oxford: SIPRI/Oxford University Press

A collection of eight papers covering Soviet national accounts, estimates of military expenditure, R&D spending, the historical perspective and future prospects. Very generous statistical and tabulated material.

10 Luckett, R. (1987) *The White Generals: An Account of the White Movement and the Russian Civil War.* London: Routledge and Kegan Paul

A revised and reprinted version first published in 1971, investigating the fortunes (or the misfortunes) of Kornilov, Denikin, Iudenich, Alekseev, Kolchak and Wrangel. A timely reprint in view of current Soviet interest in the White commanders and their political views in publications such as Denikin's *Pokhod na Moskvu.* Moscow: Voenizdat, 1989.

11 Wildman, A.K. (1987) *The End of the Russian Imperial Army: The Road to Soviet Power and Peace.* Princeton, NJ: Princeton University Press

Volume II of this magnificent history of the decline and demise of the Russian Imperial Army, the first volume of which, *The Old Army and the Soldiers' Revolt,* appeared in 1980. This present volume traces the final collapse of the army as a fighting machine, the relationships within the revolutionary government and the emergence of the Bolshevik programme for peace, enthusiastically embraced by frontline troops. See also M. Frenkin (1978) *Russkaia Armiia i Revoliutsiia 1917-1918.* Munich: Logos, to which Professor Wildman himself draws attention, and to the importance of the original archival material contained in the Frenkin volume.

12 Gervasi, T. (1986) *The Myth of Soviet Military Supremacy.* New York: Harper and Row

A massive and sustained attack on the exaggerations of Soviet military strength and claims for Soviet 'superiority', all severe misrepresentations of the East-West balance, with at least half the book taken up with nine massive appendices on the 'strategic balance', missile accuracy, theatre nuclear weapons in Europe, ground forces and satellite verification. Tom Gervasi also produced a witty and amusing annotation and correction of the Pentagon's *Soviet Military Power,* as if marking a graduate paper, originally published by Random House in 1987 and by Sidgwick and Jackson in 1988.

13 Seaton, A. and Seaton, J. (1986) *The Soviet Army: 1918 to the Present.* London: Bodley Head

A panoramic history of the Soviet Army from its earliest days as the Red Army, its political and military organisation, training, tactics and weapons, with six detailed appendices setting out the characteristics of Soviet tanks, infantry combat vehicles, anti-tank weapons, artillery, tactical missiles and infantry weapons.

14 Erickson, J. and Feuchtwanger, E.J. (1985) Editors. *Soviet Military Power and Performance.* London: Macmillan

A reprint of the 1979 edition, nine papers divided into four sections covering the system, the arms, the men and strategic perspectives.

15 Fuller, W.C.Jr. (1985) *Civil-Military Conflict in Imperial Russia 1881-1914.* Princeton, NJ: Princeton University Press

A major and original study in English of civil-military relations in the closing decades of the Russian empire, which stresses the rise of professionalism among leading members of the Russian military elite, deeply concerned with Russia's military backwardness. But this same professionalism served only to intensify disputes between the court, the civilian bureaucracy and the Ministry of War over finances and the use of troops to put down internal dissent, a historical theme with striking contemporary relevance.

16   Jones, E. (1985) *Red Army and Society: A Sociology of the Soviet Military.* Boston: Allen and Unwin

A pioneering work of considerable importance with obvious contemporary significance which examines in detail Soviet military manpower policy, conscription policy, regular officer career patterns, the 'military professional', the political officer and his role and the position of 'ethnic soldiers', 'minorities in uniform', all supported by a wealth of reference material and statistical data.

17   Treml, V.G. (1985) Editor. *High Treason: Essays on the History of the Red Army, 1918-1938* by Vitaly Rapoport and Yuri Alexeev. Durham: Duke University Press

This very unusual volume is the product of the collaboration in the 1970s of two Soviet dissidents, producing a form of 'military *samizdat*'. Bitterly anti-Stalinist, the authors or compilers have had some access to Soviet archives and to the personal files or recollections of important military figures, all to bolster their case against the Stalin clique and the 1st Cavalry Army, though guilt must be generally shared, indeed by some of the victims of the 'military purge' who should have actually conspired and taken up arms against the Stalinist regime. A strange but far from uninformed pre-glasnost work, worth close study given recent and official Soviet 'revelations'.

18   Erickson, J. (1984) *The Soviet High Command: A Military-Political History 1918-1941.* Boulder, CO; London: Westview Press

A reprint with a revised introduction of a work published originally in 1962.

19   Cockburn, A. (1983) *The Threat: Inside the Soviet Military Machine.* London: Hutchinson

Disputing the notion of absolute Soviet military efficiency and the existence of a 'massive military threat', the author surveyed Soviet military literature and tapped intelligence sources to paint a picture of a Soviet military system racked with personnel problems, race and language conflicts, corruption and nepotism within the High Command, grave supply and efficiency shortcomings with weapons and equipment, all aspects and items which are now matters for grave concern within the Soviet military establishment.

20   Scott, Harriet F. and Scott, William F. (1983) *The Soviet Control Structure: Capabilities for Wartime Survival.* New York: Crane Russak

An analysis of the Party-military control organisations, governmental agencies, the KGB, MVD and the armed forces as well as civil defence establishments which were designed to ensure survival in the event of nuclear conflict.

21   'Suvorov, V.' (pseud.) (1982) *Inside the Soviet Army.* London: Hamish Hamilton

Something of a sensation when it was first published, this account of the Soviet military system by a former Soviet major described the 'higher military leadership', the organisation of the Soviet forces, combat organisation, mobilisation, strategy and tactics, weapons and 'the soldier's lot'.

22   Duffy, C. (1981) *Russia's Military Way to the West: Origins and Nature of Russian Military Power 1700-1800.* London: Routledge and Kegan Paul

An important historical study which traces the emergence of the Russian regular army over the period 1700-1800, examining also the relative influence of Western and native Russian influences on the Russian military machine, outlining the career of Peter the Great and closing with the campaigns of Suvorov, coupled with details of the life of the

Russian soldier, the Russian officer and the Cossacks. (Published in a paperback edition in 1985).

23   'Suvorov, V.'(pseud.) (1981) *The Liberators: Inside the Soviet Army.* London: Hamish Hamilton

Announced as a 'unique document', this volume preceded *Inside the Soviet Army* and had as its centrepiece an account of the Soviet invasion of Czechoslovakia in 1968.

24   Gabriel, R.A. (1980) *The New Red Legions: An Attitudinal Portrait of the Soviet Soldier,* also *A Survey Data Source Book.* Westport, Connecticut: Greenwood

Based on extensive surveys of emigrés from the Soviet Union, men who had served in the Soviet armed forces over the period from the 1940s to the 1970s, posing 161 questions about military life and service (data duly assembled separately in the Source Book), this study aimed to provide a profile of Soviet soldiers of almost every rank and an assessment of combat effectiveness.

Military Strategy, Doctrine and Tactics

25   Cimbala, S.J. (1990) *Uncertainty and Control: Future Soviet and American Strategy.* London: Pinter

The author argues that while the superpowers have so far succeeded in coping with deterrence and crisis management, they have failed as yet to establish doctrines, procedures and technologies which would enable them to control a major war once deterrence had failed, hence the title with its counterpoint of uncertainty versus control.

26   McConnell, J. (1990) *The Transformation of Soviet Strategy in the 1990s.* Oslo: IFS-Norwegian Institute for Defence Studies

The present transformation of Soviet strategy involves nothing less than a radical break with the past, namely the abandonment of military competition with the West on the Euro-strategic, tactical nuclear and conventional levels in favour of what the Soviet command sees as the two decisive areas, strategic nuclear weapons and the militarisation of space, a development which must inevitably influence future force structures.

27   Flynn, G. (1989) Editor. *Soviet Military Doctrine and Western Policy.* London; New York: Routledge

Arguably one of the most important books on doctrine produced in the past decade. This volume, divided into two parts, deals in depth with perceptions and strategic assessments in both the East and the West, followed by a discussion of implications for Western policy both with respect to arms control and the influence of Soviet military doctrine on Western strategy. Of particular note is R. Garthoff's exposition of Soviet perceptions of Western thought and doctrine, supported by a massive appendix on Soviet source publications.

28   Moiseev, M.A. (1989) *The Soviet Military Doctrine: Orientation Towards Defense.* Moscow: Novosti

An abridged English Language version of the *Pravda* 13 March, 1989 statement on the new direction in Soviet military thinking and Soviet military doctrine by the former Chief of the Soviet General Staff, Army General Moiseev.

29   Turbiville, G.H. (1989) Editor. *The Voroshilov Lectures: Materials from the Soviet General Staff Academy.* Vol. 1. 'Issues of Soviet Military Strategy'. Washington, DC: National Defense University Press

The first of a projected six-volume series of materials derived from lectures delivered at the Soviet General Staff Academy. This first volume covers 'strategy lectures', the principles and content of military strategy, theatres of strategic military action, combat readiness, strategic deployment and the conduct of air operations. Though dated in both style and content, the lectures do convey much of the form and the institutional setting of military education for senior Soviet officers.

30   Gareev, M.A. (1988) *M.V. Frunze: Military Theorist.* London: Pergamon-Brassey

A translation of Colonel-General Gareev's original Soviet study *M.V. Frunze: Voennyi Teoretik.* Moscow, Voenizdat, 1985, regarded as a certain 'up-dating' of Soviet military thinking and a revision of the old Sokolovskii volume on military strategy published at the beginning of the 1960s.

31   Kipp, J.W. (1988) *From Foresight to Forecasting: The Russian and Soviet Military Experience.* College Station: Center for Strategic Technology, Texas A & M University System

An important and impressively documented study of the relationship between Russian and Soviet forecasting techniques as applied to strategic and operational planning, with particular reference to the development and application of the 'systems approach' (*sistemotekhnika*).

32   Scott, Harriet F. and Scott, W.F. (1988) *Soviet Military Doctrine: Continuity, Formulation and Dissemination.* Boulder, CO: Westview Press

Although somewhat overtaken by the latest flurry over current doctrinal debates over 'sufficiency' and 'reasonable sufficiency', this is a reliable guide to what can best be called the 'processes' of doctrinal formulation.

33   Johnson, N.L. (1987) *Soviet Military Strategy in Space.* London: Jane's Publishing Company

Followed by an analysis of the importance of near-Earth space, this volume examines the Soviet space effort with reference to the military applications of satellites and the first generations of offensive spacecraft, as well as projecting a possible Soviet strategy for 'space war'.

34   MccGwire, M. (1987) *Military Objectives in Soviet Foreign Policy.* Washington, DC: Brookings Institution

A 'revisionist' study which countered 'received wisdom' about the nature of the 'Soviet threat' and argued that there had been for some time a major shift, or re-structuring of Soviet strategic objectives, examined against the background of Soviet policies and commitments in potential 'theatres of military action'.

35   Simpkin, R. (1987) *Deep Battle: The Brainchild of Marshal Tukhachevskii.* London: Brassey

A posthumous volume which assembled the late Brigadier Richard Simpkin's translations of and observations upon Tukhachevskii's contributions to Soviet military science, military doctrine and modern operational ideas.

36   Baxter, W.P. (1986) *The Soviet Way of Warfare.* Novato, CA: Presidio Press; London: Brassey

A technical manual or handbook which deals with Soviet military art and military science, command/staff organisation, offensive and defensive operations, fire support and logistics and Soviet tactics in a Soviet version of 'air-land battle'.

37   Velikhov, Y., Sagdeev, R., and Kokoshin, R. (1986) Editors. *Weaponry in Space: The Dilemma of Security.* Moscow: Mir

Both a political and technical treatise. The nine chapters of this study examine several aspects of space weaponry and operations, e.g. space-based missile defence, space-based battle stations, terminal defence, attack on air and ground targets, counter-measures, US SDI research efforts. A space-based anti-missile system is not regarded in this instance as 'purely defensive' but rather as a 'novel kind of offensive weaponry' triggering a new arms race. Soviet views have since become much modified.

38 Vigor, P. (1983) *Soviet Blitzkrieg Theory.* London: Macmillan

A product of the times, when war was considered at least a likelihood, this volume sets out in brisk and unequivocal terms the Soviet theory of the blitzkrieg, often misunderstood. the Soviet position being that if properly executed, the blitzkrieg offered the possibility of winning quickly in a major war solely with the use of conventional weapons.

39 Leites, N. (1982) *Soviet Style in War.* New York: Crane Russak

Derived from a mass of Soviet material, this book set out to clarify 'how the Soviet armed forces would fight' and examined basic Soviet attitudes towards surprise, infantry operations and tactics, defence, in general the evolution of military postures during the Brezhnev era.

40 Scott, Harriet F., and Scott, W.F. (1982) *The Soviet Art of War Doctrine, Strategy and Tactics.* Boulder, CO: Westview Press

Divided into six sections, this collection of translated Soviet materials covers the early development of Soviet military thought, the Stalin era, the 'revolution in military affairs', the drive for nuclear status, controlled conflict and power projection, all drawn from significant Soviet authorities and materials.

41 Leebaert, D. (1981) Editor. *Soviet Military Thinking.* London: Allen and Unwin

Three main sections include nine papers by distinguished experts on the context of Soviet military thinking, contrasts between US and Soviet strategic thought, nuclear deterrence and strategic doctrine and the 'non-strategic dimension' (style, the Warsaw Pact and technology). Now in a revised edition.

42 Semmel, B. (1981) Editor. *Marxism and the Science of War.* Oxford: Oxford University Press

Five main sections of commentary on and excerpts from Marx, Engels, Lenin, Trotsky, Bukharin, Lin Piao, including a final section on 'Soviet Marxism and a Nuclear Strategy'.

Military Operations

PRE-1941

43 Gross, J.T. (1988) *Revolution from Abroad: The Soviet Conquest of Poland's Western Ukraine and Western Belorussia.* Princeton, NJ: Princeton University Press

Red Army operations in Poland in 1939 and Polish resistance.

44 Riess, T. (1988) *Cold Will: The Defence of Finland.* London: Brassey

In Part 1 (4), an account of Soviet and Finnish military operations in the 'Winter War' 1939-1940, Soviet order of battle, command organisation and operations, Soviet losses.

45 Coox, A.D. (1985) *Nomonhan: Japan Against Russia, 1939.* 2 volumes. Stanford, CA: Stanford University Press

A massive and unrivalled account of military operations in 1939 at Nomonhan (Khalkhin-Gol) in which Red Army troops under the command of Zhukov defeated the Japanese, a defeat which resulted in the shift of strategic emphasis in Japan away from war with the Soviet Union.

46 Drea, E.J. (1981) *Nomonhan: Japanese-Soviet Tactical Combat, 1939.* Fort Leavenworth, Kansas: US Army Command and General Staff College

A detailed tactical analysis of the Nomonhan operations, with substantial use and citation from Japanese military archives.

1941-1945

47 'Suvorov, V.' (pseud.) (1990) *Icebreaker: Who Started the Second World War?* London: Hamish Hamilton

A highly controversial but not wholly implausible analysis of Stalin's policy on the eve of the Soviet-German war in 1941, arguing that Stalin was bent on world domination and was indeed preparing to launch his own offensive war in 1941, judging by Soviet planning and preparations.

48 Adelman, J.R. and Gibson, C.L. (1989) Editors. *Contemporary Soviet Military Affairs: The Legacy of World War II.* Boston: Unwin Hyman

Seven papers reviewing the relevance of the experience of the 'Great Patriotic War' on the development of current Soviet thinking.

49 Glantz, D.M. (1989) *Soviet Military Deception in the Second World War.* London: Cass

The first highly innovative volume in the series 'Soviet Military Theory and Practice', this massive compilation examines the role of surprise and deception, particularly the latter (*maskirovka*) at all levels, strategic, operational and tactical, utilising centralised deception planning coupled with the most brutally stringent security measures and the probing of enemy psychology. Fully annotated with extensive appendices.

50 Parrish, M. (1989) Editor. *Battle for Moscow: The 1942 Soviet General Staff Study.* London: Pergamon-Brassey

An analysis of the battle for Moscow 1941-1942 prepared by Major-General Vechnyi of the Operations Section of the Soviet General Staff. Contemporary documentation.

51 Rotundo, L. (1989) Editor. *Battle for Stalingrad: The 1943 Soviet General Staff Study.* London: Pergamon-Brassey

Taken from the sixth issue of *Collection of Materials for the Study of War Experience*, the General Staff study of the battle of Stalingrad under the editorship of Major-General P.P. Vechnyi, with a list of other Soviet commanders as contributors.

52 van Tuyll, H.P. (1989) *Feeding the Bear: American Aid to the Soviet Union, 1941-1945.* New York: Greenwood

A study of Lend-Lease with special reference to the military aspects of the assistance to the Red Army and to the Soviet war machine. With 46 tables.

53 Niepold, G. (1987) *The Battle for White Russia: The Destruction of Army Group Centre June 1944.* London: Brassey

A translation by the late Richard Simpkin of General Niepold's account of the remarkable Soviet offensive in the summer of 1944 which the author witnessed at first hand. A volume in the Brassey's series 'The USSR at War'.

54 Sokolov, S. (1987) *Main Front: Soviet Leaders Look Back on World War II.* London: Brassey

Introduced with a foreword from the former Soviet Defence Minister, Marshal Sokolov, a compilation of extracts from the memoirs of Soviet commanders covering the main wartime operations.

55 Shtemenko, S.M. (1986) *The Soviet General Staff at War 1941-1945.* Moscow: Progress

A two-volume translation of the original Soviet version, *General'nyi Shtab v gody voiny*, published in various editions but cited as a 'standard Soviet work'. This translation seems to be drawn from a two-volume Soviet version published by Voenizdat in 1981 and again in 1985, though quite where one begins and the other ends is hard to determine.

56 Bartov, O. (1985) *The Eastern Front 1941-1945: German Troops and the Barbarisation of Warfare*. London: Macmillan

Based on an analysis of the records of three frontline German divisions, 12th Infantry Division, 18th Panzer and Grossdeutschland Division. This is a 'soldier's eye view' of German policies in the east, involving criminal activities which culminated in wholesale 'barbarisation' involving the German Army.

57 Harrison, M. (1985) *Soviet Planning in Peace and War 1938-1945*. Cambridge: Cambridge University Press

Published in the series 'Soviet and East European Studies', this extremely important and original volume examines in great technical detail Soviet economic planning for war, the Soviet productive effort, measures of mobilisation and the permanent lessons learned from the Second World War. Bibliography.

58 Linz, S.J. (1985) Editor. *The Impact of World War II on the Soviet Union*. Totowa, NJ: Rowman and Allanheld

14 papers divided into two sections, dealing with the war and its aftermath and its social and political consequences, together with 57 tables of data and ten figures.

59 Poirier, R.G. and Conner, A.Z. (1985) *The Red Army Order of Battle in the Great Patriotic War*. Novato, CA: Presidio Press

Including data from 1919 to the post-war years, this weighty and indispensable volume covers Red Army wartime order of battle for armies, the battle honours of corps and divisions, all corps, rifle division activations, artillery divisions, Guards divisions and rifle divisions. Chapter Four on rifle divisions and military district activations tabulates the geographical distribution of mobilisation bases.

60 Zhukov, G.K. (1985) *Reminiscences and Reflections*. 2 volumes. Moscow: Progress

A Soviet translation of the celebrated memoirs of Marshal Zhukov, published originally in Russian as *Vospominaniiai razmyshleniia* in 1974 by Novosti Press Agency, though a two-volume revised edition was published again in Russian in 1975 and presumably forms the basis for this translation. 'Presumably' is certainly relevant in view of recent discussions about the authenticity of these texts, notably the comments of V. Karpov who had access not only to the original manuscripts but also to the comments made by Zhukov himself on what the censor, a 'high-level personage', wanted changed or omitted. For more details on the writing of the memoirs and their authenticity see Volume 2 of *Marshal Zhukov: Polkovodets i Chelovek* published by APN, Moscow, 1988.

61 Fugate, B.I. (1984) *Operation Barbarossa: Strategy and Tactics on the Eastern Front, 1941*. Novato, CA: Presidio Press

A controversial but impressively documented study of 1941, designed to challenge many myths, particularly those concerned with German military planning and actual Soviet military preparations which resulted in the Soviet command, in addition to making great use of deception, sacrificing men to gain time and to exploit their three-stage line of defence. What was ultimately disastrous was not the Russian weather but lack of understanding and community of purpose within the German military command.

62 Larionov, V., Yeronin, N., Solovyov, B., and Timokhovich, V. (1984) *World War II: Decisive Battles of the Soviet Army*. Moscow: Progress

A translation of the Soviet work *Vazhneishie bitvy Sovetskoi Armii vo Vtoroi Mirovoi Voiny*, ten chapters dealing with major Soviet operations, all treated and analysed in a markedly professional tactical-technical manner which enhances its usefulness.

63   Erickson, J. (1983) *The Road to Berlin.* London: Weidenfeld and Nicolson

The second volume of *Stalin's War with Germany* following *The Road to Stalingrad*, an operational narrative from the destruction of the German Sixth Army at Stalingrad to the Red Army's storming of Berlin.

64   Glantz, D.M. (1983) *August Storm: The Soviet 1945 Strategic Offensive in Manchuria; also Soviet Tactical and Operational Combat in Manchuria, 1945.* Fort Leavenworth, Kansas: US Army Command and General Staff College

Numbers 7 and 8 in the series 'Leavenworth Papers', these two monographs represent a comprehensive examination of the 1945 Soviet blitzkrieg in the Far East and are quite invaluable for the material incorporated in the studies, including maps, terrain analysis, order of battle and bibliography.

65   Hardesty, Von D. (1982) *Red Phoenix: The Rise of Soviet Air Power 1941-1945.* Washington, DC: Smithsonian Institution Press

A major contribution to the analysis of air operations on the Eastern Front, this volume, using much Soviet material, examines Soviet air force leadership, tactics, pilot training, frontline air service, the concept of the 'air offensive', Soviet aircraft design and production, together with the roles of bomber, fighter and ground-attack aviation. See also the USAF translation in the series 'A Soviet View', *The Command and Staff of the Soviet Army Air Force in the Great Patriotic War 1941-1945*, originally published by M.N. Kozhevnikov in 1977 and subsequently revised.

66   Parrish, M. (1981) *The U.S.S.R. in World War II: An Annotated Bibliography of Books Published in the Soviet Union, 1945-1975.* 2 volumes. New York; London: Garland Publishing

With addenda of books published between 1975-1980, this bibliography is divided into five parts spread between the two volumes, covering the military campaigns, the Soviet armed forces, geographic regions at war, subject divisions (including other bibliographies, journalism, diplomacy...) and economic divisions including agriculture, the war economy, energy, labour, transport.

POST-1945

67   Garthoff, R.L. (1987) *Reflections on the Cuban Missile Crisis.* Washington, DC: Brookings Institution

An 'insider view' of the 1962 Cuban missile crisis, with an examination of the Soviet decision and its consequences. For the latest Soviet revelations and details of the transhipment of 42 strategic missiles and 40,000 men, see A. Dokuchayev on *Operation ANADYR* in *Krasnaia Zvezda* 4 February, 1990.

68   Leitenberg, M. (1987) *Soviet Submarine Operations in Swedish Waters 1980-1986.* New York; Westport; London: Praeger

Number 128 of 'The Washington Papers', Center for Strategic and International Studies, this volume examines the pattern of violations, incursions into Swedish waters and possible Soviet motives. With extensive notes and references. (See also McCormick, G.H. *Stranger than Fiction: Soviet Submarine Operations in Swedish Waters.* Santa Monica: RAND R-3776-AF 1/1990).

69   Amstutz, J.B. (1986) *Afghanistan: The First Five Years of Soviet Occupation.* Washington, DC: National Defense University

An extensive monograph on the Soviet invasion and disputed occupation of Afghanistan, with military details and a substantial bibliography.

Arms and Services, Weapons Systems, Military Technology

70 Pollock, M.A., Stubbs, K.D., Thomas, R.E., and Waddell, S.R. (1990) *Soviet Optical Data Processing and Its Suitability for Troop Control.* College Station, Texas: Center for Strategic Technology, The Texas A & M University System

A unique and innovative study in the 'Stratech Studies' series (SS90-1) which examines in great technical detail Soviet interest in optical analogue data processors, which are in many respects superior to their digital counterparts. Soviet research into optical systems is both large and comprehensive, though digital systems are not ignored, based on the Soviet view of future war which will require data processing systems with high-speed, large volume throughput and high security for troop control. Optical analogue systems seem to satisfy these requirements, though Soviet specialists have yet to solve the problem of an optical random access memory. With much technical detail and very substantial reference material.

71 Ranft, B., and Till, G. (1989) *The Sea in Soviet Strategy*, 2nd edn. London: Macmillan

A revised edition, first published in 1983, which reviews the changes in the strategic background, Soviet naval building programmes and Soviet naval missions.

72 Zaloga, S.J. (1989) *Soviet Air Defence Missiles.* London: Jane's Information Group

An examination of Soviet strategic air defence, tactical air defence, air defence radars, missile systems, systems radars, missile engagement sequences, unit organisation and deployment.

73 Everett-Heath, J. (1988) *Soviet Helicopters*, 2nd edn. London: Jane's Information Group

An examination of the design, development and production of all major Soviet helicopters, including early types from 1940 onwards, complete with photographs and line drawings. See also translation, Tishchenko, M.N. et al. *Helicopters. Selection of Design Parameters.* Moscow: Mashinostroenie, 1976.

74 Isby, D. (1988) *Weapons and Tactics of the Soviet Army.* London: Jane's Information Group

A revised edition of the 1981 version. The standard work on the Soviet Army command structure, order of battle, operational methods, weapons systems and support.

75 Cimbala, S.J. (1987) *Soviet C3.* Washington, DC: AFCEA International Press

A compendium of Soviet and non-Soviet discussions of command and control, organised into seven parts with a conclusion, comprising the philosophy and style of Soviet C3, the challenge of technology, strategic and theatre nuclear warfare, NATO and the Warsaw Pact, naval warfare, missile and space defence and 'war survival' as command and control issues.

76 Hemsley, J. (1987) *The Soviet Biochemical Threat to NATO: The Neglected Issue.* London: Macmillan

A survey in the 'RUSI Defence Studies Series' of Soviet chemical and biological capabilities, an assessment of Soviet CBW intentions and the military utility of present and future Soviet capabilities. With three appendices and 18 diagrams and illustrations.

77 'Suvorov, V.' (pseud.) (1987) *Spetsnaz: The Story of the Soviet SAS.* London: Hamish Hamilton

Controlled by GRU, Soviet military intelligence, the primary task of Soviet special forces is the destruction of tactical nuclear weapons though they have in addition an unlimited number of tasks. See also Lynn M.Hansen, *Soviet Navy Spetsnaz Operations on the Northern Flank: Implications for the Defense of Western Europe.* Stratech Studies (SS84-2).

78 Zaloga, S.J. and Loop, J.W. (1987) *Soviet Tanks and Combat Vehicles 1946 to the Present*. Poole, Dorset: Arms and Armour Press

A standard reference work which examines mechanisation, armoured vehicles production, main battle tanks, armoured infantry vehicles, mechanised artillery, air defence vehicles and combat support vehicles. With profuse illustrations and line drawings.

79 Bellamy, C. (1986) *Red God of War: Soviet Artillery and Rocket Forces*. London: Brassey

Traces the evolution of Soviet artillery and rocket forces including 1941-45 experience, artillery service and modern artillery operations.

80 Bonds, R. (1986) *Modern Soviet Weapons Illustrated Directory*. London: Salamander Books

480 pages describing more than 160 weapons in detail, covering land, sea and air.

81 Erickson, J., Hansen, L. and Schneider, W., (1986) *Soviet Ground Forces: An Operational Assessment*. Boulder, CO: Westview Press; London: Croom Helm

An analysis of changes in the Soviet ground forces after 1945, Soviet training and Soviet criteria for judging performance and the role and importance of the air element in conjunction with ground components.

82 Mason, R.A. and Taylor, J.W.R. (1986) *Aircraft, Strategy and Operations of the Soviet Air Force*. London: Jane's Information Group

Though the Soviet Air Force operates more aircraft than any other world air arm, there are problems of effectiveness and organisation, training and tactics which are examined in depth in this volume.

83 Nemecek, V. (1986) *The History of Soviet Aircraft from 1918*. London: Collins and Willow Books

An invaluable collection of archival photographs and analysis of all types of Soviet aircraft, ranging from bombers, fighters, transport aircraft, helicopters to experimental aircraft, with an enormous amount of technical detail, analysis and tabulation of specifications. First published in Czech as *Sovetska Letadla*.

84 Polmar, N. (1986) *Guide to the Soviet Navy*, 4th edn. London: Armour and Armour Press

Without doubt, the definitive assessment of the Soviet Navy in the 1980s.

85 Watson, B., and Dunn, P.M. (1986) Editors. *The Future of the Soviet Navy: An Assessment to the Year 2000*. Boulder, CO; London: Westview Press

An analysis of trends in submarine development, the 'carrier question', surface combat development and operations, amphibious forces, mine warfare and the evolution of naval strategy.

86 Chizum, D.G. (1985) *Soviet Radioelectronic Combat*. Boulder, CO; London: Westview Press

A detailed and important analysis of Soviet military and technical capabilities to exploit the electromagnetic spectrum.

87 Simpkin, R. (1984) *Red Armour: An Examination of the Soviet Mobile Force Concept*. Oxford: Pergamon

An important 'time and space' model of Soviet mobile operations, leading to a major re-examination of manoeuvre theory.

88 Hemsley, J. (1982) *Soviet Troop Control: The Role of Command Technology in the Soviet Military System*. Oxford: Brassey

An examination of the effect of automation and modelling on the effectiveness of Soviet troop control procedures.

The Warsaw Pact

89   Simon, J. (1988) Editor. *NATO-Warsaw Pact Force Mobilization.* Washington, DC: National Defense University Press

The result of a 1987 conference held at the National Defense University, Washington, this extremely important volume is concerned with mobilisation and reinforcement (a subject of continuing importance even as NATO and the Warsaw Pact change and evolve). The four main sections deal with reinforcement procedures and options, developments in the 'frontline states', communications and transportation and problems of and on the flanks. In all 18 separate papers by specialists, plus 50 figures and tables.

90   Simon, J. (1985) *Warsaw Pact Forces: Problems of Command and Control.* Boulder, CO; London: Westview Press

Ten chapters on the Warsaw Pact command structure as it developed from 1955 into the early 1980s, with two appendices on major Soviet/Pact exercises and Pact military capabilities.

91   Rakowska-Harmstone, T., Jones, C.D., Jaworsky, J., and Sylvain, I. (1984) *Warsaw Pact: The Question of Cohesion.* Ottawa: Operational Research and Analysis Department

A three-volume study dealing with the 'greater socialist army', 'military cohesion' and bibliographic/source materials, which must stand as the definitive work on the origins, development and capabilities of the Warsaw Pact in the early 1980s.

92   Clawson, R.W. and Kaplan, L.S. (1982) Editors. *The Warsaw Pact: Political Purpose and Military Means.* Wilmington: Scholarly Resources Inc.

Fourteen studies covering internal Pact political relationships, the NATO-Warsaw Pact relationship, armed forces, weapons and capabilities.

93   Lewis, J. (1982) *The Warsaw Pact: Arms, Doctrine and Strategy.* New York: McGraw-Hill

The standard handbook on the organisation, deployments and military capabilities of the Warsaw Pact to 1980/1981.

94   Ross Johnson, A., Dean, R.W., Alexiev, A. (1982) *East European Military Establishments: The Warsaw Pact Northern Tier.* New York: Crane Russak

An examination of the military institutions and military capabilities of Poland, the German Democratic Republic and Czechoslovakia at the beginning of the 1980s.

Addendum

SERIALS

95   *Soviet Military Power.* 1st edn. 1981, 9th edn. 1990. Washington, DC: Department of Defense

96   *Whence The Threat To Peace* (1981/1982 now discontinued) Moscow: Military Publishing House

English-language version of *Otkuda Iskhodit Ugroza Miru.*

COMPENDIUM

97   Woff, R. (1989) Editor. *Jane's Soviet High Command.* Coulsdon, Surrey: Jane's Information Group

Annual publication with 'Information Updates'.

BIBLIOGRAPHY

98   Smith, M.J. (1980) *The Soviet Navy, 1941-78: A Guide to Sources in English.* Santa Barbara, CA; Oxford: ABC-Clio

99   Smith, M.J. (1982) *The Soviet Army 1939-1980: A Guide to Sources in English.* Numbers 9 and 11 respectively in Burns, R.D. Editor. *The War/Peace Bibliography Series.* Santa Barbara, CA; Oxford: ABC-Clio

Extremely useful.

CHAPTER SEVEN

The Economy

Professor Robert C. Stuart
Rutgers University

Introduction: The Field

Western literature on the Soviet economy is a large and diffuse body of
scholarship, and yet it is easier to characterise this body of work than for,
say, the rather broader field of comparative economic systems. The literature on the Soviet economy can be characterised in several different
dimensions. Some familiarity with these dimensions will assist the researcher wishing quick access to basic, important, but specialised sources.

First and possibly most important is the temporal development of the
field of Soviet economics. Beginning in the 1950s, a number of major
studies of the Soviet economy addressed a wide variety of important issues attempting to build a basic understanding of the Soviet economic system, and to develop meaningful data series such that further in-depth
research could be conducted. Such studies, for example pertaining to national income, wage determination, management and taxation remain useful to the present day.

Thereafter, studies on the Soviet economy became more specialised.
Thus while typically few in number for any given sub-category, nevertheless for most of the important sub-categories of the Soviet economy specialised studies have been written. Such studies cover a variety of areas
such as labour and trade unions, management, planning, economic history, agriculture, etc. While some of these studies now pertain mainly to
the command economy rather than the transition economy, in many instances their authors have continued to publish important contemporary
articles creating a significant and continually growing body of work in
these sub-categories. Many of the sources that we will cite derive from this
background.

In the 1970s and 1980s the volume of literature expanded rapidly. To
some degree, the directions of expansion reflected topics important in a

particular era. But expansion also reflected the application of more sophisticated theoretical and econometric methods utilising gradually improving empirical evidence. However, it is important to note that throughout these years the growth of the literature was very uneven, reflecting in large part the lack of availability of Soviet materials, statistical or otherwise. Thus, for example, the literature on foreign trade expanded in many dimensions, while the literature on the Soviet financial system remains modest to the present day.

Finally, the Gorbachev era which began in 1985 presented to analysts of the Soviet economy an entirely new challenge. Although several dimensions of the scholarly response can already be identified, the literature on the Soviet economy of the Gorbachev era has yet to be fully characterised.

First, after 20 years of non-reforms in the Soviet economy, Western economists tired of the topic, a fatigue reflected in growing disinterest in economic reform during the late 1970s and early 1980s. With the rise of Gorbachev in 1985 and the subsequent events in Eastern Europe especially in 1990, economic reform, or the transition of socialist systems to a market emphasis through privatisation, is the topic centre stage in the 1990s.

Second, beyond analysis of the reform process per se, scholars of the Soviet economy obviously directed their attention at change in their particular spheres of interest, and especially the meaning of change in light of a continuing decline in the health of the Soviet economy. Thus it is now necessary and possible to analyse contemporary events by understanding the system as it operated in the pre-Gorbachev era, and the changes made during the Gorbachev era.

Third, a rather different dimension of change is that resulting from glasnost. The greater availability of and access to Soviet materials and scholars has already set in motion major new dimensions of research that are bound to alter basic conceptions of the Soviet economy, especially in the reform era. For example, direct access to the Soviet population through joint research projects allows investigation of issues such as consumer attitudes or aspects of household behaviour. Possibly most important, new data will become available and old methods, especially in areas such as national income accounting or defence spending, will be questioned and modified.

The end result of these changes will undoubtedly be a body of literature with greater theoretical sophistication and a sounder empirical base. New themes will be investigated and new views of old themes developed. This is a body of literature that has only begun to unfold as we enter the 1990s.

A rather different but useful characterisation of the literature on the Soviet economy is that which focuses on the historical evolution of the system. Typically, even in the era of perestroika and with the dominance of reform themes, we find it useful to characterise the Soviet economy in historical terms. Many would argue that in addition to inherent interest in the command system, it is impossible to understand fully the nature and difficulties of economic reform without understanding the nature of the system that is being reformed. It is this general format that we follow in the present survey, though our emphasis is on the contemporary literature.

General Surveys of the Economy

There are a number of works which provide an overall examination or survey of the Soviet economic experience at various levels of difficulty. For example, Alec Nove, *The Soviet Economic System* (3) and Paul R. Gregory and Robert C. Stuart, *Soviet Economic Structure and Performance* (1) provide both general overviews and specific details of the Soviet economy, past and present. At a similar level though without historical analysis is Michael Ellman, *Socialist Planning* (2). The Soviet experience is viewed in a general historical perspective in Roger Munting, *The Economic Development of the USSR* (6), while a simpler overview can be found in R.W. Davies, *The Soviet Economy* (Winchester, Mass.: Unwin Hyman, 1989) and James R. Millar, *The ABCs of Soviet Socialism* (7). A useful basic text, readable and focusing on performance results, is Trevor Buck and John Cole, *Modern Soviet Economic Performance* (New York: Basil Blackwell Inc., 1987). At a similar level though focusing on basic arrangements, economic reform and some special topics such as agriculture is David Dyker, *The Future of the Soviet Economic Planning System* (4). Finally, a brief but well written introduction for the non-specialist can be found in Franklyn D. Holzman, *The Soviet Economy: Past, Present, and Future* (5).

While these works provide overviews of and reference to the specialised literature, it is useful to examine the latter more closely.

The Early Years

In developing an understanding of the Soviet economy, Western economists sustain substantial interest in the pre-revolutionary Russian economy and the early years of the Soviet era (1917-1928). Both periods are important for understanding the extent to which there was economic growth and development prior to the Bolshevik Revolution, the nature of the changes which took place during War Communism and NEP and most important, the forces which influenced the major decisions made by Joseph Stalin in 1928, namely the collectivisation of agriculture and the introduction of the command economy.

A good survey of the immediate pre-revolutionary era can be found in P. Gatrell, *The Tsarist Economy, 1850-1917* (15), while the data underlying much of the analysis of these years can be found in P. Gregory, *Russian National Income, 1885-1913* (16). An excellent comparison of the Tsarist economy prior to 1917 and the Soviet economy after 1917 can be found in R.W. Davies (ed.) *From Tsarism to the New Economic Policy* (9).

Unfortunately, economists have given relatively little attention to the periods of War Communism and NEP, at least in monographs. An exception for the former is S. Malle, *The Economic Organization of War Communism, 1918-1921* (12), while a useful source covering the whole period is E. Zaleski, *Planning for Economic Growth in the Soviet Union, 1918-1932* (19).

The early years of the Stalinist command economy are of central interest and at the same time controversy. Interest focuses on why the command system was adopted, how it was adopted and with what results. Early Soviet discussion of and efforts at balance planning (dating from the 1920s) can be found in S.G. Wheatcroft and R.W. Davies, *Materials for a Balance of the National Economy, 1928-1930* (14), the chronology of events during these early years is developed in detail in R.W. Davies, *The Industrialization of Russia* Vols. 1 and 2 (18) and R.W. Davies, *The Industrialization of Russia* Vol. 3 (10).

The Soviet industrialisation drive of the 1930s is often and quite appropriately interpreted within the framework of economic development. In this context, agricultural development and especially the process and results of collectivisation have been of great importance and controversy. One of the best accounts of collectivisation as a process can be found in Moshe Lewin, *Russian Peasants and Soviet Power: A Study of Collectivization* (22).

Controversies surrounding the contribution of agriculture to early Soviet development erupted with the publication of A.A. Barsov, *Balans Stoimostnykh Obmenov mezhdu Gorodom i Derevnei* (23), in which the Soviet author challenged the traditional Western view that, simply put, the peasants paid the price for rapid accumulation through the transfer of an agricultural surplus from the rural sector to the state. The Barsov challenge was subsequently elaborated and debated in a series of articles begun by James R. Millar and collected in his *The Soviet Economic Experiment* (11). The issue is further developed in Michael Ellman, 'Did the agricultural surplus provide the resources for the increase in investment in the USSR during the First Five Year Plan?' *Economic Journal* (21), while a recent and critical appraisal can be found in David Morrison, 'A critical examination of A.A. Barsov's empirical work on the balance of value exchanges between the town and the country' *Soviet Studies* (13). Although the remainder of the 1930s deserves greater attention from economists, an excellent and very detailed survey of the early plan years, especially helpful in understanding the nature of Soviet planning at this time, is contained in Eugene Zaleski, *Stalinist Planning for Economic Growth, 1933-1952* (20). An excellent reappraisal of policies followed in the 1930s can be found in Holland Hunter and Janusz M. Szyrmer, *Faulty Foundations: Soviet Economic Policies, 1928-1940* (8).

The War Years

Until recently, little was written about the Soviet economy during the Second World War in large part due to lack of information from Soviet archives. While the era of glasnost will undoubtedly expand the information about this critical period, we already have a number of useful studies examining the command economy under wartime conditions. A broad survey of this period covering a number of issues from different viewpoints is contained in Susan J. Linz (ed.), *The Impact of World War II on the Soviet Economy* (26). The planning system is the focus of M. Harrison, *Soviet Planning in Peace and War: 1938-1945* (25) while the issue of food supplies is discussed in William Moskoff, *The Bread of Affliction: The Food Supply in the USSR during World War II* (24). The much neglected immediate post-war period is examined in T. Dunmore, *The Stalinist Command Economy* (27).

Much of the contemporary specialised literature on the pre-Gorbachev Soviet economy covers roughly the period from the 1950s through to the 1980s, an era when the basic characteristics of the Soviet economic system seemed to undergo relatively little change. There are, therefore, relatively few specialised works on, for example, the Khrushchev years except insofar as there was considerable interest in some particular and more controversial aspect of the Khrushchev legacy, for example in agriculture. Put another way, the literature on the Soviet economy beyond the 1950s does not tend to be cast in historical perspective. Rather, the literature focuses on how and how well the system functioned and to a lesser degree on largely failed attempts at reform, for example in the 1960s viewing the system as fundamentally unchanged.

Soviet Balance Planning

Cast in this perspective, contemporary literature on the Soviet economy focuses on planning – the nature of the economic system and its functioning in the various sub-sectors of the economy. Although challenged by some, the Soviet Union is widely viewed as a planned socialist system. As such, the heart of the system is the planning apparatus and the mechanisms through which plans are developed at the centre (the system of balances) and executed at the local or enterprise level. Moreover, this system has been viewed as a quantity targeted system, or a system driven largely by real as opposed to money variables. Finally, the literature on Soviet economic planning has tended to be rather distinct from the more general Western literature on the economics of planning.

The basic Soviet method of balance planning is described in a variety of sources. The best general discussions can be found in the texts cited above, while specialised aspects of planning such as tautness, ratcheting, target levels and incentive compatibility can be found in the specialised literature. Details of change through time are well charted in F. Kushnirsky, *Soviet Economic Planning, 1965-1980* (29). A useful approach to understanding balance planning is the conceptual framework of input-output analysis. A useful source which looks at this approach and the Soviet model judged by this approach is Michael P. Todaro, *Development Planning: Models and Methods* (30). It is interesting to note that there is a considerable volume of literature generally subsumed under the rubric of the economics of planning. However, much of this Western literature on planning has paid little attention to the Soviet case, and the literature which does analyse Soviet planning is not cast within the framework of macroeconomic planning models. This posture is changing in works such as that edited by Richard E. Quandt and Dusan Triska, *Optimal Decisions in Markets and Planned Economies* (28), a work in which more sophisticated theoretical tools are applied to basic economic decisions of the planned or market economy, especially microeconomic (management) decisions.

Plan Implementation: Ministers and Managers

Until recently the ministerial structure, that is roughly speaking the organisational mechanisms between the enterprise and the planner, were known to be important, but were much neglected in the Western literature. An analysis of the bureaucracy cast within the contemporary reform experience is contained in Paul R. Gregory, *The Soviet Economic Bureaucracy* (31).

At the lower end of the administrative command hierarchy, Soviet enterprise management has received considerable attention from economists. However, this is another area where approaches of researchers are changing. Although the recent literature has begun to cast the traditional hierarchical Soviet structure in a principal-agent framework using game-theoretic and other techniques of analysis, past studies of Soviet management have generally been cast within the framework of organisation theory rather than the maximisation models of Western neo-classical microeconomic theory. Building upon the early classics of Berliner, Granick, Richman and others, recent developments are analysed in W. Conyngham, *The Modernization of Soviet Industrial Management* (33) and A. Freris, *The Soviet Industrial Enterprise* (32).

The Soviet Financial System: Budgets, Prices and Investment

The Soviet manager has been of interest, obviously as a key player in the traditional planning system. The manager, however, must make decisions about inputs and must do so within a framework of limited information, especially limited monetary and financial information. Unfortunately, there is probably no aspect of the Soviet system less well understood than its financial system. In large part, this lack of understanding stems from the traditional absence of data and Soviet secrecy. However, a number of aspects of the financial system have been analysed. For a general description of the budgetary system, the reader should see R. Hutchings, *The Soviet Budgetary System* (38). For insights into the budgetary system that raise important questions about the data, see I. Birman, *Secret Incomes of the Soviet State Budget* (39). The details of Soviet pricing have been best developed in a series of articles by M. Bornstein, recent examples of which are M. Bornstein, 'Soviet price policies' *Soviet Economy* (36) with a useful update in M. Bornstein, 'Problems of price reform in the USSR', in NATO, *Soviet Economic Reforms: Implementation Underway* (34). The role of pricing as a source of inflation is investigated in Fyodor Kushnirsky, *Growth and Inflation in the Soviet Union* (35).

Although investment is a matter of great importance, it has received rather less attention than one might expect. Unfortunately, Soviet data on investment and the resulting capital stock data are messy. The result is that in the literature we tend to examine the process of investment (investment rules) or the impact of Soviet investment upon economic growth, for example through technological change. A useful assessment of investment arrangements is provided in D.A. Dyker, *The Process of Investment in the Soviet Union* (40) while standard works on technological change in the Soviet economy are J.S. Berliner, *The Innovation Decision in Soviet Industry* (41) and R. Amann and J. Cooper (eds.), *Technical Progress and Soviet Economic Development* (37).

Labour and the Household

The allocation of labour in the Soviet Union has received a great deal of attention. The nature of labour allocation is discussed in several works, most of which treat a variety of issues such as the supply of and demand for labour in the Soviet context and issues of wage policy. Useful general works include D. Lane (ed.), *Labour and Employment in the USSR* (47), M. Yanowitch, *Work in the Soviet Union* (48), Jan Adam (ed.), *Employment Policies in the Soviet Union and Eastern Europe* (46), Silvana Malle, *Employment Planning in the Soviet Union* (42) and J.L. Porket, *Work, Em-*

ployment and Unemployment in the Soviet Union (43). More specialised aspects of labour are discussed in a variety of other works. For example, the traditional Soviet practice of full employment planning is analysed in David Granick, *Job Rights in the Soviet Union: Their Consequences* (45). The matter of time allocation is discussed in W. Moskoff, *Labour and Leisure in the Soviet Union* (49) while the critical issue of trade unions is analysed in detail in Blair Ruble, *Soviet Trade Unions* (52). The Shchekino experiment, an important and early attempt to improve labour allocation in the Soviet Union is discussed in B. Arnot, *Controlling Soviet Labour* (44). There are a number of specialised dimensions of labour for which space does not permit full treatment. Worthy of mention, however, is that literature which looks at male-female earnings differentials in the Soviet Union. A useful early survey of findings is Gur Ofer and Aaron Vinokur, 'Earnings differentials by sex in the Soviet Union: a first look' in Steven Rosefielde, *Economic Welfare and the Economics of Soviet Socialism* (51). Finally, a related and important subject is that of distribution discussed in detail in Roger Skurski, *Soviet Marketing and Economic Development* (50).

It is typical in analysing the Soviet economy to treat agriculture and foreign trade as distinct and interesting sectors. The literature on both is substantial.

Soviet Agriculture

Over the years, there has been a series of conferences on Soviet agriculture all of which have made important contributions to the literature. The most recent collection dealing with the Gorbachev period is K.R. Gray, *Contemporary Soviet Agriculture in Comparative Perspective* (54). Earlier contributions include R.C. Stuart, *The Soviet Rural Economy* (58). The reader interested in Soviet agriculture should also consult the works of K.E. Wadekin, a pioneer researcher in the field. Among his recent works are *Agrarian Policies in Communist Europe: A Critical Introduction* (60), *Agriculture in Inter-System Comparison: Communist and Non-Communist Cases* (59), and *Communist Agriculture* (53).

For a critical appraisal of Soviet agriculture, see Stefan Hedlund, *Crisis in Soviet Agriculture* (56). A book that provided interesting analytical insights into Soviet agricultural policies and outcomes is D.G. Johnson and K.McC. Brooks, *Prospects for Soviet Agriculture in the 1980s* (57). For a noted Soviet viewpoint, see Z.A. Medvedev, *Soviet Agriculture* (55).

Foreign Trade

Most Western observers have noted that under the administrative command system, the arrangements of and policies for conducting foreign trade were unique. A good introduction to the basic elements of the Soviet foreign trade system is contained in H.S. Gardner, *Soviet Foreign Trade: The Decision Process* (63), while a lucid discussion of critical trade issues in planned economies is found in Thomas A. Wolf, *Foreign Trade in the Centrally Planned Economy* (61). Prior to the Gorbachev era, relatively little was known about the inner workings of the Soviet foreign trade system. Some insights, however, were to be found in V.P Gruzinov, *The USSR's Management of Foreign Trade* (64).

Soviet Economic Performance

Many would argue that the advent of perestroika in the mid-1980s was a direct result of failing Soviet economic performance, especially the growth of aggregate output, its components and the sources of this growth. Over the years, the work of Abram Bergson has in part focused upon the critical issue of productivity, for example in his *Productivity and the Social System: The USSR and the West* (71). A good survey of the growth issue is provided by G. Ofer 'Soviet economic growth, 1928-1985', *Journal of Economic Literature* (67).

There is, of course, more to economic performance than simply the growth of output. An excellent survey of major aspects of the Soviet economy before the advent of perestroika can be found in A. Bergson and H.S. Levine, *The Soviet Economy: Towards the Year 2000* (London: Allen & Unwin, 1983). Other aspects of Soviet performance have been examined in a wide variety of monographs and articles. The critical issue of income distribution is analysed in A. Bergson, 'Income inequality under Soviet socialism', *Journal of Economic Literature* (69) while more general issues of well-being are examined in A. McCauley, *Economic Welfare in the Soviet Union* (70) and M. Matthews, *Poverty in the Soviet Union: The Lifestyles of the Underprivileged in Recent Years* (68). Especially useful for analysing the issue of poverty in the contemporary period is Mervyn Matthews, *Patterns of Deprivation in the Soviet Union under Brezhnev and Gorbachev* (82).

An excellent work which analyses the peculiarities of Soviet economic results is Jan Winiecki, *The Distorted World of Soviet-Type Economies* (Pittsburgh: University of Pittsburgh Press, 1988), while the specialised but important issue of consumption is analysed, including critical issues of measurement and sectoral comparisons in Igor Birman, *Personal Consumption in the USSR and the USA* (65).

A unique contribution to our understanding of the pre-Gorbachev era are the numerous studies that have been derived from the Soviet Interview Project (SIP). An excellent collection of early results relating to a variety of (mainly) household issues can be found in J. Millar, *Politics, Work, and Daily Life in the USSR* (66).

The Gorbachev Era

Turning finally to the literature of the Gorbachev era, we have already emphasised that this literature differs from that which we have been discussing. In part it represents a continuation and an update on issues discussed earlier. But it also represents new approaches to old topics, emphasis on economic reform and new theoretical and empirical analysis not heretofore possible. We begin with a survey of the general works on perestroika turning finally to selected specialised topics.

For a detailed discussion of the initial years of perestroika, the best sources are A. Aslund, *Gorbachev's Struggle for Economic Reform* (81), and E.A. Hewett, *Reforming the Soviet Economy* (86). Aslund provides a great deal of detail about the perestroika programme, while Hewett places the reform in broad perspective, relating it to the Soviet command economy. An excellent collection of papers covering almost all aspects of the early years of perestroika is US Congress, Joint Economic Committee, *Gorbachev's Economic Plans* (90). For the general reader, Padma Desai's *Perestroika in Perspective* (73) is useful.

The literature on perestroika is substantial and growing steadily. However, it is difficult to classify this literature in any meaningful way. For example, there are numerous edited volumes, many of which are very useful because they contain timely articles on key aspects of perestroika by well-known scholars. One such useful collection covering price reform, foreign trade reform and other issues is NATO, *Soviet Economic Reforms: ImplementationUnderway* (84). A similar approach at a somewhat earlier period is D. Dyker (ed.), *The Soviet Economy under Gorbachev: The Prospects for Reform* (87) while the specialised sector of agriculture is discussed in William Moskoff, *Perestroika in the Countryside* (77). A number of scholars who have traditionally been active in discussing Soviet economic reform have also provided us with recent evidence. Among such works are M.I. Goldman, *Gorbachev's Challenge: Economic Reform in the Age of High Technology* (88) and M.I. Goldman, *The USSR in Crisis* (92), an earlier work critical of the Soviet economic system.

Selected but critical aspects of perestroika have been discussed mainly in articles. For example, an excellent survey of new organisational arrangements such as cooperatives can be found in Philip Hanson, 'Property rights in the new phase of reforms', *Soviet Economy* (76). The much discussed 500-day plan authored by S.S. Shatalin is available in translation as *Transition to The Market* Parts I and II (80). A discussion of this plan and a useful comparison to a second stabilisation and reform plan supported by Mikhail Gorbachev can be found in Padma Desai, 'Soviet economic reform: a tale of two plans', The Harriman Institute, *Forum*, December, 1990. A useful recent translation and compilation of Soviet statistical materials is Michael Ryan, *Contemporary Soviet Society: A Statistical Handbook* (79). Of special interest for the attention it has received is a study of the Soviet economy done in 1990 for the Houston summit and entitled *The Economy of the USSR: Summary and Recommendations* (74).

Soviet authors have also been active in writing about perestroika. Though not a very informative work, Gorbachev's early views on perestroika can be found in Mikhail Gorbachev, *Perestroika: New Thinking for Our Country and the World* (89). Insights into perestroika by a well known Soviet economist can be found in A. Aganbegyan, *The Economic Challenge of Perestroika* (85), and A. Aganbegyan, *Inside Perestroika* (72). An interesting discussion of the background to perestroika, the nature of and prospects for reform is Nikolai Shmelyev and Vladimir Popov, *The Turning Point: Revitalizing the Soviet Economy* (83).

Bibliography

General Surveys of the Economy

1   Gregory, Paul R. and Stuart, Robert C. (1990) *Soviet Economic Structure and Performance.* New York: HarperCollins

    Basic text treating all major aspects of the Russian and Soviet economic experience.

2   Ellman, Michael (1989) *Socialist Planning.* New York: Cambridge University Press

    A basic text dealing with the Soviet planning economy – structure, function and results.

3   Nove, Alec (1986) *The Soviet Economic System.* Winchester, MA: Unwin Hyman

    Basic text treating important themes with substantive development of the workings of the Soviet economy.

4   Dyker, David A. (1985) *The Future of the Soviet Economic Planning System.* Armonk, NY: M.E. Sharpe

    A text which covers the basics plus economic reform and specialised topics such as agriculture.

5   Holzman, Franklyn (1982) *The Soviet Economy: Past, Present, and Future* New York: Foreign Policy Association

    A brief but well-organised and readable treatment of the traditional Soviet command system.

6   Munting, Roger (1982) *The Economic Development of the USSR.* London: Croom Helm

    Discussion of the Soviet economy from an historical perspective.

7   Millar, James (1981) *The ABCs of Soviet Socialism*. Urbana, IL: University of Illinois Press

A basic survey of selected aspects of the Soviet economy by a well-known analyst of that system.

The Early Years

8   Hunter, Holland and Szyrmer, Janusz M. (1991) *Faulty Foundations: Soviet Economic Policies, 1928-1940*. Princeton, NJ: Princeton University Press

An important study simulating outcomes from possible alternative economic policies for the Soviet economy in the 1930s.

9   Davies, R.W. (1990) Editor. *From Tsarism to the New Economic Policy*. Basingstoke: Macmillan

An excellent collection of papers by noted authors comparing the late Tsarist and early Soviet economies.

10   Davies, R.W. (1990) *The Industrialization of Russia*. Vol. 3. Cambridge, MA: Harvard University Press

One of a series of works by the author, providing in-depth discussion of the events in the first year of implementation of the Stalinist planning model.

11   Millar, James R. (1990) *The Soviet Economic Experiment*, edited with an introduction by Susan J. Linz. Urbana, IL: University of Illinois Press

A collection of essays by the author dealing with important themes such as agriculture, finance and convergence.

12   Malle, S. (1985) *The Economic Organization of War Communism, 1918-1921*. Cambridge: Cambridge University Press

Detailed development of the characteristics of a period important for understanding early Soviet development.

13   Morrison, David (1985) A critical examination of A.A. Barsov's empirical work on the balance of value exchanges between the town and the country. *Soviet Studies* 34, 4, October, 570-84.

A critical examination of the original Barsov data and its manipulation.

14   Wheatcroft, S.G. and Davies, R.W. (1985) *Materials for a Balance of the National Economy, 1928-1930*. New York: Cambridge University Press

A compilation and interpretation of the important initial documents pertaining to Soviet balance planning.

15   Gatrell, P. (1982) *The Tsarist Economy, 1850-1917*. London: Croom Helm

An excellent survey of a critical period examining the nature and extent of industrialisation in the immediate pre-Soviet period.

16   Gregory, Paul R. (1982) *Russian National Income, 1885-1913*. Cambridge: Cambridge University Press

Re-estimation of important basic data series for the immediate pre-Soviet period by a well-known analyst of economic growth and development under Tsarism.

17   Nove, Alec (1982) *Economic History of the USSR*. New York: Penguin Books

An excellent general economic history of the USSR by a pioneer in the field.

18 Davies, R.W. (1980) *The Industrialization of Russia.* Vols. 1 and 2. Cambridge, MA: Harvard University Press

Volume 1 is a detailed study of the collectivisation process in 1929 and 1920 while volume 2 is a discussion of the collective farm.

19 Zaleski, E. (1980) *Planning for Economic Growth in the Soviet Union, 1918-1932.* Chapel Hill: University of North Carolina Press

A good discussion of general issues pertaining to growth and development during the early Soviet years.

20 Zaleski, E. (1980) *Stalinist Planning for Economic Growth, 1933-1952.* Chapel Hill: University of North Carolina Press

An excellent and detailed discussion of the early Soviet economic plans including methods of compilation and implementation.

21 Ellman, Michael (1975) Did the agricultural surplus provide the resources for the increase in investment in the USSR during the First Five Year Plan? *Economic Journal* 85, 4, December.

A useful overview and analysis of the whole surplus issue.

22 Lewin, M. (1975) *Russian Peasants and Soviet Power: A Study of Collectivization.* New York: W.W. Norton

An excellent account of the actual process of collectivisation by a well-known scholar.

23 Barsov, A.A. (1969) *Balans Stoimostnykh Obmenov mezhdu Gorodom i Derevnei.* Moscow: Nauka

A critical analysis of the Western view of accumulation during collectivisation done by a Soviet author and based upon archival data.

The War Years

24 Moskoff, William (1989) *The Bread of Affliction: The Food Supply in the USSR during World War II.* New York: Cambridge University Press

An important study of a neglected topic – how the Soviet population was fed during the Second World War.

25 Harrison, M. (1985) *Soviet Planning in Peace and War: 1938-1945.* Cambridge: Cambridge University Press

Focuses on a topic of great interest to economists and others - how and how well Soviet planning functioned during the Second World War.

26 Linz, Susan J. (1985) Editor. *The Impact of World War II on the Soviet Economy.* Totowa, NJ: Rowman and Allenheld

A collection of original papers by well-known authors dealing with a variety of issues relating to the Second World War.

27 Dunmore, T. (1980) *The Stalinist Command Economy.* New York: St. Martin's Press

An important study of a much neglected period – how the Soviet economy adjusted to peace at the end of the Second World War.

Soviet Balance Planning

28 Quandt, Richard E. and Triska, Dusan (1990) Editors. *Optimal Decisions in Markets and Planned Economies.* Boulder, CO: Westview Press

A collection of largely theoretical papers dealing with important issues of decision making in both planned and market economies focusing on the micro level.

29   Kushnirsky, F. (1982) *Soviet Economic Planning, 1965-1980*. Boulder, CO: Westview Press

An excellent study describing how the Soviet planning system actually worked and how it changed during the Brezhnev years.

30   Todaro, Michael P. (1971) *Development Planning: Models and Methods*. Oxford: Oxford University Press

One of the few studies of planning in development which develops the basic input-output model and applies it to the Soviet case of balance planning in a way useful for understanding the problems facing planners.

Plan Implementation: Ministers and Managers

31   Gregory, Paul R. (1989) *The Soviet Economic Bureaucracy*. Cambridge: Cambridge University Press

The first major study of the Soviet administrative structure and particularly its personnel based upon interview evidence from the Soviet Interview Project (SIP).

32   Freris, A. (1984) *The Soviet Industrial Enterprise*. New York: St. Martin's Press

A succinct, contemporary and analytical discussion of the Soviet industrial enterprise.

33   Conyngham, W. (1982) *The Modernization of Soviet Industrial Management*. Cambridge: Cambridge University Press

An excellent study of the Soviet system of industrial management, in effect updating earlier classics by Berliner, Granick, Richman and others.

The Soviet Financial System: Budgets, Prices and Investment

34   Bornstein, M. (1989) Problems of price reform in the USSR. *Soviet Economic Reforms: Implementation Underway,* edited by NATO, 130-44. Brussels: NATO

A recent account of price reform under perestroika – a topic of major importance in the reform discussion conducted by a pioneer in the field.

35   Kushnirsky, Fyodor (1989) *Growth and Inflation in the Soviet Union*. Boulder, CO: Westview Press

A study of Soviet pricing emphasising sectors where such policies have been thought to contribute to inflation.

36   Bornstein, M. (1987) Soviet price policies. *Soviet Economy*. 3, 2, 96-134.

An excellent discussion of the basics of price formation in the Soviet Union.

37   Amann, R. and Cooper J. (1986) Editors. *Technical Progress and Soviet Economic Development*. New York: Blackwell

A useful collection of articles dealing with general issues of technological change, sectoral problems and issues of technology transfer.

38   Hutchings, R. (1983) *The Soviet Budgetary System*. Albany: State University of New York Press

A basic account of a difficult topic – the structure and functions of the Soviet budgetary system.

39   Birman, I. (1981) *Secret Incomes of the Soviet State Budget*. The Hague: Nijhoff

A critical examination of the Soviet budgetary system arguing that many important components of the Soviet financial system are in fact hidden from view making Soviet official budget data of limited value for analysis.

40   Dyker, D. (1981) *The Process of Investment in the Soviet Union*. New York: Cambridge University Press

A basic and well-written survey of a very important topic – how investment allocation takes place in the Soviet Union.

41   Berliner, J. (1976) *The Innovation Decision in Soviet Industry*. Cambridge, MA: MIT Press

A classic study of the process of innovation in the Soviet Union, critical to an understanding of Soviet growth problems.

Labour and the Household

42   Malle, Silvana (1990) *Employment Planning in the Soviet Union*. Basingstoke: Macmillan

A general analysis of both the supply and demand sides of labour allocation including discussion of wage issues.

43   Porket, J.L. (1989) *Work, Employment and Unemployment in the Soviet Union*. Basingstoke: Macmillan

A broad discussion of labour allocation in the Soviet economy.

44   Arnot, B. (1988) *Controlling Soviet Labour*. London: Macmillan

A detailed discussion of the Shchekino experiment, and effort to improve labour allocation in the Soviet Union.

45   Granick, D. (1987) *Job Rights in the Soviet Union: Their Consequences*. New York: Cambridge University Press

A detailed analysis of the nature and consequences of Soviet full employment policy.

46   Adam, Jan (1987) Editor. *Employment Policies in the Soviet Union and Eastern Europe*, 2nd edn. Basingstoke: Macmillan

A collection of essays dealing mainly with labour issues in the Soviet Union.

47   Lane, D. (1986) Editor. *Labour and Employment in the USSR*. New York: New York University Press

A collection of essays covering major topics on Soviet labour policies and practices.

48   Yanowitch, M. (1985) *Work in the Soviet Union*. Armonk, NY: M.E. Sharpe

A study of attitudes and issues based on Soviet sociological and journalistic writings.

49   Moskoff, W. (1984) *Labour and Leisure in the Soviet Union*. New York: St. Martin's Press

An economic analysis of time budgeting in the Soviet household with emphasis on leisure related activities.

50   Skurski, Roger (1983) *Soviet Marketing and Economic Development*. New York: St. Martin's Press

A major study of an important aspect of the Soviet economy – the distribution system.

51   Ofer, Gur and Vinokur, Aaron (1981) Earnings differentials by sex in the Soviet Union: a first look. *Economic Welfare and the Economics of Soviet Socialism*, edited by Steven Rosefielde, 127-162. New York: Cambridge University Press

An early analysis of male/female earnings differentials in the Soviet Union using survey data.

52   Ruble, B. (1981) *Soviet Trade Unions.* New York: Cambridge University Press

The classic contemporary study of trade unions in the Soviet Union – what they are, what they do, and what they do not do.

Soviet Agriculture

53   Wadekin, K.E. (1990) Editor. *Communist Agriculture.* New York: Routledge

A survey of basic issues pertaining to collectivised agriculture by a pioneer in the field.

54   Gray, K. (1990) Editor. *Contemporary Soviet Agriculture in Comparative Perspective.* Ames: Iowa State University Press

An excellent collection of original papers devoted to various aspects of the contemporary Soviet agrcultural sector.

55   Medvedev, Z.A. (1987) *Soviet Agriculture.* New York: W.W. Norton

A discussion of agriculture in the Soviet Union by a noted Soviet author.

56   Hedlund, S. (1984) *Crisis in Soviet Agriculture.* New York: St. Martin's Press

A critical discussion of Soviet agricultural policies and institutions.

57   Johnson, D.G. and Brooks, K.McC. (1984) *Prospects for Soviet Agriculture in the 1980s.* Bloomington, IN: Indiana University Press

An excellent study of Soviet agriculture focusing upon both organisational and policy problems.

58   Stuart, R.C. (1983) Editor. *The Soviet Rural Economy.* Totowa, NJ: Rowman and Allanheld

A collection of original articles dealing with a variety of important themes.

59   Wadekin, K.E. (1982) Editor. *Agriculture in Inter-System Comparison: Communist and Non-Communist Cases.* Berlin: Duncker and Humbolt

An important attempt to analyse the effectiveness of socialist cases by careful analysis and comparison of similar socialist and non-socialist cases.

60   Wadekin, K.E. (1982) *Agrarian Policies in Communist Europe: A Critical Introduction.* Totowa, NJ: Rowman and Allanheld

A detailed study of important aspects of agriculture in the Soviet Union and Eastern Europe with emphasis on the Soviet case.

Foreign Trade

61   Wolf, Thomas A. (1988) *Foreign Trade in the Centrally Planned Economy.* New York: Harwood Academic Publishers

A brief but excellent discussion of key issues relating to trade in planned economies with a lengthy bibliography.

62   Holzman, Franklyn D. (1987) *The Economics of Soviet Bloc Trade and Finance.* Boulder, CO: Westview Press

A collection of major contributions by a pioneer in the field of trade in planned economies.

63   Gardner, H. S. (1983) *Soviet Foreign Trade: The Decision Process.* Boston: Kluwer-Nijhoff

A survey of the Soviet foreign trade system in the command economy – how it is organised, how it functions and with what results.

64 Gruzinov, V.P. (1979) *The USSR's Management of Foreign Trade.* White Plains, NY: M.E. Sharpe

An account of how Soviet foreign trade planning actually works by a Soviet author.

Soviet Economic Performance

65 Birman, Igor (1989) *Personal Consumption in the USSR and the USA.* Basingstoke: Macmillan

A comparison of consumption in the USSR and the USA covering important sectors such as food and housing including a discussion of methodological problems.

66 Millar, J. (1987) Editor. *Politics, Work, and Daily Life in the USSR.* New York: Cambridge University Press

Initial results from a major contemporary interview project – a survey of former Soviet citizens relating to a variety of issues – especially household economics.

67 Ofer, G. (1987) Soviet economic growth, 1928-1985. *Journal of Economic Literature,* 25, 4, 1767-1833.

An excellent and detailed survey of Soviet economic growth and structural change.

68 Matthews, M. (1986) *Poverty in the Soviet Union: The Lifestyles of the Underprivileged in Recent Years.* New York: Cambridge University Press

A major study of a previously neglected topic.

69 Bergson, A. (1984) Income inequality under Soviet socialism. *Journal of Economic Literature,* 22, 3, 1052-99.

One of a series of pieces on the topic of inequality in the Soviet Union by a pioneer observer of the system.

70 McCauley, A. (1979) *Economic Welfare in the Soviet Union.* Madison, WI: University of Wisconsin Press

An early and useful study of general issues of population well-being in the Soviet Union.

71 Bergson, A. (1978) *Productivity and the Social System: The USSR and the West.* Cambridge, MA: Harvard University Press

An excellent general survey of a critical issue – productivity comparisons East and West.

The Gorbachev Era

72 Aganbegyan, A. (1990) *Inside Perestroika.* New York: HarperCollins

A discussion of perestroika by a well-known Soviet economist and participant in the Soviet political process.

73 Desai, P. (1990) *Perestroika in Perspective.* Revised paperback edition. Princeton, NJ: Princeton University Press

A brief and readable discussion of basic issues pertaining to perestroika.

74 *The Economy of the USSR: Summary and Recommendations.* (1990) Washington, DC: IMF, The World Bank, Organisation for Economic Cooperation and Development, and European Bank for Reconstruction and Development

A study of the state of the Soviet economy with recommendations for reform conducted in connection with the Houston Summit of August, 1990.

75 Grossman, Gregory (1990) *The Second Economy of the USSR and Eastern Europe.* Berkeley-Duke Occasional Papers on the Second Economy of the USSR, no. 21, July.

A bibliography of the second economy literature by a long-time observer of the Soviet economy.

76 Hanson, Philip (1990) Property rights in the new phase of reforms. *Soviet Economy* 6, 2 (April-June), 95-124.

An excellent discussion of changing property arrangements in the Soviet Union, for example in the cooperative sector.

77 Moskoff, W. (1990) *Perestroika in the Countryside.* Armonk, NY: M.E. Sharpe

A collection of articles dealing with issues of economic reform in Soviet agriculture – organisational change, leasing, trade, etc.

78 Plokker, Karin (1990) The development of cooperative and individual labour activity in the Soviet Union. *Soviet Studies* 42, 3, July, 403-28.

An excellent survey of the development of private and cooperative activity in the Soviet Union with emphasis on labour allocation.

79 Ryan, Michael (1990) *Contemporary Soviet Society: A Statistical Handbook.* Brookfield, VT.: Edward Elgar

A wide variety of Soviet data made available to those who cannot access such data directly.

80 *Transition to the Market* (1990) Parts I and II. Moscow: Cultural Initiative Foundation

The 500-day plan authored by S.S. Shatalin as the leader of a group formed by Gorbachev and Yeltsin. Covers the basic plan and draft legislation for implementation.

81 Aslund, A. (1989) *Gorbachev's Struggle for Economic Reform.* Ithaca, NY: Cornell University Press

An excellent and detailed account of the nature of perestroika.

82 Matthews, Mervyn (1989) *Patterns of Deprivation in the Soviet Union under Brezhnev and Gorbachev.* Basingstoke: Macmillan

An excellent and recent discussion of the issue of poverty in the Soviet Union including survey results and treatment of contemporary policies.

83 Shmelyev, Nikolai and Popov, Vladimir (1989) *The Turning Point: Revitalizing the Soviet Economy,* translated by Michele A. Berdy. New York: Doubleday

A survey of the Soviet economy, past, present and future by two well-known Soviet authors.

84 *Soviet Economic Reforms: Implementation Underway.* (1989) Brussels: NATO

An excellent collection of articles by well-known authors dealing with central issues of reform – pricing, legal issues, trade policies, ruble convertibility, etc.

85 Aganbegyan, A. (1988) *The Economic Challenge of Perestroika.* Bloomington, IN: Indiana University Press

A broad discussion of reform in the Soviet economy – the background, reform alternatives, impact and possible outcomes written by a well-known Soviet economist.

86 Hewett, E. (1988) *Reforming the Soviet Economy.* Washington, DC.: Brookings Institution

An early study of perestroika especially useful for understanding the reform process in the Soviet Union as it unfolded, and how it relates to the command system.

87 Dyker, D. (1987) Editor. *The Soviet Economy under Gorbachev: The Prospects for Reform*. London: Croom Helm

A useful collection of articles dealing with various aspects of economic reform in the Soviet Union.

88 Goldman, M. (1987) *Gorbachev's Challenge: Economic Reform in the Age of High Technology*. New York: W.W. Norton

An early discussion of perestroika by a well known analyst focusing on the issue of technology and the problems of technological change in the reform process.

89 Gorbachev, M. (1987) *Perestroika: New Thinking for Our Country and the World*. New York: Harper and Row

The original work on perestroika by Mikhail Gorbachev which would probably not be read were it not for the identity of the author. Now interesting in historical perspective.

90 United States Congress, Joint Economic Committee, (1987) Editor. *Gorbachev's Economic Plans*. Washington, DC.: US Government Printing Office

One of a series of publications by the JEC – covers a wide variety of important topics researched by specialists and excellent as a basic introduction to perestroika.

91 Bergson, A. and Levine H.S. (1983) Editors. *The Soviet Economy: Towards the Year 2000*. London: Allen and Unwin

An excellent collection of original articles discussing important aspects of the Soviet record.

92 Goldman, M. (1983) *The USSR in Crisis*. New York: W.W. Norton

Written well before perestroika, a critical analysis of the Soviet economic system and its problems.

CHAPTER EIGHT

Business

Tania Konn
Glasgow University

Business Information

The English-language business literature of the pre-Gorbachev era reflected the relatively stable conditions under which business with the Soviet Union was conducted. Centralisation of foreign trade in the hands of relatively few foreign trade organisations and close control of relationships with foreign firms ensured that trade negotiations followed well-understood channels, and that openings for individual entrepreneurial initiatives were extremely limited. Business information needs in this situation were predictable and largely of a kind to satisfy bureaucratic demands. The English-language information sector servicing this area was characterised by relatively few well-established information agencies, lethargic marketing of information services, and a steady output of unremarkable literature.

The dramatic events of perestroika and glasnost transformed this static situation. On the Soviet side a new business information era began on January 1st, 1987, when foreign trade regulations were reformed. On that date 21 ministries and around 70 industrial enterprises were granted the right to operate directly in foreign markets (9). Currently some 20,000 enterprises have the right to engage in foreign trade. The new policy of actively encouraging contact and cooperation with external firms, associated with a drive towards a less constrained and more responsive internal economy, inevitably involved considerable modification of Soviet attitudes towards business information production and use.

Externally perestroika encouraged the belief that Soviet markets offered untapped potential. Foreign firms wishing to take advantage of changing conditions in the Soviet Union required information for their assessments of possibilities and risks. Normal information requirements for such purposes were complicated by persisting political volatility, by un-

settling differences between official pronouncements and business realities, and by continuing obstructive formalities seemingly inseparable
from Soviet business dealings.

The scale and nature of the Soviet business information sector since
1987 have been transformed by the operation of these factors upon information demand and supply. Both printed publications and electronic services have grown considerably in numbers and in diversity. Publishing of
Soviet business material has become intensely competitive, attracting
numerous newcomers. The resulting literature, reflecting both opportunities of market orientated business and the unusual volatility of Soviet
business conditions, combines high volume with utilitarian aims and
ephemerality. Hardly anything written before 1987 remains worth reading
for its original information purpose.

Coming to Terms

Market economy managers routinely seek out standard types of information when evaluating and taking organisational decisions. The requirements are well enough understood to produce diversified networks of
specialist information suppliers – on, for example, consumer preferences,
influential contacts, company profiles, regulatory constraints, investment
prospects, debt repayments, competitive bids, risk assessments, market
potential, productivity.

In pre-1987 Soviet Union most of these forms of business information
rarely emerged as organisational necessities. The prevailing political and
economic philosophy favoured economic centralisation and close control
of consumer choices. This situation severely circumscribed managerial responsibility and rendered independent organisational information gathering superfluous when it was not simply forbidden. The business and
economic information that was produced and made available often reflected bureaucratic and political, rather than operational, imperatives (12:
p.36). Data were frequently employed to disguise economic realities.
Many commentators have pointed to the inadequacies of Soviet economic
data and their presentation (13, 17). The deeper analyses and significance
of such practices are of more interest to economists than businessmen.
The extent and effects of statistical incompetence, and of attempts to mis-
lead, upon ordinary business life are best captured by journalists. A readable and vivid account is to be found in *The Hard Road to Market*, by
Robert Boyes (1).

Following the reform of foreign trade laws in 1987, the inrush of
foreign businessmen quickly confirmed the existence of an information
gap of substantial proportions. Frequently, demanders of information
found that what they sought was not available, badly presented, or unre-
liable. It was obvious that improvements in the collection and presenta-

tion of business data were needed. It was essential, too, for Soviet information providers and businessmen to appreciate the crucial role of information in organisations within market economies. One of the benefits of
glasnost was that it allowed criticisms of inadequacies to be expressed
publicly. An illuminating, concise record of the statistical debate has been
compiled by Treml (2). As a result of such pressures, improvements have
been recorded and further progress is expected. One development of note
is the cooperation of Dun and Bradstreet and Goskomstat to produce
USSR Import and Export Trade Statistics (93). External statistical sources,
such as *East European Statistics Service* (92) and *Comecon Data* (91), also
benefit from the more open approach to statistics.

Developments

Organisational information demands consist of numerous interdependent
and interacting components. Too many to receive detailed consideration
in a chapter of this type. However, within the broad developments out-
lined above, it is possible to indicate the main classes of business literature and services that have drawn most attention in recent years. These
may be represented by seven, non-exclusive groups:

* General Context and Analysis.

* General Business Information and Analysis.

* Practical Guidance.

* Legalities and Joint Ventures.

* Finance and Banking.

* Sectoral Information.

* Contact Information.

General Context and Analysis

Business enterprises of the market economy type require a constant inflow
of general intelligence. That is, sifted and evaluated background information relating to factors likely to have a bearing upon their operations. This
material provides the essential political and economic context for understanding present and possible future business activities. Such intelligence
contributes importantly to strategic business thinking. For example, it is
essential for forward planners to appreciate the significance of political
shifts, to be able to balance the nuances of official statements and the practical extent of central government authority, to be aware of future govern-

mental intentions, of attitudes towards foreign investment, of payment records, and accurately to assess risk factors.

Gaining and evaluating business information is not a straightforward process at the best of times. When operating across national boundaries this process becomes even more problematical. Additional effort and resources have to be expended upon the acquisition and processing of information, and much greater attention paid to its analysis and interpretation. Something of the importance of this process may be gauged by the high prices charged for some types of information in this category.

The general descriptive and interpretative literature of glasnost and perestroika of interest to thinking managers is formidable in volume. Examples of the genre are to be found in other chapters and will not be discussed here. Little need be said, either, of the intense interest in Soviet affairs shown by the media generally. These are important agencies for transmitting information with business implications and for influencing attitudes, but are outside our scope.

There are numerous printed, periodical sources of information (3, 4, 5), but for present purposes it is more useful to call attention to the efforts of electronic services to reflect the growth of general interest in Soviet topics. These services, like the paper counterparts upon which they are largely based, provide the latest political, social and economic information about the Soviet Union on a frequent and regular basis. In doing so they have considerably enlarged their coverage of the Soviet Union with special reference to business matters (6, 7, 8). Electronic services of this type make it easier to monitor a wide range of newspapers, magazines, reports and other information sources with speed and flexibility. The growing investment in this medium suggests that, for businessmen particularly, it will become a major form of 'literature' capturing the latest information and trends.

Glasnost has produced conditions relatively tolerant of independent news agencies. As a result, new internal news services have appeared. Such agencies are useful for the balancing glosses they provide to official pronouncements and explanations, and for their willingness to handle subjects not thought fit for public discussion by the authorities. However, information liberalisation is not always allowed free rein. The discussion of certain topics can still cause official displeasure powerful enough to ensure the return of repressive measures. Recently, for example, the news agency Interfax was compelled to close down for a time because coverage and treatment of events offended official susceptibilities. Current events (March, 1991) indicate that the future of independent news agencies is far from secure.

General Business Information and Analysis

In line with increasing numbers of foreign business relationships, the volume of publications devoted to general considerations of Soviet business issues has expanded substantially in recent years. The justification for this type of literature is the belief that 'a clear and concise review of the major elements of the reform programme are essential for any Western business which has trade links with the country or is contemplating the vast market' (15: p.6).

The type of work falling into this category describes the impact of economic and legal reforms upon business interests, examines specific aspects of trade, considers national economic implications and, usually, attempts to predict future developments. Most try to tease out the implications of reform for their own country, their own business interests as well for the Soviet Union. Sometimes titles in this group also offer practical advice of the 'how to do business with the Russians' variety. In a few cases the essentials of reform may be set out without complicating analysis and interpretation (9).

As with business literature generally the aim of works in this class is utilitarian, with presentational styles ranging from management popular to heavy academic. However they are written, the pace of change within the Soviet Union ensures a short shelf-life for most books in this group. As a result analysts are responding in print with increasing speed and facility to the latest events. The uncertainties of economic life force many commentators into the stratosphere of generalisation, and to resort to repetition of the obvious. For example, to be informed 'that the future path of reforms is highly uncertain', or that the 'leadership is worried about the likely social conflicts', or that 'the population is increasingly disillusioned about the meagre economic effects of perestroika' (14: p.15, 11) hardly advances the understanding of businessmen constantly exposed to instant media punditry, which is usually pitched at the same level of generality.

Lindsay's work *International Business in Gorbachev's Soviet Union* (15) is a good example of the type of work intended to appeal to businessmen – readable, interesting in its interpretations and authoritative in its judgments. Ellman's survey *The USSR in the 1990s* (13) is balanced and presented in the concise, clear manner preferred by businessmen. More nationally pugnacious in its tone and assessments is *US Commercial Opportunities in the Soviet Union* (10). This work reviews various ways in which American firms might operate to advantage in the Soviet Union and examines some of the obstacles to success. As with a number of other books of this type the situational analysis carries a political message – 'Western firms trading with the Soviet Union or setting up co-production facilities there may eventually incur a near-universal cost, the gradual weakening of the very free market mechanisms that have upheld the capitalist system itself' (10: p.174). This wariness of too precipitate business dealings with the Soviet Union is characteristic of a number of American publications on the theme of West-Soviet economic relations. International organisations and agencies usually adopt more measured tones, even when the message is much the same (12). The constant hazard associated with titles of this type lies in the volatility of Soviet circumstances. Changes can invalidate elaborate analyses, attitudes and intentions captured so permanently in book form. Since change and uncertainty are the characterising features of the Soviet scene it is inevitable that book-bound authors, involved in protracted publishing cycles, can be embarrassed by unexpected events. The swiftness of developments means that businessmen cannot rely solely upon infrequently issued books to replenish their capital of working information. The requirement to keep abreast of latest developments is essential. To meet this need weekly, fortnightly, monthly and quarterly publications have appeared in increasing numbers.

Typically, publications of this kind highlight current dominant business, industrial and financial concerns. They monitor legal changes relating to business, review sector developments, indicate opportunities, assess risk factors, analyse latest joint venture developments, provide contact information. Within the group there are interesting variations of style, format, authority and purpose. At one end of the scale are grouped relatively modest publications which simply digest and report business news without frills. Some way up the scale are the growing number of glossy management style magazines with feature articles supported by snippets of business news and expressed in the punchy style characteristic of the genre. Still further along the scale are market reports and in-depth analyses of markets and opportunities. Along this scale, differences in costs can be startling. Given the rapidity of changing events in the Soviet Union, weekly publications have an obvious edge in reporting terms – a fact of importance highlighted by the number of services increasing their frequency of publication. Monthly and quarterly publications offer the possibility of more considered judgments.

One striking feature of the titles in this body of literature is the high degree of editorial individualism displayed. It is very rare to find comparable publications focusing on the same issues for editorial treatment. This may be taken to be one sign of the volatility of the field. The situation also reflects the variety of sources and contacts from which such publications draw their information. Periodicals now constitute an area of intense publishing endeavour and competition with established information suppliers having to fend off the market encroachments of numerous incomers. A consequence of these conditions is the growing difficulty in assessing the quality of new provision. The numbers of publications appearing on the market are an obstacle to systematic, objective evaluation. It is also the case that many services have been established for too short a time to present a reasonable corpus of work for judgment.

Of special significance in this important group of business information sources are publications originating in the Soviet Union, especially those inclined to editorial independence. For example *Commersant* (26) appeared, or rather reappeared, in 1990. Issued in both Russian and English versions this weekly deals with business topics in a lively, non-deferential style. Despite glasnost the position of the publication is delicate, as is illustrated by differences between the English and Russian versions. What can be said in English is not always thought appropriate for a more conservative Russian readership. However, its success to date ensures it a reputation that cannot be ignored by business analysts.

Regional business news services, reflecting the new sense of regional enterprise and independence are now appearing, such as *Delovaia Sibir*. These titles contrast markedly with the older established, staider, official Soviet business information sources. Even these are changing, however. *Foreign Trade USSR* (34), the organ of the USSR Ministry of Foreign Economic Relations, appears in five languages in glossy format, and *Business Contacts* (21) has an upmarket management appearance. Both are intended to encourage trade with the USSR and present information in a relatively lively style.

A number of Soviet business information sources are published and distributed abroad. For example *Ecotass* (33), the economic and commercial bulletin of the Soviet News Agency Tass, is published by Pergamon Press in the UK, while the *Bulletin of Commercial Information for Foreign Businessmen* (20), of the USSR Chamber of Commerce and Industry, is published and distributed by International Trade Press in the USA. Both, despite such associations, are modestly produced publications, a fact that does nothing to diminish their informativeness and utility.

As might be expected, the greater contribution to the expansion of English-language sources has occurred outside the Soviet Union. *Business Eastern Europe* (22) from Business International is the undisputed market leader. The UK is well represented in this field with *East European Markets* (28), a highly respected newsletter. The contributions of the Economist Intelligence Unit to this category have achieved wide recognition, based on established services and the continuing publication of new, authoritative publications (27, 29, 32). A significant example of British-Soviet cooperation is evidenced in the publication of *Arguments and Facts International* (18), a highly informative periodical based on Russian sources.

The contribution of US sources to this form of information provision is highly significant, as is the increasing English-language provision of European sources. From the US *PlanEcon Report* (38), *PlanEcon Business Report* (37) and *Comecon Reports* (25) are services of high standing. As an example of closer US-Soviet information contacts we may note that, at the end of 1990, a Russian-language version of *Business Week/USSR* (24) was distributed in the Soviet Union as a joint venture between McGraw Hill and Kniga Publishers of Minsk. The influence of continental Europe may be illustrated by reference to *Business in the USSR* (23), a recent French-Soviet project, *East West: Fortnightly Bulletin* (30) produced in Belgium, and *Glasnost* (35) produced in Denmark. There are numerous other titles in this area. Since it is possible only to mention a few it is advisable to consult available guides for fuller coverage (96, 97).

The unremitting need for up-to-date information is often best met by resorting to the use of online services. Many publications of the type mentioned above are available in electronic form, and online services are further widening their coverage of business information through cooperative ventures. For example in 1990 Maxwell Online announced a contract with VINITI to make business information available, and GBI agreed to the production and marketing of databases with ICSI. A more recent development has seen the American-based Telebase System Inc. combine with the Soviet-Swiss joint venture Lesinvest to offer Soviet businessmen access to its information network at substantial discounts. In addition, this grouping of information interests intends to gather commercial information in the USSR to create databases to be used by Western clients. A number of electronic services provide statistical data (94). The flexibility of such provision is well illustrated by the deducible statistical facility offered by *Tradstat* (95) for the manipulation of official trade figures.

Practical Guidance

Perestroika may have had the aim of liberalising the economy, but the more obvious result has been a considerable increase in the degree of uncertainty associated with conditions of business. Most commentators on the business scene have called attention to this phenomenon. For example, Lindsay points out that 'even those reforms which have been codified and are being actively pursued are often muddled and unclear, subject to pressure to pull back from the more radical elements... perestroika does not mean an easy market for Western business. Instead, it has led to confusion and uncertainty on both sides, as the various changes to laws and rules are still being applied and in some cases only slightly understood... there may be considerable obstacles to overcome in even the most simple of deals' (15: p.2,148).

This situation has created a market for guidance literature which offers practical advice on how to initiate and carry on business in the Soviet Union. The degree of detail presented by these publications varies, but their intentions are broadly similar. They claim to guide their readers through the maze of legalities and local practices surrounding foreign business in the Soviet Union. Encouragement is provided by frequent references to the huge potential of the Soviet market. Balance is maintained by repeated stressing of possibilities of disaster if local conditions are not fully understood. The complications of provided explanations quickly bring about the realisation that perestroika initially did not represent a programme to secure the establishment of a Western style capitalist economy: 'the Soviet economy is to remain centrally planned and managed. Indeed the target is to boost the efficacy and role of central planning and management in fulfilling the strategic goals of economic development, determining its rates, ratios and balance' (9: p.12).

There are numerous examples of this genre. Titles may be general in coverage (44, 47, 48, 50, 51), or they may concentrate on such specifics as contracts (45). They have in common an inevitable sameness of content, an adherence to conservative business wisdom and, to put it at its best, an uninspiring presentational style. In qualification it may be said that such works have to be written quickly for a very utilitarian purpose. An interesting, and highly informative, example of the type is *Moscow Business Survival Guide*, by P.E. Richardson and D.F. Kolley (49). It is informative in that it is written by businessmen with experience of Soviet trading. It is also evidence of the importance of English as the language of business. It is produced in Norway. The volatility of the economic and political situation means that published information of this factual nature can be rendered misleading or obsolete quickly and unexpectedly. The frequent changes of business requirements encourage the emergence of a continuing stream of new publications presenting the latest developments and changes, sufficient in number to illustrate the point that informing businessmen of Soviet market requirements is recognised by publishers as a promising area for exploitation. Interestingly, Soviet publishing houses have also grasped the potential of this type of publication. Such titles as *How to Make Your Way to the Foreign Market, How to Become a Prosperous Businessman, Business Papers, Model Contracts* etc, parallel Western works. In the Soviet market, however, these are the only titles of their type. They appear to have been sellouts despite following the Western practice of charging high prices for business books and manuals. The adoption of Western practices in regard to other forms of business literature in the Soviet Union has not always been as successful however. Many new ventures have collapsed (*Commersant*, 4/1/1991: p.16). The number of these practical works also confirms the importance of up-to-date information. While some publishers recognise the need to cater for this requirement through new editions, others prefer to bring out new titles. Some choose the more flexible method of regular updating of a basic text through monthly and quarterly supplements. The standard setting *Doing Business With Eastern Europe* (46), for example, provides monthly updates for those subscribing to its full range of services.

The range of material in this category of practical guidance literature can be extended by referring to many institutions and organisations, such as banks, government departments, chambers of commerce, that produce publications of advice for their clients. These are often free, but should not be neglected for that reason. Although, by their nature, less than comprehensive they provide helpful advice to entrepreneurs.

Legalities and Joint Ventures

The willingness of the Soviet Union, from 1987, to consider joint ventures in trade and business aroused considerable interest throughout the world. However, despite initial enthusiasm joint ventures represent a fraught area of economic activity, with only a small minority of engaged enterprises making a profit. Further, it is an activity embedded in legalities and vacillating support from the authorities. It is clearly an area favouring long-term strategies. As might be expected in these circumstances a special branch of guidance literature, concentrating upon joint ventures and their legal requirements, has emerged as a growth area. Typically these works discuss such topics as the legal status of a joint venture enterprise, the various procedures to be undertaken when setting up a venture, franchising, permitted activities, currency, tax and labour issues. Some offer advice on methods of negotiating with the Soviets, listing the favoured ploys of contract negotiators. All these works stress the problems to be expected; all counsel patience and the need to look well ahead for worthwhile returns. *Eastern Bloc Joint Ventures* (57) provides substantial recognition of the breadth and depth of interest in the legal aspects of joint ventures. A number of other works bring different legal aspects into focus (52, 53, 54, 55, 56). The complex and changing state of business law in the USSR, the state of 'law war' between the republics and Moscow, and developing interest in business arrangements other than the joint venture, offer scope for periodical publications to record and discuss latest developments. Recent examples of the eagerness to cater for such needs are *Soviet Business Law Digest* (60) and *Soviet and East European Business Law Bulletin* (59), both launched in 1990, and *East European Business Law* (58) appearing in 1991.

Finance and Banking

As with joint ventures, the reform of Eastern European and Soviet banking and allied financial activities such as insurance has produced a crop of English-language publications to inform and monitor developments. In 1990 and 1991 the United Kingdom and Ireland produced five new titles between them – *Central European Finance and Business* (61), *East Euro-*

pean Banker (62), *East European Finance Update* (63), *East European Insurance Report* (64), *Finance East Europe* (65). Apart from confirming the rise of a more open information economy and the intense competitiveness of the information market so created, there is little to be said about individual titles at this stage. They are intent upon establishing their positions in a variety of ways but it is too early to say whether circumstances and demand will allow them all the success they desire.

Sectoral Information

Market, product and production information is highly valued by businessmen. The very high prices charged for publications and services that provide reliable data in these fields attest to their potential worth. Nonetheless, provision in this area is patchy. In the early years of perestroika data were often out of date, or known to be inaccurate. In many instances specific data were simply not available. The situation, as elsewhere, is changing however. Improvements in official Soviet statistical methods have been noted. Independent Soviet agencies have appeared employing market survey techniques to provide analyses and assessments of markets. In addition, Western consultants are producing an increasing number of specialised Soviet Union market reports. The aim of this type of publication is to provide data and analysis needed to assess the potential of a given market and to survey current developments and trends. Such information rarely comes cheaply. In addition to such specialised sources sectoral data are provided in the general business sources noted above.

The leading information service in this area is *East European Industrial Monitoring Service* (67) which provides data and analyses over 21 industrial sectors. It is especially useful for the attention paid to information carried in the provincial and technical press of key Soviet republics. Chemicals, as befitting a major industry, are well covered by *PlanEcon Soviet Chemical Review* (69) and *East European Chemical Monitor* (70) among others. Indicative of recent Western interest is the publication of *East European Health Care Markets* (72) and *USSR: Pharmaceutical Market Outlook* (76), both appearing in 1990. The latter are examples of reports specially commissioned to estimate the potential of Soviet markets. Other specialised sector information sources are becoming available as outside businessmen scan the Soviet economy for specialist niches to exploit (71, 73, 74, 75, 77).

Contact Information

For business and trading organisations contact information is vital. At the immediate practical level it is necessary to know what other organisations, or sections of the public, might be customers for goods and services offered. At a different level it may be helpful to know the names and other details of chief negotiators, or of influential middle men, or the profiles and prospects of firms likely to offer benefits through cooperation or merging of interests. This kind of information is often acquired on an informal, experiential basis, but it is another area in which published sources can be extremely helpful. This is a need long recognised in market-orientated economies both at formal and informal levels. As a result a large contact information sector, of which advertising is only the most obvious example, has developed in such economies.

The position in pre-perestroika Soviet Union in regard to contact information never paralleled that in Western economies. In a country in which even ordinary telephone numbers were difficult to ascertain there was little scope for producing contact publications independently. However, from 1987, it became increasingly apparent that organisations wishing to trade in the Soviet Union, as well as Soviet enterprises exploring possible external ventures, were finding it difficult to establish essential business contacts. As a result of changed attitudes considerable efforts have been made to produce and distribute contact information. Names, addresses, telephone and fax numbers, product interests of individuals, organisations and ministries spill from the presses. Since the numbers involved are large, and directories have much in common, only a few titles will be mentioned to illustrate developments. Reference may be made to standard bibliographical aids for a broader selection.

As in other sectors of the business information economy, the familiar features of cooperative ventures and recent incomers are in evidence. For example *Trading Partners USSR* (84), The *USSR Business Guide and Directory* (86), *Euro-Soviet Trade Directory* (82), *USSR and Eastern Europe Yearbook* (85) are all products of cooperative arrangements. A further interesting joint venture, between Moskovskii Rabochii and Blaue Horner Publishing, has resulted in the reappearance of *All Moscow* (*Vsia Moskva*) last published in 1936 (78). The importance of Moscow as the centre of Soviet decision-making invests this volume with special significance and utility.

The potential of the contact information market has been appreciated and acted upon by numerous likely, and unlikely, publishers. Full confirmation of possibilities is received when established companies such as Dun and Bradstreet, in association with Goskomstat, propose to enter the market with three new directories – *Directory of Operational Joint Ventures*, *Directory of the Largest 500 Machinery Enterprises in the USSR, Di-*

rectory of USSR Enterprises Involved in Export, and by the interest of the British-Soviet Chamber of Commerce (79) in the field. Specialised directories concentrating upon specific sectors of the economy are appearing (81). Electronic sources of contact information, such as *Zapisnaia Knizhka*, are now also available (90). External publishers have shown a keen interest in Soviet contact data. It is also an area of information supply increasingly represented by Soviet publications.

The importance of advertising as a form of contact information is evidenced by the increasing number of magazines carrying adverts, and by the appearance of specialist advertising magazines such as *Perspective* (87).

The numerous recent additions to this class of publication inevitably raise the question of opportunism for, undoubtedly, the quality and utility of a number of compilations are in doubt. It is an area of competitive exploitation with products that cannot easily be pre-judged in terms of value, and which avoid the process of critical appraisal to which other types of business literature are subjected. Perhaps judgment should be reserved, for the previous dearth of contact data means that a great information void has had to be filled and all contributions to the English-language pool of data should be welcomed. There is no knowing when such ventures, products of a tentative openness, may be required to adapt to less favourable conditions for carrying out their information trade.

Conclusion

The literature of business may lay no claim to style. It may not even embody many original ideas. The overriding aim is the transmission of functional data; often of an ephemeral nature. Eager publishers have ensured that a great deal of such data has appeared on the market, often at eyebrow-raising prices. One problem arising from this massive influx of new material and services is the difficulty of assessing the quality and reliability of the data and interpretations provided. Events have moved so quickly, and the number of publications has increased so dramatically, that objective overall assessments are impossible. Subjective evaluations, however, suggest that although there are excellent titles and services on offer in the business field, there are also contributions of a more opportunistic nature. Value for money is not an easily applied concept in this field except, perhaps, to the established proven services and titles. A recession, and perhaps events in the Soviet Union, may well diminish the appeal of Soviet business ventures and so effect a subsequent shake-out of titles and services. This may be no bad thing; currently too many publications appear to be optimistically targeting the same markets. Whatever the outcome, however, it has to be accepted that the Soviet business information sector has been transformed by events of recent years. Current political events suggest a future fraught with uncertainty, and the possibility, even, of a return to pre-glasnost and pre-perestroika days. To balance such views it may be that the momentum of business developments has carried the business information sector beyond the point where a total return to past information practices is possible.

Bibliography

Coming to Terms

BOOKS

1   Boyes, R. (1990) *The Hard Road to Market: Gorbachev, the Underworld and the Rebirth of Capitalism.* London: Secker & Warburg

Unabashed journalism, but highly informed and perceptive. Glib assumptions about a liberalised and decentralised Soviet economy need to be tested against the more complicated realities portrayed in this work.

2   Treml, V.G. (1988) Perestroyka and Soviet statistics, *Soviet Economy* 4, (1), 65-94.

Examines changes in Soviet methods of gathering and manipulating economic and social statistics. Concludes that needed improvements in the quality and reliability of official statistics are slow in appearing. Includes a useful chronology of significant statistical events and a list of new and resumed statistical compendia. The chronology and compendia lists have been updated and published separately as V.G. Treml, *A Chronology of Perestroyka of State Statistics in the USSR Spring 1985-Present*, Washington, DC: Center for International Resources, US Bureau of Census, 1990.

General Context and Analysis

PERIODICALS

3   *Current Digest of the Soviet Press.* Oxford: Blackwell

Digests and translates into English items from 95 Soviet newspapers and journals. Valuable source of current information. Also available via Dialog and Nexis.

4   *Report on the USSR.* Munich: Radio Liberty/Radio Free Europe

A weekly analytical report of Soviet broadcasts. Like SWB, very useful for keeping abreast of developments.

5   *SWB: Summary of World Broadcasts.* Part 1: The USSR. Reading: BBC Monitoring

This weekly monitor presents broadcast, and some printed, reports. Items are classified for ease of reference. Few other aids have the same immediacy.

ELECTRONIC

6   *Profile Information.* Sunbury-on-Thames: *Financial Times*

Includes general and business information drawn from the *Financial Times*, as well as such important sources as TASS, Associated Press Newswire and BBC Summary of World Broadcasts.

7   *Reuters Textline*. London: Reuters

Currently provides the most extensive online coverage of news sources within Eastern Europe and the Soviet Union. Textline is updated four times a day.

8   *SINT (SOVINFO NOVOSTI TEXT)*. Munich: GBI (German Business Information)

Full text reports on business in the Soviet Union.

General Business Information and Analysis

BOOKS

9   Bubnov, B. (1987) *Foreign Trade with the USSR: A Manager's Guide to Recent Reforms*. London: Pergamon

A modest work notable for its early appearance. This now tells against it, for the world of perestroika and practical responses to theoretical economic liberalisation have moved on. Nonetheless still a useful guide to early intentions.

10   Carnouvis, C.C. and Carnouvis, B.Z. (1989) *US Commercial Opportunities in the Soviet Union: Marketing, Production, and Strategic Planning Perspectives*. London: Quorum Books

An interesting analytical treatment of business and trade issues. Soviet economic reforms are discussed together with the range of possible implications for the USA. A work with wider interest than the American bias might suggest.

11   *Economic Reforms in the European Centrally Planned Economies*. (1989) Geneva: UN

Produced in association with the Vienna Institute for Comparative Economic Studies. General analyses of economic reforms to date. Not much said that would surprise a regular newspaper reader.

12   *The Economy of the USSR: A Study Undertaken in Response to a Request by the Houston Summit*. (1990) Washington, DC: IMF

Important for the balanced treatment of weaknesses in the Soviet economy and for a review of needed reforms. Sets the scene for long-term management thinking.

13   Ellman, M. (1989) *The USSR in the 1990s: Struggling Out of Stagnation*. London: Economist Intelligence Unit

A breezy analysis of the economic situation and prospects of the Soviet Union. An excellent example of the clarity and compression aimed for by the better business publications.

14   Friedlander, M. (1990) Editor. *Foreign Trade in Eastern Europe and the Soviet Union: The Vienna Institute for Comparative Economic Studies – Yearbook II*. London: Westview Press

Short summaries of business, economic and financial topics. Useful as first approaches to specific issues. The broad geographical sweep of many of the papers ensures treatment at a very high level of generality.

15   Lindsay, M. (1989) *International Business in Gorbachev's Soviet Union*. London: Pinter

Sets out to describe the legal and regulatory circumstances governing trade and business. An interesting treatment of the main themes – the State Enterprise Law, Foreign Trade Reform, Joint Enterprises, Banking and Credit Reform, Prices and Wages Reform, Cooperatives, Political Reform. Includes a useful appendix of biographical detail of key figures.

16 *Perestroika: Changing Perspectives in the USSR and Eastern Europe.* (1990) London: Euromonitor

An example of a business report presented by one of the established agencies of economic data and analysis. It well illustrates the point that authoritative economic analysis does not come cheaply. In this case £495 for 120 pages.

17 Shelton, J. (1989) *The Coming Soviet Crash: Gorbachev's Desperate Pursuit of Credit in Western Financial Markets.* London: Duckworth

The Soviet need for foreign credit and capital is examined against the background of economic performance and political aims. The author has little sympathy with programmes of Western assistance. The Soviet Union should 'work to have something worthwhile to trade. If they want to acquire hard currency they should concentrate on developing ways to earn it... It is time for them to grow up and play by the rules'. This is a fairly common American view.

PERIODICALS

18 *Arguments and Facts International.* Hastings, East Sussex: Arguments and Facts International

A monthly publication based on the highly successful Soviet newspaper *Argumenty i Fakty* with a claimed subscription of over 33 millions. Started in 1990 as a generally informative magazine it now concentrates on business issues providing contacts 'hitherto impossible to obtain', 'hard information...impossible to find elsewhere' and features of 'unchallengeable authority'. Most other periodicals claim the same. In the short time of its existence it has come to be highly regarded for its acute analysis.

19 *BLOC: The Soviet Union and Eastern Europe Business Journal.* New York: Eastern Information Resources Inc.

Published six times a year this management glossy appeared in 1990 with the usual mix of hard news and contact data. Intended to inform Western businessmen so that they are better able to take advantage of opportunities in Eastern Europe.

20 *Bulletin of Commercial Information for Foreign Businessmen.* [Of the USSR Chamber of Commerce and Industry.] San Francisco: International Trade Press

Established in 1989 as a monthly but recently changed to a bi-monthly publication. Highlights important business events and provides a forum for Soviet firms searching for partners. Advertising agencies, exhibition organisers, amongst others, publicise skills and services likely to interest Western firms. Modest but useful.

21 *Business Contacts.* Moscow: USSR Chamber of Commerce

Appearing since 1990 in seven European-language versions, as well as in Russian, the magazine is intended to facilitate the exchange of information about firms, goods and services and to establish mutually beneficial business contacts. Monthly.

22 *Business Eastern Europe: A Weekly Report to Managers of East European Operations.* London: Business International

A long-established weekly (1972-) which enables readers to keep abreast of current developments. Short, pointed, analytical features supplemented by the usual mix of business news about licensing, cooperation, exhibitions, etc. Considered to be one of the leaders in this field.

23 *Business in the USSR.* Paris: Business in the USSR

The product of a cooperative venture between SOCPRESSE, the Moscow Joint Stock Innovation Bank and Progress Publishers. Its glossy appearance, and style, mimic current Western management magazines. The business and economic content is serious enough. It will be interesting to see whether this title, and others of a similar nature, survive the current recession. Monthly available since 1990.

24   *Business Week/USSR.* New York: McGraw Hill; Moscow: Kniga

The Russian-language edition of *Business Week.* A monthly publication which started in January 1991. Too early to pass judgment on the venture, but it appears to have powerful backing.

25   *Comecon Reports: Economic and Financial Intelligence Commentaries From the Soviet Bloc.* New York: World Reports Ltd.

A substantial quarterly which devotes much space to Soviet business and economic issues. Lengthy analytical articles, often critical of Soviet policies and intentions, characterise this review. A major publication with stamina – established in 1980.

26   *Commersant (Kommersant).* Chicago: Refco; Moscow: Kommersant

A weekly business newspaper re-established in 1989 (it last appeared in 1917). It is produced in English and Russian, although the different language editions are often dissimilar in content and emphasis. The English version is breezy in style, displaying a refreshing willingness to adopt independent critical approaches. A valuable Soviet source of current business information.

27   *Country Report USSR: Analysis of Economic and Political Trends Every Quarter.* London: Economist Intelligence Unit

Succinct analytical surveys of political and economic events combined with the presentation of statistical economic indicators make this a highly regarded, if modestly produced, title. Subscribers also receive an annual supplement which provides background economic and political information. One of the most successful quarterlies, running since 1952.

28   *East European Markets.* London: *Financial Times*

Apppearing fortnightly, in newsletter format, this title provides country information and statistical indicators. A useful publication for its conciseness and relative currency. A relatively venerable service for the field – established since 1981.

29   *East European Risk Service.* London: Economist Intelligence Unit

Assessing likely future risks is an unavoidable management task. This is an example of the kind of publication now being produced to assist the process. Political and economic events are examined and trends projected. Financial issues are closely reviewed. Warning signs, when needed, are quickly hoisted. Published as two main reports a year with two updating supplements.

30   *East West: Fortnightly Bulletin of Business Developments with the Central and Eastern European Countries and the USSR.* Brussels: East West Publications

One of the longer established newsletters (1969-) with a record of reliability and highly informative analysis. The mix is similar to that of later competitors – short features, notes and brief references to business events.

31   *East-West Business Analyst.* Oxford: Debos Oxford Publications

Content consists of expected information – business events, trends, recent legislation, contact data, etc. Monthly, first appearing in 1990.

32   *Eastern Europe and Soviet Union Forecasting Service.* London: Global Forecasting Service, Economist Intelligence Unit

Analyses political, economic and business factors likely to have a bearing upon the medium-term business future. Main forecasts balanced by alternative scenarios. The annual service includes two main and two updating reports. A new, 1990 venture.

33 *Ecotass: The Economic and Commercial Bulletin of the Soviet News Agency Tass.*
Oxford: Pergamon

A long-established (1964) weekly, and valuable for that reason. Sober, and modestly
produced, but provides excellent coverage of the official side of business – joint
ventures, national economic contacts, activities of foreign firms, contracts gained, etc.

34 *Foreign Trade USSR.* Moscow: USSR Ministry of Foreign Economic Relations

Official monthly giving details of recent trade contracts, Chamber of Commerce Reports,
etc. Carries articles on foreign trade by officials.

35 *Glasnost: The First Word in Business.* Arhus: Continental Information Denmark

A monthly in 1989, but from June 1990 became a fortnightly publication in response to
the pressure of events. A slight publication, usually eight pages, with a distinctive
personality. Lively in style and in editorial expression. Covers much the same ground
as other titles of this nature.

36 *Interflo: A Soviet Trade News Monitor.* Maplewood, NJ: Interflo

A well-established monthly first issued in 1981. Summaries and excerpts of items that
have appeared in the public record. Modestly produced and, for the field, reasonably
priced. Offers good value for money. No editorial material.

37 *PlanEcon Business Report: A Bi-Monthly Newsletter on Eastern Europe and the Soviet
Union.* London: PlanEcon Inc.

Reviews current events and developments in the business world: 'the emphasis is on
business: how to do it, who is doing it, where it is being done, where the serious money
is going – all with facts and figures, comment, analysis and forecasts'. One of the latest
additions, 1991, to a growingly competitive field.

38 *PlanEcon Report: Developments in the Economies of the Soviet Union and Eastern
Europe.* Washington, DC: PlanEcon Inc.

An excellent weekly report which provides stimulating analyses of specific foreign and
domestic problems; for example, of the size of Soviet and East European markets.

39 *Russia Express: Executive Briefing.* Monmouth, Gwent: International Industrial
Information

Another recent (1989) addition to the competitive newsletter field. Published every two
weeks. Better produced than many, but the format is the same. Short editorials are
followed by brief notes about business events and rounded off with lists of exhibitions,
opportunities, contracts, etc.

40 *Soviet and East European Foreign Trade.* Armonk, NY: M.E. Sharpe

A quarterly presenting translations of Soviet and East European items from the press
generally. Modestly priced and affording access to information not always easy to
obtain in English. First issued in 1965.

41 *Soviet and Eastern European Report: A Monthly Newsletter on Developments in
Business, Law and Finance.* Wendens Ambo, Saffron Walden, Essex: Gostick Hall
Publications

A new publication, 1990, which is difficult to assess at such an early stage, but its aims
are similar to other competitors.

42 *Soviet Business Review.* Copenhagen: Dhalfelt International

A monthly newsletter produced by a Western consulting company with offices in
Moscow. Standard newletter format – short items of business news, joint venture
opportunities, financial information, analysis of sectoral developments. Another
product of perestroika optimism appearing in 1989.

43   *Soviet Business Survey.* Moscow: VNIKI Institute; Colchester: Lloyd's List International

An interesting newcomer, 1990, to the list of business monthlies. Produced cooperatively by the All-Union Market Research Institute (VNIKI) and Lloyd's List International. The format is more polished than many others of this type, and the involvement of VNIKI ensures excellent contacts with Soviet specialists. Covers economic and technological trends, investment opportunities, and provides a digest of the Soviet press and professional publications.

Practical Guidance

BOOKS

44   *Business and Investment in Eastern Europe.* (1991) London: Eurostudy

This 750-page book claims to be the most comprehensive, up-to-date collection of information on business in Eastern Europe, including the Soviet Union. Covers joint ventures laws, foreign investment laws, company law, and international trade rules.

45   *Contract System.* (1990) Sverdlovsk, USSR: AKTSEPT Association

Practical guide to forms and the preparation of business contracts applicable to a variety of Soviet organisations and institutions.

46   *Doing Business with Eastern Europe.* London: Business International

A standard reference set of ten volumes in loose-leaf form, updated monthly. One volume deals with Operating Techniques, another concentrates on Comecon. The remaining country volumes (400 pages each) cover a wide range of business issues. Nothing quite compares in scope and depth.

47   *Economist Guides: The USSR.* (1990) London: Hutchinson

Aimed at businessmen. Provides general coverage of business matters, including 'business etiquette'. In addition helpful travel advice. Received rave reviews.

48   Knight, M.G. (1987) *How to do Business with Russians: A Handbook and Guide for Western World Business People.* New York: Quorum Books

A curious mixture of good advice, descriptions of official requirements and an odd collection of business telephone conversations and correspondence in English. It is difficult to divine the practical purpose of the latter. Has to be treated warily because of its publication date.

49   Richardson, P.E. and Kolley, D.F. (1990) *Moscow Business Survival Guide.* Narvik: Soviet Information Service

The first of a three-volume set of business guides to the USSR. Vol.2 will cover business legislation. Vol.3 is planned as a directory of joint ventures and foreign representatives operating in the USSR. The set will be updated and republished bi-annually.

50   Starr, R. and March, S. (1990) *Practical Aspects of Trading with the USSR.* London: Worldwide Information

Received good reviews for clarity of exposition and practical usefulness. It is indicative of book production problems in this field that certain sections are already out of date. Still regarded as one of the better examples of the genre.

51   Warren, Andrew, Charkham, R., Louis, N. and Mamut, A. (1990) *A Guide to Doing Business in the USSR.* London: Kogan Page Ltd.

A 200-page guide which provides an overview of recent changes and covers the basic legal and economic structure of the USSR. Joint venture rules and regulations are examined.

Joint Ventures

BOOKS

52 *East-West Joint Venture Contracts.* (1990) Geneva: UN

Covers economic, business, financial and legal aspects. Full guidance on drawing up contracts. Includes model contracts.

53 *East-West Joint Ventures.* (1990) Geneva: UN

Comprehensive information about rules of competition, registration, co-ordination with host country authorities, trade rights, currency transfers, accounting, taxation.

54 Hober, K. (1989) *Joint Ventures in the Soviet Union: A Legal Treatise with Forms and Commentaries.* Ardsley-on-Hudson, NY: Transnational Juris Publications Inc.

Complete and comprehensive manual on joint ventures in a loose-leaf format to allow for supplements.

55 *Joint Ventures and International Associations in the USSR.* (1990) London: Intershelf

This publication is the product of a joint venture between a British company and the Moscow Institute of Civil Engineering. Provides practical guidance for those proposing to engage in joint ventures. A field in which it pays to heed advice that encourages caution.

56 *Joint Ventures in the USSR.* (1989) Montreux: Worldwide Information

One of a series of practical guides for those interested in doing business in the Soviet Union. Covers every aspect of joint venture activity. Series edited by Robert Starr. Withdrawn because legal aspects are now outdated.

57 Winter, David (1990) Editor. *Eastern Bloc Joint Ventures: A Collection of Papers Delivered at the International Bar Association Regional Conference Warsaw ... 1990.* London: Butterworths

Following law changes in the Soviet Union and Eastern Europe certainly keeps lawyers active. Even when sense has been made of the last round of changes there is every likelihood that circumstances will have rendered such sense irrelevant. At the time of writing this work constitutes a useful overview of legal aspects of joint ventures.

Legalities and Joint Ventures

PERIODICALS

58 *East European Business Law.* London: *Financial Times*

First of 11 annual issues appeared in March, 1991. The declared aims might be applied to all journals of this type: 'will mainly concentrate on bringing...news of legal changes, but it will also aim to set these in context and assess the increasingly diverse legal situation for doing business in the countries of Central and Eastern Europe'.

59 *Soviet and East European Business Law Bulletin.* London: Butterworths

Quarterly. First issue November, 1990.

60 *Soviet Business Law Digest.* Montreux: Worldwide Information

A bi-monthly journal launched in 1990.

Finance and Banking

PERIODICALS

61 *Central European Finance and Business.* London: Euromoney Publications

First issue appeared in March, 1991. Intends to provide sectoral surveys with the usual mix of macroeconomic statistics, changes in laws and regulations, news of latest deals and personnel changes. Monthly.

62 *East European Banker: The Financial Industry's Monitor on East and Central European Affairs.* Dublin: Lafferty Publications

Covers banking activities, interviews with officials, financial developments and news analysis, future events, provides contact data and bank profiles. Began as a bi-monthly in 1990, now appears monthly.

63 *East European Finance Update.* London: Business International

Formerly *Countertrade Update: Eastern Europe* but the 1991 version has changed emphasis. Quarterly updated reference service in three parts which covers East European country finance, international finance in Eastern Europe, and strategies for East European countertrade.

64 *East European Insurance Report: The Review of East and Central European Insurance and Reinsurance.* London: *Financial Times*

A monthly first appearing in November, 1990. News, analysis and events are collected under country headings. Occurrences of insurance significance are listed, as are recent joint ventures. Monthly issues are intended for cumulation in a ring binder. No aesthetic imagination wasted on appearance.

65 *Finance East Europe.* London: *Financial Times*

Launched in March 1991, and set to appear twice a month, this 12-page newsletter provides financial, banking and business 'news, speculation and analysis'.

Sectoral Information

PERIODICALS

66 *East Europe and China Agriculture and Food: The Monthly Newsletter on Developments in Agriculture and Food in Eastern Europe, USSR and China.* London: Agra Europe

This title is from a well-established source. Data tend to struggle after events.

67 *East European Industrial Monitoring Service.* London: Business International

One of the undoubted market leaders in this field. Covers 21 industrial sectors in terms of future expectations, export and import figures, problems, and much else on a monthly basis. Authoritative.

68 *PlanEcon Energy Report.* Washington, DC: PlanEcon Inc.

Quarterly updates on energy developments in the Soviet Union and Eastern Europe. Rich in data. PlanEcon also publish PlanEcon Long-Term Energy Outlook as an annual but with supplementary services at extra cost.

69 *PlanEcon Soviet Chemical Review.* Washington, DC: PlanEcon Inc.

An annual providing data, forecasts and analysis. Difficult to envisage strategic thinking without such a publication.

ELECTRONIC

70   *East European Chemical Monitor.* Vienna: Business International

An example of a database available only electronically. Material is culled from a wide selection of the popular, commercial and trade press about companies, their market performance and prospects, etc.

REPORTS

71   *Approaching the Soviet PC Market.* (1990) London: Business International

A good example of the type of publication offering advice focused upon a particular sector. Analyses the state and extent of the Soviet PC market. Exploitative possibilities are examined and operational problems considered.

72   *East European Health Care Markets.* (1990) London: ABHI

The need to assess the potential of markets is crucial. In some areas possibilities are obvious, in others they have to be researched. This is an example of the latter category. It was commissioned by the Association of British Health Care Industries and produced by AGB Business International to provide and assessment of future trends and market opportunities.

73   *East European Motor Industry.* (1989) London: Economist Intelligence Unit

A report which examines prospects and developments for the motor industry. Covers the Soviet Union.

74   *A Profile of the East European Paint Industry.* (1991) London: Information Research Ltd

Production and industry distribution statistics and glosses are provided. Tackles the chancy business of predicting how privatisation will affect the market.

75   *Tourism in Eastern Europe: Prospects for Growth and New Market Opportunities.* (1990) London: Business International

A regional overview, followed by individual country analyses (including the Soviet Union), completed with an assessment of prospects for the tourist industry.

76   *USSR: Pharmaceutical Market Outlook.* (1990) London: Strategic Forecasting Services

Another special study of health care provision in the Soviet Union conducted by Research Consultants International. The value of such data may be gauged by the asking price – $15,000.

77   *USSR Telecommunications to the Year 2000.* (1990) Hastings, East Sussex: Arguments and Facts International

The drive to improve telecommunications has opened a huge market for Western firms. This study of possibilities from the Telecommunications Research Centre provides market forecasts for each of the 15 Soviet republics, but warns against over-optimistic estimates.

Contact Information

DIRECTORIES

78   *All Moscow (Vsia Moskva).* (1990/91) Marburg: Blaue Horner Publishing House; Moscow: Vsia Moskva

The importance of Moscow as the centre of Soviet economics and business invests this volume of addresses, names and telephone numbers with special significance.

79   *British-Soviet Trade and Investment Opportunities, 1991.* (1991) London: Caversham Press

Produced with English and Russian texts, this publication represents the glossier end of directory publishing. Contains, in succinct form, a great deal of advice on trading with the Soviet Union, brief reviews of recent business trends, short pieces on sectoral developments and profiles of companies with interests in Soviet markets. Adverts and contact data are included.

80   *Business Moscow.* (1991) Moscow: Sovero.

Interesting in that this is the production of a Soviet foreign trade advertising agency. Lists addresses, telephone and fax numbers of USSR business ministries and those of international and foreign commercial groups, as well as descriptions of Soviet organisations and business representation.

81   *Directory of Soviet Engineering.* (1990) London: Flegon Press

Provides addresses and information on 10,000 engineering units.

82   *Euro-Soviet Trade Directory.* (1990) Monmouth, Gwent: International Industrial Information Ltd

Useful for individuals and organisations wishing to advertise in the Soviet Union. This directory is published and distributed in the Soviet Union. Provides profiles of Western firms wishing to enter into trading and business agreements with Soviet organisations.

83   *Soviet Foreign Trade Directory.* (1989) London: Flegon Press

Contains around 25,000 names and addresses of Soviet businesses.

84   *Trading Partners USSR.* (1990) Abingdon, Oxon: Sovinform Ltd.

A wide-ranging directory of Soviet enterprises wishing to trade with Western firms. Corporate information is provided on 1,500 Soviet firms, and over 1,300 'opportunities' are detailed covering over 2,500 products. To be published twice yearly.

85   *USSR and Eastern Europe Yearbook.* (1990) London: Soviet Marketing

A useful listing of over 2,000 Soviet enterprises engaged in foreign ventures. Aimed at cooperating foreign partners. Compiled by the All-Union National Market Research Institute and published and distributed by Market Knowledge, an American agency.

86   *USSR Business Guide and Directory, 1991.* (1990) Downers Grove, IL: Market Knowledge

This work lists 2,100 major Soviet businesses involved in foreign economic activities with the intention of facilitating contact with Western firms wishing to conduct business in the Soviet Union.

PERIODICALS

87   *Perspective.* Sevenoaks, Kent: Skyset Ltd.

Quarterly industrial advertising magazine first published in 1989. For UK manufacturers who wish to advertise their products in the Soviet Union. Articles are also included. The publication appears under the Mir imprint in the Soviet Union.

ELECTRONIC

88   *SINU (SOVINFO NOVOSTI UNTERNEHMEN).* Munich: GBI (German Business Information)

Directory-type information for about 600 organisations and enterprises in the Soviet Union.

89   VNIIKI. Munich: GBI (German Business Information)

Directory-type information for about 1,000 exporting Soviet firms.

90 *Zapisnaia Knizhka* (Notebook). Moscow: FAKT

Provides contact data – addresses of trade missions, banks, foreign firms, Soviet trade organisations, telephone, fax and telex numbers, etc. Subscribers can enter their own data.

Statistical Sources

PERIODICALS

91 *Comecon Data,* edited by the Vienna Institute for Comparative Economic Studies. London: Macmillan

The latest 1988 edition of this standard annual (first published in 1969) has over 400 pages of statistics in what is described as a 'pocket book'. The data covering such fields as consumption, foreign trade, domestic finance, production and population are derived from over 50 statistical yearbooks and periodicals produced by East European countries. Needs careful handling in the light of recent revelations of statistical manipulation. Also available in electronic form through Reuters.

92 *East European Statistics Service.* Brussels: East-West Publications

A monthly now in its 15th year. A long record for this area. Presents the latest statistics from a variety of sources with acute analysis.

93 *USSR Import and Export Trade Statistics.* New York: Dun & Bradstreet Corporation

First version produced in 1991. A reference publication containing annual historical Soviet import and export trade statistics for 1988, 1989 and 1990. Quarterly data for 1991 onward are provided. The data are provided in a time series format.

ELECTRONIC

94 *Eastern Bloc Countries Economic Data Base.* Vienna: Wiener Institut fur Internationale Wirtschaftsvergleiche

English labelled statistical database. Standard time series include production, employment, wages, finance, imports and exports.

95 *Tradstat: World Trade Statistics Database.* London: Tradstat Ltd.

Although the service does not currently carry Soviet trade figures, it is possible to assess developments in Soviet trade through the trade statistics of other countries. Tradstat allows this to be done with relative ease.

Guides

96 Konn, Tania (1990) *USSR Business Information.* Headland, Cleveland: Headland Press. (Business Research Guide, no.7)

A 50-page guide to the major English language sources of business information which also provides contact data.

97 East European business information. (1990) *Business Information Review,* 7 (2), 3-32.

A 'special report' on East European information sources. Selective, with special emphasis on electronic sources.

CHAPTER NINE

Science and Technology

Dr Stephen Fortescue
University of New South Wales

The treatment of Soviet science and technology in the English-language literature cannot be described as exhaustive. Perhaps inevitably, given that research is not centrally planned, the literature reflects the accidental, even haphazard interests of authors working in the field. While there have been major extended research projects, it is not possible to describe the literature as a whole in terms of an integrated process of intellectual development. This means that the field has to some extent lacked, on the one hand, new work being eagerly received and driving further development along the same lines and, on the other hand, books appearing that have aroused controversy and new research to prove them wrong. The problem is not one of the poor quality of researchers. Perhaps it is simply that there are not enough researchers in the field and, as a result, we are not forced to work in the close proximity needed to produce either consensus or conflict.

A major problem in writing on science and technology is the matter of definition and boundaries. There is the old problem of the boundary between science and technology. Given that my brief is to cover both, the problem on this occasion is the relatively minor one of internal structure and categorisation. More difficult are the two extreme boundaries of the science and technology continuum. When does the study of science become the much broader study of intellectual development, a matter of politics, philosophy and the history of ideas, culture and society? The problem is clearly much more difficult if we include the social sciences in our definition of science. I happily do not have to do so here, and so feel that the problem has been kept under control. The other boundary is at the technology end of the spectrum. When does a concern with Soviet technology become a concern with the broader topic of the Soviet economy and industrial development? Studies of innovation often have less to do with technology and R&D than with micro- and macroeconomics, management and labour. I have been narrow in my interpretation and have usually excluded works that are primarily concerned with the factory rather than the institute or design bureau (an exclusion which is made easier by the relatively small factory R&D sector in the USSR) and works of a technical economic nature (those that have mathematical formulae!).

I have included some major works which are no longer in print but which are still important and useful enough to be worth searching for in a quality university library. A number of the best publications in the field are multi-author compilations on a variety of topics. The format makes it difficult to give them their due in an essay of this type. I have therefore tried to highlight them in the annotated bibliography.

The modern era of Western research into Soviet science and technology can be dated from the publication in 1969 of the OECD's *Science Policy in the USSR* (31). Although published in Paris a number of the authors were from the University of Birmingham, in the UK. Their contributions established the tradition of dense, detailed empirical work at that university. The results of this subsequent work appeared as three compilations, edited by Amann, Cooper and Davies (46) and Amann and Cooper (35, 43). Although based on sector-by-sector case studies, the three volumes combined provide an invaluable overall picture of the state of Soviet technology. The first volume was specifically concerned with measuring the comparative performance of Soviet technology; the second with explaining the reasons for the generally poor levels of performance found. The third volume continued the consideration of both these issues.

Other sectoral studies have been concerned, sometimes implicitly, often explicitly, with the same issues. These include Robert W. Campbell's *Soviet Energy Technologies* (45), Kelly, Shaffer and Thompson's *Energy Research and Development in the USSR* (37), ZumBrunnen and Osleeb on the iron and steel industry (39) and, not strictly a sectoral study, Hill and McKay's *Soviet Product Quality* (33).

These works have established, most would consider conclusively, that while Soviet science and technology might show occasional patches of world-class performance, on the whole it lags seriously behind the West. The Soviet lag is also evident, virtually by definition, in the extensive literature on Soviet technology imports. The mere fact that the topic is always imports, not exports, in itself indicates a problem. Much of this literature suggests that the technology, once imported, is not put to good use. The literature includes Sutton's three-volume historical study (52), Holliday's *Technology Transfer to the Soviet Union* (51), books authored by Hanson and Bornstein (50, 47), and books edited by Smith and Parrott (49, 48).

It could be said that the rest of the literature, whether consciously or unconsciously, is concerned with establishing the reasons for poor Soviet performance. Four basic areas of study can be identified. The boundaries between them cannot always be clearly maintained and the allocation of works to particular categories in this survey will inevitably be somewhat arbitrary.

Before allocating publications to the different categories it is worth devoting some attention to the sorts of books we are dealing with. They do vary considerably in terms of methodological approach and basic source material. The bulk of the literature is typical Western Sovietological research. That is, it is research done essentially in the reading room of a library or in an office, using almost exclusively published Soviet sources. One might at first fear that such an approach would produce too rosy a view of Soviet performance. Experience tends to suggest the reverse. Soviet published sources – in particular the press – have always tended to be highly critical of specific aspects of the Soviet system. Soviet science has not escaped such treatment, particularly under glasnost. The fear then becomes how much can one rely on what are usually pretty tendentious accounts of apparently isolated instances in order to draw conclusions on the general situation. The Soviet press has always been presented accurately, in this author's opinion, as having an educational rather than a news function. The assumption, therefore, has been that a story critical of the state of affairs in a particular institute is an expression of concern that a general problem exists. This, however, has never been more than an assumption. To add to the danger, the Soviet press has been as susceptible to campaigns as any other sector of Soviet society. Usually centrally directed, a campaign on a particular issue might be designed to overcome an existing difficulty, but equally could be a prophylactic measure or even part of a purely political manoeuvre. Whatever the reason, a distorted view of the actual situation could be presented.

Most researchers have been aware of these dangers, and therefore work hard to find as many references as possible to provide corroboration for any particular point they might be making. This can lead to overloaded footnotes, but would appear to be a necessary part of the research process.

Another approach, the one we have already noted in reference to the 'Birmingham school', is to search hard for quantitative data. This raises the well-known problems of Soviet statistics – those of quality and availability. It also raises the issue of whether Western scholarship has been dragged in the direction of those fields which are well served with data or which are well suited to statistical analysis. This has meant in practice a relative neglect of science in favour of technology.

All researchers are very well aware that some of the difficulties of traditional Sovietological research are, somewhat paradoxically, increasing under glasnost. The first, most immediately obvious problem is the information explosion. The number of Soviet newspapers and journals, even in such a narrow field as science and technology, is expanding rapidly and taxing the budgets of libraries and the reading time of researchers.

More important is the question of the quality and reliability of the sources. The Soviet press has never been characterised by objectivity; nor has it been as uniform in its bias as one might expect. Nevertheless, in the past one could be confident that anything that appeared in the press was at least tolerated by the political leadership, and this provided a benchmark for analysis. Now anyone can say anything they like – with no press council and poorly developed libel laws. The fragmentation of authority and heightened tensions in the USSR, including within the scientific community, ensure that the press is tendentious and highly erratic in its tendentiousness. At the same time one cannot be confident that 'campaigns' have disappeared. While they might not be centrally directed now, fashion seems to have taken over the directing role. One sometimes wonders whether science is not a victim of just such a fashion at the moment.

All the dangers of traditional Sovietology have encouraged researchers whenever possible to use sources of information additional to routine published Soviet sources. One such source is what could be called non-routine Soviet information. An example is fiction. Soviet literature has traditionally been no less educational and documentary than the press, but nevertheless it does sometimes provide a different angle. Soviet fiction dealing with science has been well surveyed by Rosalind Marsh (38).

A very large biography, memoir and autobiography literature exists in Russian. Unfortunately, very little of this corpus has been translated into English – biographies of the physicists Landau, Kurchatov, Khokhlov and Kapitza are exceptions (22, 23, 19, 20). Soviet biographies all too often tend to be formulaic and hagiographical. However even the worst, and those that have been translated are by no means the worst, often provide useful information.

The big opportunity for alternative sources of information came with the large-scale emigration of Soviet Jews. A considerable proportion of those leaving had worked in the areas of science and technology, and Western researchers wasted no time interviewing those they could find. The major survey directed specifically at science and technology was carried out in a Harvard University project by Mark Kuchment and Harley Balzer. The results have been presented in book form by Balzer (32). This survey, and others, have confirmed the view of a lagging Soviet science and technology, although perhaps not as forcefully as might have been expected. The impact of emigrés has also been seen in a number of books of memoirs and analysis written by former Soviet citizens. These books will be described later.

One of the problems of Soviet science and technology has been its relative isolation from the world. However, particularly since the death of Stalin and then détente, the degree of isolation has lessened. We therefore have access to information from Western scientists who have visited and worked in Soviet laboratories, or who have received Soviet scientists in their laboratories in the West. In the case of the US-Soviet scientific and technical exchange agreements of the détente era, reports were received by the National Academy of Sciences from all the participants. These and other data were used by Ailes and Pardee in their 1986 publication (34). In that same year NATO displayed considerable initiative in bringing together Sovietologists specialising in science and technology and Western scientists with direct experience of Soviet laboratories and research. The proceedings of the conference were published under the editorship of Craig Sinclair (26).

One source that has been rarely used in the past has been direct contacts with Soviet *naukovedy* (those who study science). That is quite clearly changing now, as links between Soviet and Western *naukovedy* rapidly develop at both the formal and informal levels. The published results, it is hoped, will not be long in coming.

The foregoing titles represent the basic sources available to those studying Soviet science and technology. To what use have they been put?

History

There is no Western general history of Soviet science and technology. The closest to the full sweep is Alexander Vucinich's history of the Academy of Sciences from 1917 to 1970, *Empire of Knowledge* (4). This volume is a continuation of his earlier two volumes on the pre-revolutionary period (11) and is primarily an intellectual rather than organisational history of the Academy of Sciences.

Other historical works are limited to specific periods and issues. Three books, by Bailes (8), Lampert (6) and Fitzpatrick (5), deal with the origins and development of the technical intelligentsia in the pre-Second World War Soviet Union. Robert Lewis deals with the structural development of industrial R&D over the same period (7). There are the already mentioned works on technology imports in the historical era, by Sutton (52) and Holliday (51).

As previously noted there are a number of Soviet biographies which have been translated into English. These provide some valuable historical details, although as usual what is left out is often more interesting than what is left in. To the Soviet historical biographies we can add Kendall Bailes' biography of Vernadsky, a book which succeeds well in describing an era – or rather a number of eras – through the life of one man (14). Of fascinating historical interest are the letters of Petr Kapitza to his wife, reproduced in the book edited by Badash (18). Bailey's biography of Sakharov provides what little readily accessible information there was on Sakharov's scientific career (16). Sakharov's own memoirs add little to our knowledge (15).

Ideology

There is another group of biographies or semi-biographies dealing with one particularly controversial scientific issue that deserves a section of its own. This concerns the role of Lysenko in Soviet science, including in particular his influence on the fate of the geneticist Nikolai Vavilov. The standard account is still David Joravsky's *The Lysenko Affair* (10), but that excellent work is well complemented by Zhores Medvedev's account (12), the translation from the French of Dominique Lecourt's book (9), and then the translation from Russian of the biographical treatment of Vavilov by Mark Popovsky (3).

There are other broader accounts of the role of ideology in Soviet science. David Joravsky describes the historical process of the infiltration of Marxism-Leninism into the natural sciences (13). Loren Graham's *Science, Philosophy, and Human Behavior in the Soviet Union* (1), an update of the original 1972 edition, tries to demonstrate the positive use made of the materialist view of the world by a number of Soviet scientists. Hoffman and Laird summarise the history and significance of the concept of the scientific-technical revolution (2).

Structure

The greatest concentration of published work has been on the structure of contemporary Soviet science and technology. Some of these works are simply handbooks, describing structures with little attempt at analysis. The most extreme (and highly useful) example is the volume in the Longman series on science and technology throughout the world. It was edited by Michael Berry of the University of Birmingham (25). The far older volumes, one written by Cocks (27) and one edited by Thomas and Kruse-Vaucienne (29), although broader in approach, are still essentially descriptive. The most recent book which tries to provide a comprehensive survey, albeit briefly, of the structure of Soviet science (with little on technology) is Fortescue's 1990 publication (24).

Other books provide rich detail on the structures of science in general, in the process of examining narrower issues. Fortescue is specifically concerned with the interaction between the party apparatus and the science sector (36). Kneen provides considerable detail on structure while trying to put Soviet science into a social and political context (41). Balzer's recent presentation of the results of the Harvard survey of emigrés provides a brief but comprehensive account of structures along the way (32). Zhores Medvedev's early book brings the insights of an emigré to a pretty comprehensive survey (28). Raymond Hutchings deals with the basic science and technology structures, but with special and unique emphasis on Soviet design (30). The volume edited by Smith, Maggs and Ginsburgs (44), and the one written by Swanson (40), provide details on the legal aspects of research, in particular intellectual property rights, and technology assimilation and transfer. The publication prepared by Ailes and Rushing is essentially a collection of statistics on scientists and engineers, with a strong comparative approach (42).

Behaviour

Over the years structural analysis has tended to dominate the field to the disadvantage of behavioural analysis. This bias is to be explained primarily by the availability of sources. When talking about behaviour at the top levels of the science sector, i.e. about policy-making processes, supporting sources have been virtually non-existent. One can sometimes imply or guess how decisions are made on the basis of often equally scantily documented suppositions about other sectors of the Soviet system, usually being guided in the process by some theoretical preconceptions such as totalitarianism, pluralism, etc. We then have odd scraps of information from the memoir literature. The results, while valuable and interesting, have never inspired total confidence. An exception, although one which is broad in its approach, is Parrott's history of technology policy-making (53).

The data on behaviour in the laboratories have been treated with a similar lack of confidence. Items in this area have traditionally been one-off 'horror' stories in the Soviet press, supplemented in more recent times by memoir and emigré accounts and some Soviet sociological data. Most Western researchers have been very wary of all these sources. Lubrano has summarised the sociological literature in her *Soviet Sociology of Science* (56), and edited a book with Solomon that attempts a behavioural approach (54). Fortescue has chanced his arm with the whole range of data in the last part of his 1990 volume (24). However, the bulk of the accounts of behaviour within Soviet institutes and laboratories are derived from the experiences of emigrés. Those that have appeared in English are by Mark Azbel (21), Raissa Berg (17), Mark Popovsky (55) and Zhores Medvedev (57). The first two are autobiographies, Popovsky's is a combination of reminiscences, eye-witness accounts, gossip and apocalyptic comment from a former Soviet journalist. The last is a very detailed and personal account of the role of censorship and control of international communication in Soviet science.

The Future

There appear to be three areas in the field which have been well covered – institutional structures, analysis of the technological level of most of the major industrial sectors, and technology transfer. This is not to say that these areas can now be abandoned. Many of the major works are ten years old or more, and these are all fields of actual or potential rapid change. However an excellent base has been laid for future updating.

There are two areas in particular where one can hope for major developments as far as structural analysis is concerned, both based on broader and deeper contact between Western and Soviet *naukovedy*. Firstly, there is the potential for vast improvement in the availability and quality of statistical data. Contacts are already well established between the Soviet State Committee for Statistics and the US National Science Foundation, and one can confidently expect interesting new publications to arise out of these and other contacts. The second area of great potential is that of comparative analysis. Western studies of Soviet science and technology, particularly science, have rarely been specifically comparative – partly because many of the researchers involved have a background in general Soviet studies rather than science studies; partly because of the objective difficulties of data and methodology involved; and partly because of the dangers of bias or accusations of bias. Despite these difficulties the lack of comparative analysis has been a major shortcoming. The opportunity would now seem to be there for a determined effort to overcome that shortcoming.

The opportunities for further research and publication in the history of Soviet science and technology are clearly enormous. As more archival material, one hopes, becomes available, the historical topics begging for attention become limitless, from the immediate effect of the October Revolution on scientists' lives and work, to the transformation of science into an instrument and focus of national security in the post-Second World War period. This author is particularly attracted to the idea of gaining a greater understanding of the way Soviet scientists worked in the past, through the exploitation of the great biographical resources that are already or potentially available.

As our historical knowledge and understanding increase and improve, the opportunity will arise for further analysis of the role of ideology in Soviet science (ideology being used here in the widest of senses to embrace 'vulgar' Marxism-Leninism through the broader materialist conception of the world to any world-view at all). In terms of the mind sets and world-views of scientists themselves, this question will become more, not less, important as Marxist-Leninist ideology loses its official status. Will that loss of official status make any difference to Soviet science? Has the official ideology effectively been dead for so long that its formal decease will have no effect? Alternatively, will there still be scientists making use of Marxism and materialism in their search for scientific truth regardless of its official status? If the official ideology is truly dead, will some other ideology take its place in the minds of scientists? Will it turn out that the negative authoritarian aspects of Soviet science did not in fact derive from the ideology, but from other historical, structural and psychological factors, and therefore could well continue into an ideology-free future?

In looking at the role of ideology one feels that there is considerable room for further analysis of and theorising about the general relationship between science and the state and between science and society. The place of the intelligentsia in Soviet society, both the intelligentsia in general and the scientific-technical intelligentsia in particular, has long been a major topic for students of the historical and contemporary Soviet Union. In the contemporary Soviet Union, with the movement of the intelligentsia into positions of power (usually, it is true, the social sciences and humanities intelligentsia) and the possible hardening of class differences, these issues become fundamental for the whole future of the Soviet Union.

The final area of opportunity is that of behaviour. As already described, the scientific process has been relatively neglected in the existing literature. The reasons for that neglect may now be losing their validity. New opportunities for access will shine much greater light on both policy-making processes and everyday life in the laboratory. It should also become easier to evaluate the quality of the data on which we have relied (or chosen not to rely) in the past. All the vast range of techniques of the Western sociology of science, for better or worse, could be applied to the Soviet case. The opportunities for comparative research are enormous.

These essentially optimistic conclusions are based on the assumption that the current opening-up and de-ideologisation of Soviet society will continue. They are further based on the knowledge that there are capable Western researchers, as demonstrated in the existing literature, able to take advantage of the new opportunities.

Bibliography

History and Ideology

1   Graham, Loren R. (1987) *Science, Philosophy, and Human Behavior in the Soviet Union*. New York: Columbia University Press

An update of the original 1972 edition (entitled *Science and Philosophy in the Soviet Union*), with an extremely interesting new chapter on the life sciences. The rest of the book is an account of the influence on, and use made by, a number of Soviet scientists, primarily physicists, of Marxism-Leninism and the materialist approach in general. The theme is still a controversial one, particularly since to a significant degree it is developed in isolation from political and organisational history. However the scholarship is impressive and the content fascinating.

2   Hoffman, Erik P. and Laird, Robbin, E. (1985) *Technocratic Socialism: the Soviet Union in the Advanced Industrial Era*. Durham: Duke University Press

The book is not primarily devoted to science and technology issues, but rather to a detailed examination of the various aspects of Brezhnev's concept of mature socialism. However sections of the book are directly concerned with the concept of the scientific-technical revolution and Soviet ideas on the place of science in modern society and the nature of science management. The treatment is theoretical rather than empirical.

3 Popovsky, Mark (1984) *The Vavilov Affair.* Hamden, CO: Archon Books

A biography of Lysenko's main victim, the biologist Nikolai Vavilov. The author is a former Soviet journalist specialising in science who left the USSR in 1977. He succeeded in early 1965 – that brief period of ideological relaxation after the fall of Khrushchev – in getting access to Vavilov's police file. He managed to preserve and smuggle out of the USSR the notes he took. They form the basis of the chilling final chapters of the book. Material of this sort is now being published in the USSR, but Popovsky's work remains a useful English-language source.

4 Vucinich, Alexander (1984) *Empire of Knowledge: The Academy of Sciences of the USSR (1917-1970).* Berkeley, CA: University of California Press

A history of the Academy of Sciences in the Soviet era (with an excellent introductory chapter covering the period before 1917). The accent is on intellectual rather than institutional history, and the book is generally more descriptive than analytical. It lays a good basis, but leaves plenty of room for further publications on the Academy.

5 Fitzpatrick, Sheila (1979) *Education and Social Mobility in the Soviet Union, 1921-1934.* Cambridge: Cambridge University Press

Although not strictly a treatment of science and technology the book makes such an important contribution to the history of the intelligentsia in the first decades of the Soviet era that it is justifiably included here. The book is essentially about the *vydvyzhentsy,* the workers and peasants who were pushed through higher education in their thousands and then went on to become the new Soviet technical and managerial intelligentsia. Fitzpatrick does not ignore the old intelligentsia and its offspring, who managed to cling on through the travails of the period, although she does leave room for future work in that particular field.

6 Lampert, Nicholas (1979) *The Technical Intelligentsia and the Soviet State: a Study of Soviet Managers and Technicians, 1928-1935.* London, Basingstoke: Macmillan

Strictly applied classificatory considerations suggest that this work should not be included in this chapter since it deals with the technical intelligentsia in factories. However, the work contributes to our understanding of the development, values and treatment of the larger group of people from which the scientific community was drawn.

7 Lewis, Robert A. (1979) *Science and Industrialisation in the USSR.* London: Macmillan; New York: Holmes and Meier

A history of the development of the Soviet industrial R&D sector up to 1940. A number of chapters break up the period into shorter time spans of roughly a decade. Other chapters deal with particular issues, such as planning and factory-based R&D, over the whole period. The study was written explicitly with the intention of shedding light on the origins of current R&D structure and performance. The relevant conclusions are well presented in the final chapter.

8 Bailes, Kendall (1978) *Technology and Society under Lenin and Stalin: Origins of the Soviet Technical Intelligentsia, 1917-1941.* Princeton, NJ: Princeton University Press

A prize-winning account of the Soviet technical intelligentsia. Excellently researched, using a wide variety of published sources plus Soviet and Western archives, the book provides an impressive mix of description and empirical data on social origins, education, career structures, management-labour relations, etc. The last two chapters, on R&D and aviation, do not quite fit into the narrative but are interesting all the same. The book is particularly strong on the late 1920s and early 1930s – lack of data presumably contributed to some fading away in the second half of the 1930s.

9   Lecourt, Dominique (1977) *Proletarian Science? The Case of Lysenko.* London: New Left Books; Atlantic Highlands, NJ: Humanities Press

A translation from the French. As one would expect in a series edited by Louis Althusser, the book is primarily concerned with the ideological and intellectual aspects of Lysenkoism rather than politicial and organisational history.

10   Joravsky, David (1970) *The Lysenko Affair.* Cambridge, MA: Harvard University Press

A classic account of the destruction of Soviet genetics. Joravsky is primarily an historian of ideas and the intellectual-ideological aspects of the affair receive considerable attention. But the author by no means falls into the trap of attributing all causes and events to ideology. The political and organisational machinations are also well described. Although glasnost has led to a flood of new Soviet publications on Lysenko's main victim Vavilov, Joravsky's book has not been left behind by events.

11   Vucinich, Alexander (1963-1970) *Science in Russian Culture.* 2 vols: Vol. 1 – A history to 1860 (1963); Vol. 2 - 1861-1917 (1970). Stanford, CA: Stanford University Press

Beautiful histories of Russian science before the Revolution. The stress is on intellectual history, but institutional development and the struggle of free thought with political authority are not neglected.

12   Medvedev, Zhores A. (1969) *The Rise and Fall of T.D. Lysenko.* New York: Columbia University Press

An interesting account of Lysenko's career by an emigré Soviet scientist. The history starts in 1929 and carries through to 1966. The story of Lysenko's revival under Khrushchev and then rapid fall once the First Secretary was removed is particularly valuable.

13   Joravsky, David (1961) *Soviet Marxism and Natural Science, 1917-1932.* New York: Columbia University Press; London: Routledge, Kegan Paul

A classic account of the early history of the Soviet Marxist philosophy of science, essentially the history of the great struggle between the mechanists and the Deborinites. What was mainly a struggle between philosophers had little direct influence upon science itself. However, as Joravsky describes so well in the book's 'sequel', his volume on Lysenko, direct influence was to come later. The oldest book in this survey is still one of the best.

Biography and Memoirs

14   Bailes, Kendall (1990) *Science and Russian Culture in an Age of Revolutions: V.I. Vernadsky and His Scientific School, 1863-1945.* Bloomington, IN: Indiana University Press

An excellent biography of the great Russian geologist-chemist-ecologist Vladimir Vernadsky, completed just before Bailes' untimely death. Vernadsky was already a major scientific and political figure before the Revolution, so the great strength of the book is that through the life of its subject we get an invaluable picture of the adaptation (in this case) of the old intelligentsia to the new regime. It provides excellent material for any reflections on the relationship between the scientist and the state.

15   Sakharov, Andrei (1990) *Memoirs.* New York: Knopf

The memoirs of one of the truly heroic characters of the twentieth century. To be honest they do not read like the memoirs of a hero, but rather of the mild and modest man that Sakharov apparently was. He does not concentrate on his scientific work and is particularly coy about his weapons research. A great deal has been published on this latter aspect in recent months.

16 Bailey, George (1989) *The Making of Andrei Sakharov*. London: Allen Lane

Only a small proportion of the book is devoted to the work or even the life of Sakharov. Most of it is devoted to what the author sees as the long historical and intellectual antecedents of Sakharov, starting with the ancient Greeks but with particular emphasis on Galileo. There is a potted, and very unfriendly, history of socialism, in both its Western and Russian varieties. It is not to my taste, but others might find its eclecticism stimulating.

17 Berg, Raissa L. (1988) *Acquired Traits: Memoirs of a Geneticist from the Soviet Union*. New York: Viking

The very interesting autobiography of a Soviet geneticist emigré, originally published in Russian (in the West) in 1983. Berg is the daughter of the famous academician Lev Berg. She spent much of her working life in Novosibirsk. She is very good when describing growing up in an intelligentsia family in the early years of the Soviet regime (she was born in 1913) and working in a Soviet research institute. She draws out well the value conflicts to which scientists, including careerist managers, were subjected during the dissident era.

18 Badash, Lawrence (1983) *Kapitza, Rutherford and the Kremlin*. New Haven; London: Yale University Press

The letters of the Soviet physicist Petr Kapitza to his wife in the period immediately after he was refused permission to return from the Soviet Union to his laboratory in Cambridge. The letters provide a fascinating insight into the character of Kapitza and the regime he was now forced to serve. Badash's introduction is modest but excellent.

19 Grigor'ev, V.I. (1985) *Rem Khokhlov*. Moscow: Mir

A translation of a Soviet biography of the popular physicist and late rector of Moscow University. The book was well reviewed in the West partly, one suspects, because the Western scientist reviewers knew and liked Khokhlov, and partly because he was spared political dramas in his life and so censorship was not a big issue.

20 Kedrov, F.B. (1985) *Kapitza: Life and Discoveries*. London: Central Books

To publish a complete biography on Kapitza in the Soviet Union when this one appeared would have been virtually impossible. Some Western reviewers were upset by the glaring gaps in Kapitzsa's eventful life. This reader found the signs of the censor's pencil so evident that he concluded the author had deliberately done no editing so as publicly to absolve himself from responsibility. The book does have the usual shortcomings of Soviet biographies – primarily what we would see as an excessively tactful attitude to the subjects's personal life and personality. However, as usual, there is useful and interesting information to be gleaned from it.

21 Azbel, Mark Ya. (1981) *Refusenik: Trapped in the Soviet Union*. Boston: Houghton Mifflin

The memoirs of a physicist in the Institute of Theoretical and Experimental Physics of the Soviet Academy of Sciences turned Jewish refusenik. An interesting account of life both inside and outside the Institute.

22 Livanova, Anna (1980) *Landau: A Great Physicist and Teacher*. Oxford: Pergamon

A well-received Soviet biography of the great physicist. The book provides more detail on his scientific research than on his private life – his character, the difficult period in 1937, the tragic accident that brought his career to an end. This coyness is typical of Soviet biographies and derives partly from a sense of decency and partly from political control.

23 Golovin, I. (1969) *Igor Kurchatov*. Moscow: Mir

An interesting Soviet biography of the head of the Soviet atomic and hydrogen bomb, nuclear power and fusion programmes by his long-time colleague and assistant. It is not surprisingly less than fully open and frank, but provides useful information nevertheless.

General Structure

24 Fortescue, Stephen (1990) *Science Policy Making in the USSR*. London: Routledge

The first part of this book is devoted to straightforward structural issues – funding, personnel, institutions and planning. The second half attempts an examination of behaviour, with chapters on management style and rank-and-file behaviour.

25 Berry, Michael J. (1988) Editor. *Science and Technology in the USSR*. Harlow: Longman

A handbook in the Longman World Series. While it contains good, concise introductory chapters on the overall structure of Soviet science and technology, the bulk of the book consists of lists of Soviet institutes working in all the major disciplines and brief accounts of their specific areas of research. The volume contains masses of useful information for Western scientists, such as addresses, lists of journals translated into English, advice on access to the literature, etc. More for scientists than Sovietologists.

26 Sinclair, C. (1987) Editor. *The Status of Soviet Civil Science*. Dordrecht: Nijhoff

The proceedings (with some papers in French) of a NATO conference on Soviet civilian research. The novelty of the conference was that it brought together Sovietologists and Western scientists with direct experience of Soviet research. The result was a lively debate which, however, is not reflected in the published proceedings. The book is patchy, both in quality and coverage, but useful and still relevant insights can be gleaned from it. The Sovietologists concentrate on organisational structures and communication flows (both internal and external); the scientists describe Soviet work and their impressions of it in a wide variety of fields.

27 Cocks, Paul (1980) *Science Policy USA-USSR. Vol. 2: Science Policy in the Soviet Union*. Washington, DC: National Science Foundation

This volume was never easy to obtain, and by now it is presumably impossible. That is a pity because for a long time it was one of the best general overviews of Soviet science and technology. The approach is essentially structural, but contains some interesting information on decision-making procedures.

28 Medvedev, Zhores (1978) *Soviet Science*. Oxford: Oxford University Press; New York: W.W. Norton

An historical survey of science under the Soviet regime by an emigré biologist. The book was written with a general audience in mind, and lacks a 'scientific' apparatus. It is largely neutral and objective in tone. It reads easily and has something to offer even today.

29 Thomas, John R. and Kruse-Vaucienne, Ursula (1977) Editors. *Soviet Science and Technology: Domestic and Foreign Perspectives*. Washington, DC: George Washington University Press

A collection of 19 papers plus commentary presented to a National Science Foundation conference in 1976. It is a large book covering a very wide range of topics, including structures, political interactions, technology transfer and historical case studies. At the time of publication the book represented an invaluable source of information. Many of the papers are still well worth reading.

30 Hutchings, Raymond (1976) *Soviet Science, Technology and Design: Interaction and Convergence*. Oxford: Oxford University Press

Provides a great deal of straightforward information on the structure of science and technology, in chapters and appendices on organisation, planning, expenditure, personnel, etc. This sort of information can now be obtained from more up-to-date publications. But what makes this book unusual and still interesting are the chapters on design, based partly on the author's brief visit to the All-Union Research Institute for Technical Aesthetics in 1971.

31   Zaleski, E., Kozlowski, J.P., Wienert, H., Davies, R.W., Berry, M.J., and Amann, R. (1969) *Science Policy in the USSR*. Paris: OECD

A pioneering work of mixed French-British authorship. It brings together a mass of quantitative data and balanced analysis, and covers all aspects of science and technology. Once one gets used to its unusual presentation (each paragraph is numbered), and learns to find one's way around the huge number of tables and appendices, it is still a useful source of definitions and information.

Specialised Topics

32   Balzer, Harley (1989) *Soviet Science on the Edge of Reform*. Boulder, CO: Westview Press

The published account of the survey of Soviet emigrés with science and technology backgrounds conducted by Harvard University. The interesting results of the survey take up about half the book. The remainder contains a general account of Soviet science and technology, including an understandably patchy last chapter on current developments.

33   Hill, Malcolm R. and McKay, Richard (1988) *Soviet Product Quality*. London; Basingstoke: Macmillan

This is a very technical book (with chapters on general purpose machine tool standards, 'squirrel cage' electrical motors, automobiles and their components, domestic refrigerators and cameras), but an excellent introduction and conclusion put such technicalities in context. The authors test the assumption that Soviet quality is poor (they are talking about technical quality rather than economic utility). They note some successes and some improvements, but their general conclusion is that the assumption is correct.

34   Ailes, Catherine P. and Pardee, Arthur, E. (1986) *Cooperation in Science and Technology: an Evaluation of the US-Soviet Agreement*. Boulder, CO: London: Westview Press

An examination of the US-USSR Agreement on Cooperation in the Fields of Science and Technology (1972-1982). Consideration of technology transfer and commercial relationships is specifically excluded. The book provides, in its first part, analysis of the background objectives and organisational arrangements, and an exhaustive quantitative analysis of all aspects of the Agreement. The second part deals with the 11 specific working groups individually. The third part sums up the effectiveness of each working group and the Agreement as a whole. A careful, almost pedantic, analysis which provides a good basis for drawing up new programmes of cooperation.

35   Amann, R. and Cooper, J. (1986) Editors. *Technical Progress and Soviet Economic Development*. Oxford; New York: Blackwell

Strictly speaking this work cannot be regarded as the third in the series of Birmingham University publications. It has a different publisher, is more modest in scale, and has more general chapters than its predecessors. However, it very competently continues the tradition of detailed empirical sector-by-sector analysis, with chapters on civilian production in the defence industry, computing, biotechnology and product quality. There are useful general chapters on overall Soviet technological and economic performance, technology transfer and planning reforms.

36 Fortescue, Stephen (1986) *The Communist Party and Soviet Science*. London; Basingstoke: Macmillan; Baltimore, MD: John Hopkins University Press

An examination of the relationship between the science sector and the party apparatus, from the Politburo to primary Party organisations. Although put in a basic theoretical framework (totalitarian versus pluralist models), and containing one chapter on the ideology of Soviet science, the work is essentially an empirical examination of institutional relationships.

37 Kelly, William J., Shaffer, Hugh L., and Thompson, J. Kenneth (1986) *Energy Research and Development in the USSR: Preparations for the Twenty-First Century*. Durham: Duke University Press

A large book containing chapters on all major (and some minor) sources of energy. There is a good introductory chapter on the energy R&D sector, and chapters on energy modelling and prediction. A series of appendices containing the texts of plans and details on institutes and scientific councils, plus good indexes, make the book a very useful and accessible one.

38 Marsh, Rosalind J. (1986) *Soviet Fiction since Stalin: Science, Politics and Literature*. London; Sydney: Croom Helm

A survey of Soviet fiction dealing with science. The analysis is straightforward and not particularly exciting, but there is a wealth of empirical data. It would appear from the fiction surveyed that Soviet science receives somewhat more positive attention in literature than in the press. It would also appear that literature has not been used to slip in information on real-life situations that could not be directly reported for censorship reasons.

39 ZumBrunnen, Craig and Osleeb, Jeffrey, P. (1986) *The Soviet Iron and Steel Industry*. Totowa, NJ: Rowman and Allanheld

An application of a linear programming model devised by the authors to the soviet iron and steel industry, designed to determine the optimal allocation of inputs and outputs. As such the book is highly technical, but in the process of the exposition much can be gleaned about the technological processes used by the Soviets.

40 Swanson, James M. (1984) *Scientific Discoveries and Soviet Law: A Sociohistorical Analysis*. Gainesville: University of Florida Press

Relates the history of the development in law of the Soviet approach to recognition of a scientist's rights over his or her discoveries. It provides a history of the issue, including analysis of the 1959 and 1973 Statutes on Discoveries, and an examination of how the system works in practice. There is also a more theoretical discussion of the Soviet legal approach to such issues. This is a field of major current debate and developments. Swanson's book provides good background for understanding the current situation.

41 Kneen, Peter (1984) *Soviet Science and the State*. London; Basingstoke: Macmillan; Albany: SUNY Press

The author deals with three themes: Soviet natural scientists as a social group, the institutions in which they work, and the political context of science. These themes are dealt with esentially at the work-place level, i.e. the overall structure of the science sector is dealt with only briefly. The bulk of the author's attention is given to demographic analysis of research personnel. Work-place relations are dealt with primarily through citation analysis. The analysis of the relationship between science and the party-state is modest but useful.

42 Ailes, Catherine P. and Rushing, Francis, W. (1982) *The Science Race: Training and Utilization of Scientists and Engineers, US and USSR*. New York: Crane Russak

Essentially a collection of quantitative data on scientific and engineering personnel, explicitly compared to US data. It has been a useful reference work, but one suspects that new Soviet data and, most importantly, new methodological analysis will make it redundant.

43   Amann, R. and Cooper, J. (1982) Editors. *Industrial Innovation in the Soviet Union.* New Haven; London: Yale University Press

After measuring the level of technological performance in their 1977 volume the 'Birmingham school', in this massive work, undertakes to describe the innovation process and thereby to contribute to an explanation of relatively poor performance. There are excellent general chapters, followed by sectoral analyses of machine tools, group technology, chemicals, management automation, industrial control instrumentation, defence innovation and technology imports. One of the most impressive contributions to the field.

44   Smith, Gordon B., Maggs, Peter B., and Ginsburgs, George (1981) *Soviet and East European Law and the Scientific-Technical Revolution.* New York: Pergamon

Many of the chapters deal with the scientific-technical revolution in very broad terms, and therefore have no direct connection with the natural sciences or technological processes. These chapters are more concerned with general developments in Soviet law and the legal profession. There are, however, chapters on the legal aspects of technology assimilation and transfer. No book, no matter how recently published, could hope to be up-to-date in these fields at the moment, but this one still retains historical interest.

45   Campbell, Robert W. (1980) *Soviet Energy Technologies: Planning, Policy, Research and Development.* Bloomington, IN: Indiana University Press

A detailed empirical analysis of a wide range of energy technologies, with the findings being used to present some gloomy conclusions on Soviet potential for technological development. Many of the areas examined have undergone considerable change since the book was written, but the current situation might suggest that the author's conclusions were broadly correct even if much of his data is obsolete.

46   Amann, R., Cooper, J., and Davies, R.W. (1977) Editors. *The Technological Level of Soviet Industry.* New Haven; London: Yale University Press

The first of the classics of the 'Birmingham school'. A massive volume which is explicitly devoted to comparing Soviet technological performance to that of other industrialised nations, through the collection of detailed empirical data in a number of sectors. The sectors covered include iron and steel, machine tools, power transmission, chemicals, industrial process control, computers, military and rocket technology and passenger cars. Introductory chapters clearly explain the methodology and summarise the findings – essentially a large and persistent Soviet lag.

Technology Transfer

47   Bornstein, Morris (1985) *East-West Technology Transfer: the Transfer of Western Technology to the Soviet Union.* Paris: OECD

The Soviet volume in a series of studies on East-West technology transfer under the auspices of the OECD Committee for Scientific and Technological Policy. The book differs from most others on the topic by not adopting a sector-by-sector case study approach. Bornstein examines the reasons for Soviet demand for Western technology, constraints on the level of transfer, and its impact on the Soviet economy. There is also a chapter on Soviet foreign trade. Since the Soviet requirement for technology imports shows no sign of diminishing, the issues so ably set out here continue to be relevant.

48   Parrott, Bruce (1985) Editor. *Trade, Technology and Soviet-American Relations.* Bloomington, IN: Indiana University Press

Contains a useful combination of overview and sector-by-sector chapters. The sectors covered include: automobiles, computers, energy, defence industry and agriculture. The overview chapters include economic aspects, assimilation, and political issues from Soviet and American perspectives. The authors are all leaders in their fields and the overall quality is extremely high.

49   Smith, Gordon B. (1984) Editor. *The Politics of East-West Trade.* Boulder, CO: Westview Press

Another in the considerable literature on East-West trade, indeed with many of the same authors as in other volumes. But the names are good ones, and the chapters, both the general and the specialised, are of high quality. The content is devoted to Soviet-US trade, and policy disputes in the US over it, so do not be misled by the title.

50   Hanson, Philip (1981) *Trade and Technology in Soviet-Western Relations.* London; Basingstoke: Macmillan; New York: Columbia University Press

A detailed empirical examination of technology transfer to the Soviet Union, primarily in the 1960s and 1970s. With the exception of a one-chapter case study of the mineral fertiliser industry, the approach is not sectoral. One of the author's intentions was to put the debate on technology transfer on much firmer ground by defining terms, measuring flows, etc. But the author's particular concern was to measure the effectiveness of the assimilation of Western technology into the Soviet economy. His findings are, as he admits, imprecise, but the issues discussed, as clearly as one would expect from this excellent author, are vital to the debate, even today when the empirical data in the book are increasingly out of date.

51   Holliday, George D. (1979) *Technology Transfer to the Soviet Union, 1928-1937 and 1966-1975: the Role of Western Technology in Soviet Economic Development.* Boulder, CO: Westview Press

By examining technology transfer to the Soviet Union over two very different periods, the author tries to demonstrate that the Soviet Union has adopted more recently a strategy of gradual but definitive movement towards greater technological interdependence with the West, interdependence presumably being a euphemism for dependence. The author is well aware of the continual debate over this issue within the Soviet Union – indeed he devotes considerable valuable attention to it – so his analysis is more nuanced than my bald summary might suggest. The empirical analysis is concentrated on the automobile industry – the GAZ plant in the earlier period, and VAZ and KamAZ more recently.

52   Sutton, Antony (1968-1973) *Western Technology and Soviet Economic Development.* 3 vols. Vol. 1: 1917 to 1930 (1968); Vol. 2: 1930 to 1945 (1971); Vol. 3: 1945 to 1965 (1973). Stanford, CA: Hoover Institution Press

A massive research effort. It is primarily empirical rather than analytical (the conclusion consists of 12 out of 1,120 pages of text, and half of that is a resume of the empirical findings). However, the author's themes are clear: the USSR has always relied heavily on Western technology and will have to do so as long as it maintains a centrally planned economy; that reliance guarantees Soviet backwardness; and the West has usually been prepared to provide technology despite dubious benefits. The weight of the evidence is impressive, although some would claim to be able to make a case, using the same and other data, for opposite conclusions.

Policy-Making and Behaviour

53   Parrott, Bruce (1983) *Politics and Technology in the Soviet Union.* Cambridge, MA: MIT Press

A detailed examination over the whole Soviet period of the struggle within Soviet politics between those who have had an optimistic faith in the superiority of the Soviet approach to technological development, and those who have argued for a pragmatic readiness to borrow from and deal with the West. An impressive piece of research that makes a major contribution to our understanding of Soviet technology policies and policy-making in general.

54 Lubrano, L.L. and Solomon, S. Gross (1980) Editors. *The Social Context of Soviet Science*. Boulder, CO: Westview Press; Folkestone: Dawson

A book which consciously tried to move away from the usual structural orientations of Western work on Soviet science towards the behavioural dimension. There are, nevertheless, structural chapters (and very good ones too). The behavioural element is represented by chapters on working life in institutes and the social composition and attitudes of scientists. There are then 'case study' chapters on the Kol'tsov Institute and genetic engineering. Although the promise of a consistent behavioural theme is not fulfilled, the individual contributions are all good enough to make the book an excellent one.

55 Popovsky, Mark (1979) *Manipulated Science: The Crisis of Science and Scientists in the Soviet Union Today*. Garden City: Doubleday. [Published in the UK by Collins and Harvill with the title *Science in Chains*].

Popovsky was a journalist specialising in science and technology matters before emigrating from the USSR in 1977. He provides an extremely unflattering view of Soviet science, particularly its institute directors and managers. While some might find the work tendentious and 'unscientific', there is little in it that cannot be found in the Soviet press every day. The book does not attempt to be exhaustive or even systematic in its coverage, but deals with a number of scattered topics.

56 Lubrano, Linda (1976) *Soviet Sociology of Science*. Columbus, OH: AAASS

A survey of the Soviet discipline of *naukovedenie*, providing summaries of the work of the major Soviet writers. On the whole Lubrano lets the authors speak for themselves, leaving her interpretations brief and to the point. Most of the work dealt with is theoretical rather than empirical, presumably reflecting the balance in the Soviet discipline at the time.

57 Medvedev, Z. (1971) *The Medvedev Papers*. London: Macmillan

Medvedev, a dissident emigré biologist, concentrates on the difficulties put in the way of cooperation and communication between Soviet and foreign scientists. There is an interesting combination of purely personal experiences (including his long battle with the Soviet postal service) and more general descriptions of travel procedures and censorship. One hopes and believes that the book is now mostly out of date, but one can never be sure.

CHAPTER TEN

General Reference

Dr Wojciech Zalewski
Stanford University

Introduction

During the 1980s electronic information technology became firmly established in the world of bibliography and data services. The process of adaptation has been rapid. It is possible to project that during the 1990s the majority of bibliographic citations of current English language publications, as well as a significant proportion of earlier publications, will be available in machine-readable formats. This facility transforms the concept of reference and bibliographical services, especially in regard to comprehensiveness and search methodology.

At the end of the 1980s bibliographic and information sources were produced in three major formats – printed, online, and CD-ROM (Compact Disk Read Only Memory). Often these formats are employed simultaneously. Trends, however, are indicating a change in the balance of outputs. A diminishing reliance upon paper formats is now paralleled by a growth in electronic forms of publishing. There is an increase of original publications available only on CD-ROMs, optical disks are more frequently employed, and full text files in machine-readable form are common.

These developments have bibliographic significance for those researching Soviet materials. The internationalisation of databases is inevitable. Technological differences between Soviet and Western bibliographic facilities, an obstacle in the past, will be overcome. Data created by such institutions as the All-Union Book Chamber (Vsesoiuznaia Knizhnaia Palata), the Institute of Scientific Information in the Social Sciences (Institut Nauchnoi Informatsii po Obshchestvennym Naukam), as well as work done by Soviet libraries, will become available through Western networks. Consequently, discussions of available information sources must embrace both machine-readable and print forms of information services. They must also indicate how these converging forms relate to each other currently within the information sector. In addition, and importantly because of the pace and profundity of change, means of keeping abreast of bibliographical developments must be considered.

Printed Sources

There is a wealth of general publications which contain materials on the Soviet Union. Familiarity with such sources is taken for granted. This section concentrates upon bibliographies and reference works more closely applicable to Soviet studies. Excluded from our purview are statistical sources and business directories, which are discussed elsewhere in this volume.

Guides to Bibliographical Aids

Works in this category are designed to provide the first step in the quest for information. They list standard reference works which lead to more specialised sources. In addition to bibliographies they list encyclopedias, dictionaries, statistical materials, directories, standard texts and similar reference materials. For beginners in the field it is advisable to initiate a bibliographic search with such guides to make use of the systematising work of other specialists.

A search for English-language references could begin with E.P. Sheehy's *Guide to Reference Books* (1). The latest edition has increased substantially the coverage of Russian/Soviet materials. The availability of such guides, and there are others, makes it unnecessary to comment on all the works cited. Indicated titles not highlighted in the bibliography may be traced for full descriptions in the standard reference works. Guidance in systematic searching from general to more specialised reference materials in Soviet studies is provided by Zalewski's *Fundamentals of Russian Reference Work in the Humanities and Social Sciences* (4). Data sources and reference materials are covered in G. Walker's more circumscribed *Official Publications* (3). As in so many other fields the need to keep up-to-date is paramount. Continuing bibliographic and reference updates are provided in the annual bibliographic surveys compiled for *The Russian Review* and *Slavic Review*.

The most important bibliography of bibliographies, which provides a key to Russian-language publications, is the work by B.L. Kandel', *Otechestvennye Ukazateli Bibliograficheskikh Posobii* (2). It has to be mentioned here, as an exception to the inclusion specification, because of its significance as a guide to the field.

General Bibliographies

English-language publications in Russian/Soviet and East European area studies are registered in two bibliographies which aspire to be as comprehensive as possible. They are *The American Bibliography of Slavic and East European Studies (ABSEES)* (6), and the *European Bibliography of Soviet, East European and Slavonic Studies (EBSEESS)* (9). Both are annual publications organised by subject to include monographs, articles, reviews and special interest items. They exclude newspapers from their coverage, as well as general interest journals (for coverage of the latter see the electronic bibliography section below). A useful supplement to these standard works is published annually in *Canadian Slavonic Papers* as 'Canadian Publications on the Soviet Union and Eastern Europe', by J. McIntosh. An interesting project, now with an uncertain future due to the death of its initiator, is S.M. Horak's *Russia, the USSR, and Eastern Europe* (10). Horak has produced a series of annotated bibliographies of monographic publications covering the period 1964 to 1985. Translated material from the Russian, sponsored by the US government, is listed in *Transdex Index: Index to JPRS* (14).

Lists of English-language journals and series relevant to Soviet studies are not readily available. Titles, however, can be drawn from the lists of journals searched for *ABSEES* and *EBSEESS* material. These listings form useful bibliographies of journals relevant to the field. A practical approach to the task of identifying major journals in Soviet Studies is provided by the comprehensive subscription lists of the Library of Congress. This is made possible through the work by J. Hoskins: *The USSR and East Central and Southeastern Europe: Periodicals in Western Languages* (11). A list of monographic series published in the West is included in Zalewski's *Fundamentals* (4).

An important forthcoming bibliographic event will be the publication of *The Soviet World 1948-1988* (Inter Documentation Company) in microfiche form. This work, to be published in 1991, will index the contents of 300 Western and Soviet newspapers and journals. The compilation will be produced by the staff of the Institute for Soviet and East European Studies of the University of Amsterdam. Advance notices suggest that it will prove a most useful addition to our bibliographical armoury.

Existing general bibliographies do not adequately cover the area of Russian literature published abroad, while bibliographic search and retrieval through library and dealer catalogues is cumbersome. Specialist bibliographies are available. Some of these items provide English annotations and so merit mention. An overview of the bibliographic situation in this area is provided by Mark Kulikowski in an aptly entitled article 'A neglected source: the bibliography of Russian emigré publications since 1917' (12). Other major bibliographic contributions bring us to the opening years of our review period. These are described in the bibliography (7, 8, 13, 15). Valuable for its work in abstracting current journals is *Abstracts of Soviet and East European Emigré Periodical Literature* (5), compiled by L. Khotin. The provision of English-language annotations widens the utility of this service.

Subject Bibliographies

The majority of subject bibliographies published in the West are 'hidden' in monographs. There are also separately published bibliographies devoted to special subjects at the level of specific events or individual authors, for example, glasnost, nuclear weapons policy, Afghanistan. This latter group of bibliographies is receiving fewer new titles because of escalating publishing costs, limited markets and possibilities of retrieval of desired information from electronic databases. The following discussion excludes both these categories to concentrate upon bibliographies relevant to disciplines rather than specific subjects.

Major bibliographic resources for both Western and Russian-language publications are the *MLA International Bibliography of Books and Articles on the Modern Languages and Literatures*, New York: Modern Languages Association of America, 1921-, and the *Year's Work in Modern Language Studies*, London: the Modern Humanities Research Association, 1931-. The former title substantially increased its coverage of Slavic-language materials during the 1980s. Both are standard works in the field, with long-established reputations and so covered in Sheehy. The series of bibliographies prepared by G.M. Terry under the title *East European Languages and Literatures* (24) also offer broad coverage of language, literature and related subjects as expressed in articles, conferences and collective works. A useful way of gaining a rapid overview of recent periodical publication is through the use of contents listings. One such is produced by the Bayerische Staatsbibliothek, in Munich. The tables of contents of leading Slavic linguistic and literary journals are published under the title *New Contents: Slavistics* (19).

In history, bibliographical activity over the last decade has produced notable additions to our stockpile of aids. For example, *A Researcher's Guide to Sources on Soviet Social History in the 1930s*, by L. Viola and S. Fitzpatrick (21), is an important bibliographical event which also sets new methodological standards. Other useful contributions have been made with *Bibliography of Articles on East-European and Russian History*, by M. Späth (23) and *Russia and Eastern Europe, 1789-1985: A Bibliographical Guide*, by R. Pearson (20).

Subject bibliographers have ranged widely over the field of Soviet studies to produce works of varying ambition, coverage and utility. A few titles have been selected to indicate something of this variety. The increasing importance of law, as relations with the Soviet Union have been liberalised, is recognised by the publication of *Soviet Law in English*, by I.I. Kavass (17). The persistence of the nationality issue is reflected in S.M. Horak's *Guide to the Study of Soviet Nationalities* (16). Less ambitious works, nevertheless useful in filling bibliographical lacunae, are *Bibliography for Soviet Geography*, by J. Sanchez (22), *Russian-EnglishDictionaries with Aids for Translators*, by W. Zalewski (25) and J. Leyda's 'Seventy-five years of Russian and Soviet films, 1907-1982: a select list' (18).

Non-Bibliographic Reference Sources

GUIDE TO ARCHIVES

During the 1980s an unprecedented effort was made in the West to describe Russian/Soviet archival resources. The guides published, taken together, facilitate access to all major Western repositories of consequence. Although not all holdings have been converted to machine-readable form as yet, it should be noted that major cataloguing networks such as OCLC and RLIN also include archival materials.

A comprehensive guide to archival sources in the United States is provided by *The Russian Empire and the Soviet Union*, by S.A. Grant and J.H. Brown (26). Examples of geographically limited guides are *Scholar's Guide to Washington, D.C. for Russian/Soviet Studies*, by S.A. Grant (27), and R.A. Karlowich's *A Guide to Scholarly Resources on the Russian Empire and the Soviet Union in the New York Metropolitan Area* (32). European counterparts are available. For example, R.C. Lewanski's *Eastern Europe and Russia/Soviet Union: A Handbook of Western European Archival and Library Resources* (34) and J.M. Hartley's *Guide to Documents and Manuscripts in the United Kingdom* (31).

The two most important Russian/Soviet archival holdings in the United States have good guides. The Hoover Institution Archives has issued a general guide to its resources by C. Palm and D. Reed (35), followed by two special guides. The latter consist of a description of Russian and Soviet materials (33) and of the Nicolaevsky collection (29). The Columbia University Bakhmeteff Archive has a guide prepared by E. Scaruffi (36). The relatively new Russian archive in Leeds, England, has issued several lists describing its holdings and acquisitions. An example of a European institutional guide is that produced by the International Institute of Social History, Amsterdam (30). The general guide is published in English and covers materials relevant to Soviet studies.

In the context of repositories mention should be made of the collecting activities of the Center for Research Libraries which is a resource for rarely held titles in academic libraries. Information about its holdings is provided by *Soviet Serials Currently Received at the Center For Research Libraries* (37).

The number of archival guides available invests a guide to guides with a special value. A bibliography of guides to Soviet archives, as well as information about Soviet archives, is found in various works by P.K. Grimsted. Her *Handbook* (28), an international guide to archives and libraries, is especially noteworthy.

ENCYCLOPEDIAS AND DICTIONARIES

Due to a lack of a solid English-language encyclopedia on Russia/Soviet Union, Western scholars undertook the challenging task of translating the third edition of the *Bol'shaia Sovetskaia Entsiklopedia*. The results have appeared in the 30-volume *Great Soviet Encyclopedia* (43). The contents are subject to the verdict of history but, at the more practical level, the rather confusing arrangement due to the vagaries of translation should be noted. The *Cambridge Encyclopedia of Russia and the Soviet Union* (39) is intended for general readers but its contributors maintain a high standard of scholarship. Although not encyclopedic in nature, wide coverage statistical compendia can be included in this category. In some areas they can be used to update information provided in available encyclopedias. *USSR Facts and Figures Annual* (52) provides a useful factual survey of current developments in many major sectors on an annual basis.

While general encyclopedias on the Soviet Union, in the English language, are few in number and are inadequately complemented and supplemented by universal encyclopedias, the position regarding subject encyclopedias is changing. Several key subject encyclopedias have been published, or are in the process of preparation. Significant contributions to this sector are being made by the Academic International Press. This publishing house has issued *The Modern Encyclopedia of Russian and Soviet History* (47), *The Modern Encyclopedia of Russian and Soviet Literature* (48), *The Modern Encyclopedia of Religions in Russia and the Soviet Union* (49), *The Military-Naval Encyclopedia of Russia and the Soviet Union* (46) and its companion volume *Soviet Armed Forces Review Annual* (51). For good measure the annual *Facts and Figures* also appears under this imprint. A further contribution to history is J. Paxton's basic *Companion to Russian History* (50), two encyclopedias on the Russian Revolution by H. Shukman (38) and G. Jackson (41). The situation in literature has been improved by the appearance of two excellent compilations – *Handbook of Russian Literature*, by V. Terras (44), and a translation of the well-received German work *Dictionary of Russian Literature since 1917* (45). The strong movement in subject publishing may be illustrated further by reference to political economy and law. In the former field M.I. Volkov's *A Dictionary of Political Economy* (40) deserves mention, as does the *Encyclopedia of Soviet Law* (42).

BIOGRAPHICAL DICTIONARIES

The search for biographical data in Soviet sources presents notorious diffi-culties. There are signs of change brought about by glasnost, and as a re-sult certain types of biographical data are more accessible than in the past. Indicative of this movement is S. Chainikov's *Who's Who in the Soviet Government* (64), and a number of other similar publications issued or prepared in the Soviet Union. It is hoped that the Soviets will eventually publish general, academic, cultural and special interest biographical dic-tionaries not currently available. Despite the increase in Soviet publishing in this area, primary reliance still has to be placed upon Western sources. These focus on political figures and are decidedly sketchy for other sectors of activity. An effort is being made to provide current biographical data by the Central Intelligence Agency in a series of publications (55). Radio Free Europe/Radio Liberty are also sponsoring biographical services (56, 57, 58). Commercial enterprise has contributed to filling gaps in biographical knowledge with *SovietBiographicalService* (60), *The Tauris Soviet Direc-tory: The Elite of the USSR Today* (61), *Who's Who in the Soviet Union: Political and Military Leaders*, by U-J. Schultz-Jorge (66), and *The Soviet Nomenklatura*, by A.L. Weeks (63).

One of the difficulties with biographical dictionary publishing is maintaining titles in a state of up-to-dateness. The rapid changes in the Soviet Union in recent years have exacerbated this problem as new per-sonalities emerge and others recede into the background. Older diction-aries may lose some of their immediacy but still retain historical significance. In this class, for example, we may include *Who's Who in the Soviet Union* (65) and *Biographical Dictionary of Dissidents in the Soviet Union* (53). Examples of more specifically historically orientated diction-aries are *The Soviet Biographic Archive, 1954-1985*, from Chadwyck-Healy (59), *Soviet Government Officials, 1922-1941: A Handlist*, edited by R.W. Davies (54), and *Biographical Dictionary of the Soviet Union, 1917-1988* (62). It is worth noting that very useful information about biographi-cal sources is to be found in the *The Modern Encyclopedia of Russian and Soviet History* (47) (Vol. 4, 140-164) in an article entitled 'Biographic aids for the study of Russian history', by A.E. Graham.

DIRECTORIES

The up-to-dateness of directories has been severely tested by recent events. For example, many new institutions have been created, street names have altered and administrative structures changed. The situation has brought a positive response from publishers of all kinds in a growing variety and volume of directories to aid businessmen, scholars and tour-ists. Only an illustrative selection of this output can be indicated here.

A directory of the Soviet Academy of Sciences has been prepared by B.A. Ruble and R. Mdivani – *A Scholar's Guide to Humanities and Social Sciences in the Soviet Union* (69). C. Rose's *The Soviet Propaganda Net-*

work: A Directory of Organizations Serving Soviet Foreign Policy (68) is important for political activists. The new openness in the Soviet Union facilitates greater contact with foreigners. Organisations seeking such contacts are listed in *Neformalniye: A Guide to Independent Organizations and Contacts in the Soviet Union* (67).

Of general interest in this category are *USSR: Yearbook* (70), published by the Novosti Press Agency and *Vsia Moskva* (71) which revives, to a limited extent, the pre-revolutionary tradition of city directories.

Machine-Readable Bibliographies and Data Sources

English-language academic and cultural publications, monographs, journals and indexes to major newspapers and journals produced over the last decade are almost all bibliographically registered in one or another variety of electronic formats. Currently the majority of bibliographic institutions such as Wilson, Bowker, Gale and the Modern Language Association issue their products in paper and electronic formats. The comprehensiveness of the process of registration means that a substantial amount of English language treatments of Soviet themes is covered by these services. In addition some electronic services also include selected Soviet vernacular publication, but none of the Soviet-produced electronic files is available in the West at the time of writing.

Electronic services are available either through original publishers, such as H.W. Wilson Company, or through mediating vendors. Of the latter the most popular for the social sciences and humanities and relevant Soviet studies are DIALOG and its less expensive derivate KNOWLEDGE INDEX (DIALOG Information Services Inc., Palo Alto, CA), BRS and its shorter and inexpensive spin-off, BRS/AFTERDARK (BRS Information Technologies, Latham, NY), and INFOTRAC (Information Access Company) which is a laser disc database for newspapers and magazines. There are, of course, many other services but of only limited application to Soviet studies. The European vendor of importance is QUESTEL which includes FRANCIS (Centre National de la Recherche Scientifique, Institut de l'Information Scientifique et Technique, Sciences Humaines et Sociales, Paris). Some ten per cent of FRANCIS, a database with a wide coverage of the human, social and economic sciences, is devoted to materials dealing with the Soviet Union and Eastern Europe.

Vendors publish lists of the files they offer customers. These lists can serve as subject guides and are useful information tools. Details of such lists can be found through the titles discussed in the Database Directories section below.

Bibliographic Databases

General bibliographies are published in a number of forms. They may be (a) format-orientated, e.g. confined to books or articles, or to non-print materials, or to specified languages; (b) limited by geographic boundaries, e.g. publications of the USA; (c) limited by chronological considerations, e.g. annual registers. The subject matter of documents is subordinated to these organising principles. This type of general bibliography satisfies a number of functions. Increasingly, because of their comprehensiveness and flexibility through their electronic forms, they reduce the need for separately published subject or specialised bibliographies. Already special bibliographies can be drawn from online databases by skilful search and use of available technical facilities. In this development, associated with the decline in the number of bibliographies compiled and published in traditional formats, may be seen the emergence of a new era in the bibliographical world.

MONOGRAPHS

Monographs are registered in library catalogues and in formal bibliographies. Both traditional forms are under pressure from electronic sources. Library catalogues online are replacing the card catalogues. The advantages of the change are obvious in the ease with which the electronic form can include the holdings of a number of libraries and the choice of searching methods that are available – author, title, keyword, subject, call number, series, and in some case imprint.

In the United States several cataloguing networks were established in the 1970s. Developments have progressed to the point where a systematic effort is being made to convert older records into machine-readable form. Among the leading networks are the OCLC (Online Computer Library Center) and RLIN (Research Library Information Network) owned by the Research Library Group (RLG). These networks make available all materials, domestic and foreign, archival, non-print and electronic, catalogued by the libraries which utilise them. The Library of Congress records are also loaded into these networks. The *National Union Catalog* of the Library of Congress has appeared in microfiche form since 1983. As a consequence of this process of library automation, production of printed catalogues has ceased almost entirely. An exception is the *Bibliographic Guide to Soviet and East European Studies* (Boston, G.K. Hall, 1978-) which, despite its title, annually registers books catalogued by the Library of Congress and the research collection of the New York Public Library.

The movement to automate cataloguing systems, both within and between libraries, is well advanced in the United Kingdom also. Systems such as BLCMP are well established, and centralised catalogue records are available through BLAISE. The Joint Academic Network (JANET) was formally inaugurated in 1984. Conceived initially as a communication system linking universities through their central computer facilities, JANET was later extended to include their libraries, research councils, polytechnics, the British Library, and other organisations concerned with academic research. The link makes available to each academic library the catalogues of others. These developments have been given added impetus by the Consortium of University and Research Libraries (CURL) which encompasses the seven largest university libraries – Cambridge, Oxford, Manchester, London, Leeds, Edinburgh and Glasgow. This group has expressed a close interest in securing the benefits of cooperation through automation and in making available records of special collections and older materials. BNBMARC, the national register of monographs and first issues of serials deposited with the British Library by British publishers, is available online via BLAISE-LINE, while the *British National Bibliography* is available on CD-ROM.

Developments are continuing in this field. For example, cataloguing networks are experimenting with mounting subject bibliographies in their systems, but no bibliography relevant to Russian/Soviet area studies has been included so far. However it is of interest that RLG is exploring the feasibility of sharing databases with the Institute of Scientific Information in the Social Sciences in Moscow.

General bibliographies of monographs and lists of periodicals are made available in a number of formats – machine-readable, paper-based, and on CD-ROM. The basic publications, such as *Cumulative Book Index*, *Books in Print*, *Ulrich's International Periodical Directory*, *Dissertation Abstracts*, *British National Bibliography*, are too well known to require comment in addition to what can easily be found in general reference guides. However, it should not be forgotten that their comprehensiveness ensures coverage of Soviet topics.

Government documents generally are not catalogued by libraries, but they are loaded into networks, for example RLIN. Thus items registered in the Monthly Catalog, which records United States government publications, are made available in a flexible manner.

PERIODICALS

This bibliographic sector consists of listings of titles, indexes of contents, abstracts and the text itself in newspapers and journals.

No listing of English-language journals dealing specifically with the Soviet Union is available online. However, *Ulrich's* facility in allowing searches to be conducted by descriptor and geographic codes may provide some help in this direction. Similarly, there are no online indexes exclusively devoted to Soviet studies. The *Current Digest of the Soviet Press* (72) could be considered an exception because it provides full text and, due to its keyword search capability, it serves as a workable index to the press. Broadcast information is important, and has affinities with periodical publications. Useful in keeping check on what has been said is

Daily Report: Soviet Union: Index: Foreign Broadcast Information Service (73) which is available on CD-ROM. The dearth of special indexes to periodicals compels the use of major general indexes. Among these *World Affairs Report*, *Public Affairs Information Service (PAIS International)*, *Current Contents*, *World Translation Index*, and the text file *Facts on File World News Digest* have special relevance for Soviet studies. They are all available on DIALOG, KNOWLEDGE INDEX, and NEXIS, and some already exist on CD-ROM.

An important index for newpaper articles is the *National Newspaper Index* (76) available on DIALOG, KNOWLEDGE INDEX, ORBIT and NEXIS, which contains INFORMATION BANK (available from Mead Data Central) with abstracts of leading newspapers. The full text of *The New York Times* is available on DIALOG. Journal articles can be identified by using the *Magazine Index* (75), which is searchable through DIALOG and INFOTRAC. For government documents there is the *Index to U.S. Government Periodicals* (74). The H.W. Wilson Company, among its bibliographies on WILSONLINE, offers the *Reader's Guide to Periodical Literature*. This service is also available on CD-ROM as WILSONDISC. All these sources, although general in nature, provide access to English language material relevant to many aspects of Soviet studies.

SUBJECT BIBLIOGRAPHIES

Computerisation of bibliography permits the creation of large databases comprehending broad fields of knowledge and encompassing all bibliographical forms and subjects. Currently the only file dealing solely with the Soviet Union is *Soviet Science and Technology*. But, as has been emphasised above, researchers will find significant amounts of material relating to the Soviet Union in the general subject bibliographies available online. Further examples of such files are *Social Science Citation Index*, *Sociological Abstracts*, *Economic Literature Index*, *Arts and Humanities Citation Index*. Indexes of this kind have their paper counterparts, but they are more readily searched online through such hosts as DIALOG and KNOWLEDGE INDEX. Importantly, it should be remembered that new databases are being created and made available. It is essential, therefore, to consult database directories (see below) in preparation for systematic searches. From such general services it is possible to compile narrowly focused bibliographies of English-language materials but, with the exception of the MLA service, vernacular literature is not satisfactorily represented in such indexes.

Non-Bibliographic Databases

To date, only limited use can be made of non-bibliographic resources in electronic form applicable to Soviet studies. What is available, however, is interesting and indicative of future potential. The Machine-Readable Data

Files (MDF) contain a variety of data in social sciences including public opinion surveys, censuses, etc. Most of these are available online only. When purchased by a library they are mounted in its cataloguing system. Information about their availability is provided by the Inter-University Consortium for Political and Social Research (ICPSR) (Ann Arbor, MI) in the form of *Guide to Resources and Services* (78). *The Soviet Interview Project, 1979-1983* is an example of the interesting material contained in this file. The *Biography Master Index* (77) is noteworthy because its worldwide biographical index coverage includes Soviet figures. *SOVSET* (79) stands in a category of its own. It is the equivalent of an electronic bulletin board. It links those interested in Soviet studies so facilitating the exchange of ideas and the maintenance of scholarly contact and communication. *SOVSET* also carries a data library component which contains *Radio Free Europe Daily Reports*, in full text, as well as other social data.

Database Directories

Database directories, in printed form, provide information about individual databases – their content, subject coverage, data elements (author, title, editors, pagination, etc.), producers, contacts, vendors, prices, formats. They are usually updated annually, so it is important to consult the latest available issue when initiating a search. Through their subject indexes it is possible to determine the databases most likely to be of use. Because of their strong similarities only a small selection of titles, from a very competitive publishing field, have been selected for notice. In addition, since many of the descriptive elements in different directories are similar, annotations have been kept short. For an overview of database problems, reference may be made to *Issues in Online Database Searching*, by C. Tenopir (86).

The following listing of directories provides a basic introduction to electronic bibliographical resources applicable to materials on the Soviet Union. The *Information Industry Directory* (85) has established a formidable presence in the field, but there are other contributors. The *Directory of Online Databases* (82) and *Computer-ReadableDatabases* (80) are international in scope. The latter provides, in addition to details of online services, information on available CD-ROMs. *Database Directory* (81) is broadly similar, but provides no information about CD-ROMs. To this group of representative works may be added the internationally orientated *Online Bibliographic Databases: A Directory and Sourcebook*, by J.L. Hall (84). Details of full text services are listed in *Fulltext Sources Online: Bibliodata for Periodicals, Newspapers, Newsletters and Newswires* (83).

Conclusion

The computerisation of libraries and bibliography has opened a new era in information transfer and searching. At this point, however, the Western and Soviet bibliographical worlds have not been fully linked, neither has the enormous task of converting older bibliographical records into machine-readable form been completed. Full searching capacity through electronic media is still some way off. Currently paper-based bibliographies are cheaper to use, more secure and better delineated. However, the advantages of electronic services, such as speed of search, up-to-dateness, size of database, and the larger number of indexes which can be searched at a time, have given notice that the situation is changing and will continue to do so.

In the West, bibliographic registration is no longer carried out manually. This change, the basis of electronic databases, makes it necessary for scholars to develop new bibliographical skills to exploit such databases. This requirement is given added force by the speed with which electronic bibliographies and databases are incorporating increasing amounts of data relating to the Soviet Union. It is likely that Soviet databases will grow and that exchanges of electronic bibliographic and other data will be arranged. There are signs that we are on the threshold of this new era of information exchange.

I should like to express my gratitude to Professor Terence Emmons, Anthony Angiletta, Molly Molloy and George Klim for their comments, advice and editorial contributions. I should also like to thank the students in my Slavic Bibliography class for being catalysts of this project.

Bibliography

Printed Sources

GUIDES TO THE BIBLIOGRAPHICAL/REFERENCE SYSTEM

1   *Guide to Reference Books* (1986), 10th edn. edited by E.P. Sheehy. Chicago: American Library Association

    Selective for Soviet materials but identifies major works of reference and provides descriptive annotations. A necessary tool for beginning a search.

2   Kandel, B.L. (1990) *Otechestvennye Ukazateli Bibliograficheskikh Posobii*, 2nd edn. Leningrad: Ministerstvo Kultury RSFSR, Gos. Publichnaia Biblioteka im. M.E. Saltykova-Shchedrina

    An annotated listing of 1,072 bibliographies of bibliographies published in Russia and in the Soviet Union in all subjects and disciplines. An advisable first consultation in a bibliographic search.

3   Walker, G. (1982) Editor. *Official Publications of the Soviet Union and Eastern Europe, 1945-1980: A Select Annotated Bibliography.* London; New York: Mansell

Lists and describes official sources covering a wide range of activities: law, international relations, military, economic, social and cultural affairs, etc. English-language materials have been listed where available. A major work now in need of updating.

4   Zalewski, W. (1985) *Fundamentals of Russian Reference Work in the Humanities and Social Sciences.* New York: Russica. (Russica Bibliography Series, no. 5)

Designed as an introduction to search methodology and to major reference works which lead to expanded bibliographic and data searches. Updated version is now available on disk from the author.

GENERAL BIBLIOGRAPHIES

5   Khotin, L. (1981-) Editor. *Abstracts of Soviet and East European Emigré Periodical Literature.* Pacific Grove, CA: ASEEEPL

The only current index to major emigré journals. Organised by disciplines, subdivided by broad categories. Well indexed by subjects, names, titles and authors. Selective and annotated. Four issues a year.

6   *The American Bibliography of Slavic and East European Studies.* (1956-) Washington, DC: AAASS

Currently compiled at the Library of Congress and published annually. Attempts the comprehensive registration of all English-language material published in the United States and Canada. Ethnic and emigré materials are covered on a selective basis. Recent files are computerised and searchable in this form at the editorial office.

7   Bakunina, T.A. and Volkoff, A.M. (1976/77) *L'Emigration Russe en Europe: Catalogue Collectif des Périodiques en Langue Russe.* Paris: Institut d'Etudes Slaves (Bibiliothèque Russe de l'Institut d'Etudes Slaves, t.40). Vol. 1, 1855-1940, by Bakunina, contains 1,405 titles. Vol. 2, 1940-1970, by Volkoff, contains 490 titles.

A union list of Russian-language emigré journals found in the libraries of Europe. Organised by title according to the Cyrillic alphabet, with an index of titles in Romanised form and with a name index.

8   *L'Emigration Russe: Revues et Recueils, 1920-1980: Index Général des Articles.* (1988) compiled by T.L. Gladkova et al. Paris: Institut d'Etudes Slaves (Bibliothèque Russe de l'Institut d'Etudes Slaves, t.81)

An index of over 25,000 entries drawn from 45 journals and 16 collections published between 1920 and 1980 in various world centres. Weeklies, dailies and specialist periodicals are excluded. The most extensive index to Russian-language emigré journals available.

9   *European Bibliography of Soviet, East European and Slavonic Studies.* (1977-) Paris: Institut d'Etudes Slaves

Published annually, but with the disadvantage of a five-year delay. Latest volumes include publications on Soviet and East European studies published in European countries. The product is the result of a cooperative effort of bibliographers based in dispersed European centres. Less comprehensive than its American counterpart.

10   Horak, S.M. (1987) *Russia, the USSR and Eastern Europe: A Bibliographic Guide to English Language Publication, 1981-1985.* Littleton, CO: Libraries Unlimited

Restricted to monographic publications. Material arranged by discipline and subject. Annotated mainly by quoting from reviews.

11 Hoskins, J. (1979) *The USSR and East Central and Southeastern Europe: Periodicals in Western Languages*, 4th revised edn. Washington, DC: Library of Congress

An annotated list of Western-language journals in the humanities and social sciences received by the Library of Congress.

12 Kulikowski, M. (1989) A neglected source: the bibliography of Russian emigré publications since 1917. *Solanus* 3 (New Series), 89-102.

A crucial bibliography of bibliographies presented in the form of a bibliographic essay.

13 Stevanovic, B. and Wertsman, V. (1987) *Free Voices in Russian Literature, 1950s-1980s: A Bio-Bibliographical Guide*. New York: Russica. (Russica Bibliography Series, no. 4)

Provides details on over 900 Soviet authors whose writings, because of censorship, appeared only in the emigré press. Selective lists of Russian emigré periodicals and serial editions are included. Newspapers are excluded from the survey. Sketchy biographies of authors are in English. Useful although not a comprehensive guide to Russian emigré and samizdat literature.

14 *Transdex: Index to JPRS*. (1975-) Wooster, OH: Micro Photo Division, Bell and Howell

Bibliographic index to United States Joint Publications Research Service translations. There is a useful annual cumulation of monthly publications. Microfiche.

15 Woll, J. and Treml, V.G. (1983) *Soviet Dissident Literature: A Critical Guide*. Boston, MA: G.K. Hall

A selective introduction to the literature, broadly interpreted, produced by Soviet authors in the West.

SUBJECT BIBLIOGRAPHIES

16 Horak, S.M. (1982) *Guide to the Study of Soviet Nationalities: Non-Russian Peoples of the USSR*. Littleton, CO: Libraries Unlimited

An annotated bibliography of predominantly English-language (60 per cent) monographic contributions. 1,346 entries in all. Organised by ethnic groups and subdivided by subjects.

17 Kavass, I.I. (1988) *Soviet Law in English: Research Guide and Bibliography, 1970-1987*. Buffalo, NY: W.S. Hein

Includes 1,600 books and articles. Most of those published in the last two decades are included. Organised in three parts – Researching Soviet Law, Subject Bibliography and an annotated Author Bibliography.

18 Leyda, J. (1983) *Kino: A History of the Russian and Soviet Film*, 3rd edn. Princeton, NJ: Princeton University Press

Contains a bibliographic essay – 'Seventy-five years of Russian and Soviet films, 1907-1982: a select list' (p.414-475). The section is indexed.

19 *New Contents: Slavistics*. (1976-) München: O. Sagner.

Tables of contents from about 400 leading journals in Slavic languages and literature. Prepared by the Bavarian State Library.

20 Pearson, R. (1989) *Russia and Eastern Europe, 1789-1985: A Bibliographical Guide*. Manchester: Manchester University Press. (History and Related Disciplines Select Bibliographies)

A listing of books suitable for undergraduate students and general readers. History and related areas, such as religion, education, science, culture, national minorities, are covered in selective fashion.

21   Fitzpatrick, S. and Viola, L. (1990) Editors. *A Researcher's Guide to Sources on Soviet Social History in the 1930s.* Armonk, NY: M.E. Sharpe

Essays on various disciplines within the social sciences with references to key bibliographic and reference sources and to important subject monographs.

22   Sanchez, J. (1985) *Bibliography for Soviet Geography: With Special Reference to Cultural, Historical, and Economic Geography.* Chicago: CPL Bibliographies. (Council of Planning Librarians Bibliography, no. 152)

Lists and annotates 38 maps and atlases. Includes a brief section on basic reference aids.

23   Späth, M. (1981) *Bibliography of Articles on East-European and Russian History: Selected from English Language Periodicals, 1850-1938,* edited by W. Philipp. Wiesbaden: Harrassowitz (Bibliographische Mitteilungen des Osteuropa – Instituts an der Freien Universität Berlin, 20)

Over 2,500 entries organised by subject and indexed by author. Selective.

24   Terry, G.M. (1978) *East European Languages and Literatures: A Subject and Name Index to Articles in English-Language Journals, 1900-1977.* Oxford; Santa Barbara, CA: ABC-Clio Press

Lists over 10,000 articles culled from over 800 periodicals. Journals published in Eastern Europe are excluded. In addition to coverage of language and literature includes some material on related cultural areas such as folklore, theatre, cinema, opera, etc. Subsequent volumes carried the coverage into the late 1980s – Vol. 2, 1978-1981, Nottingham, Astra Press, 1982; Vol.3, 1982-1984, Nottingham, Astra Press, 1985; Vol.4, 1985-1987, Nottingham, Astra Press, 1988.

25   Zalewski, W. (1981) *Russian-English Dictionaries with Aids for Translators: A Selected Bibliography.* New York: Russica. (Russica Bibliography Series, no. 1)

Records bilingual, multilingual and English/Russian dictionaries with a glossary to Russian terms. Also contains bibliographies, guides, monolingual dictionaries and special purpose dictionaries for abbreviations, pseudonyms, etc. It focuses on subject dictionaries.

NON-BIBLIOGRAPHIC REFERENCE SOURCES

Guides to Archives

The function and content of archival guides are evident from their titles. Those covering broad geographic areas are organised by institution with name and subject indexes, and routinely provide information about addresses, accessibility, contact persons, and descriptions of holdings. Because of these relatively standard features, annotations of the individual entries seems superflous. However, special archives will receive some comment.

26   Grant, S.A. and Brown, J.H. (1981) *The Russian Empire and the Soviet Union: A Guide to Manuscripts and Archival Materials in the United States.* Boston: G.K. Hall

27   Grant, S.A. (1983) *Scholar's Guide to Washington, D.C. for Russian/Soviet Studies: The Baltic States, Belorussia, Central Asia, Moldavia, Russia, Transcaucasia, the Ukraine,* 2nd edn. revised by B.P. Johnson and M.H. Teeter. Washington, D.C.: Kennan Institute

for Advanced Russian Studies of the Woodrow Wilson International Center for Scholars, Smithsonian Institution Press. (Scholar's Guide to Washington, DC, no.1)

28 Grimsted, P.K. (1989) *A Handbook for Archival Research in the USSR*. New York: International Research and Exchanges Board

An exhaustive introduction to archival issues, with discussions of general reference aids and major archives. A listing of guides to the latter is provided. An essential key to Soviet archives. Grimsted's other guides to archives can be traced through this work.

29 *Guide to the Boris I. Nicolaevsky Collection in the Hoover Institution Archives*. (1989) Part I compiled by A.M. Bourguina and M. Jakobson. Part II compiled by M. Jakobson. Stanford, CA: Hoover Institution Press. (Hoover Bibliography Series, no.74)

One of the largest single collections in the Hoover Archives. About 400 boxes of materials on Russian pre-revolutionary and emigré movements, organisations and personalities.

30 Van der Horst, Atie and Koen, Elly (1989) Editors. *Guide to the International Archives and Collections of the IISH, Amsterdam*. Amsterdam: Institute of Social History

An international collection with holdings measuring about 6,000 linear meters. About 22 per cent of the collection deals with Russia. There are personal as well as organisational documents. Entries provide biographical, or historical, data as well as brief descriptions of holdings.

31 Hartley, J.M. (1987) *Guide to Documents and Manuscripts in the United Kingdom relating to Russia and the Soviet Union*. London: Mansell

32 Karlowich, R.A. (1990) *A Guide to Scholarly Resources on the Russian Empire and the Soviet Union in the New York Metropolitan Area*. Armonk, NY: M.E. Sharpe

33 Leadenham, C.A. (1986) *Guide to the Collections in the Hoover Institution Archives Relating to Imperial Russia, the Russian Revolutions and Civil War, and the First Emigration*. Stanford, CA: Hoover Institution Press. (Hoover Bibliographical Series, no.68)

34 Lewanski, R.C. (1980) *Eastern Europe and Russia/Soviet Union: A Handbook of Western European Archival and Library Resources*. New York: K.G. Saur. (Joint Committee on Eastern Europe. Publication Series no.3)

35 Palm, C.G. and Reed, D. (1980) *Guide to the Hoover Institution Archives*. Stanford, CA: Hoover Institution Press. (Hoover Bibliographical Series, no.59)

Describes the contents of 676 collections. Organised by subject, with an alphabetical list of collections and an index.

36 Scaruffi, E. (1987) Editor. *Russia in the Twentieth Century: The Catalog of the Bakhmeteff Archive of Russian and East European History and Culture*. The Rare Book and Manuscript Library, Columbia University. Boston, MA: G.K. Hall

Archives of Russian emigré writers, scholars, literary critics and journalists, institutions and organisations, most of them emigré and materials documenting historical events.

37 *Soviet Serials Currently Received at the Center For Research Libraries: A Checklist*, (1990) 4th edn. compiled by S.I. Ignashev. Chicago: Center For Research Libraries

List of 1,287 titles of Soviet periodicals, serials, annuals and numbered monographic series received at CRL as of June 1, 1990. Updated periodically.

Encyclopedias and Dictionaries

38 Shukman, H. (1988) Editor. *The Blackwell Encyclopedia of the Russian Revolution.* Oxford; New York: Blackwell

Part One has subject articles, Part Two biographies. In addition to discussing pertinent current issues it also provides historical and cultural background. Further reading recommendations are provided.

39 *Cambridge Encyclopedia of Russia and the Soviet Union.* (1982) Cambridge; New York: Cambridge University Press

Written by accomplished scholars but intended to interest the general reader. Descriptive rather than analytical.

40 Volkov, M.I. (1985) Editor. *A Dictionary of Political Economy.* Moscow: Progress

Translation of *Politicheskaia Ekonomiia.* Moskva: Politizdat, 1981.

41 Jackson, G. (1989) Editor. *Dictionary of the Russian Revolution.* New York: Greenwood

'Guide to the major institutions, people, and movements associated with the Russian Revolutions of 1917-1921' (Preface). Includes chronologies, maps, name and subject indexes and bibliographies at the end of articles.

42 *Encyclopedia of Soviet Law.* (1985) 2nd edn. revised by F.J.M. Feldbrugge and others. Dordrecht: Nijhoff (Law in Eastern Europe, no. 28)

Articles are relatively long, based on subject headings selected according to usages in Soviet legal encyclopedias as well as terms familiar to Western lawyers. The broadly classified approach is supported by an extensive bibliography covering English and Russian publications.

43 *Great Soviet Encyclopedia.* (1973-) New York: Macmillan

A volume-by-volume translation of the 30-volume standard Soviet version *Bol'shaia Sovetskaia Entsiklopedia.* (3rd edn). Format compels use of index

44 Terras, V. (1985) Editor. *Handbook of Russian Literature.* New Haven: Yale University Press

Primarily for English-speaking readers. Wherever possible bibliographies refer to English-language materials. Treatment of literary subjects is better than for individual writers.

45 Kasack, W. (1988) *Dictionary of Russian Literature since 1917*, translated by M. Carlson and J.T. Hedges. New York: Columbia University Press

Translation of *Lexikon der Russischen Literatur ab 1917* and of *Lexikon der Russischen Literatur ab 1917, Ergänzungsband.* Munich: Otto Sagner, 1986. Full treatment of Russian authors. More authors are covered than in (41) and (48). Relatively less emphasis upon literary topics, literary critics and criticisms, genres, etc.

46 Jones, D.R. (1978-) Editor. *The Military-Naval Encyclopedia of Russia and the Soviet Union.* Gulf Breeze, FL: Academic International Press

Established as a basic source. The publishers claim that 'nearly half of the entries have never before appeared in any reference work'.

47 Wieczynski J.L. (1976-1987) Editor. *The Modern Encyclopedia of Russian and Soviet History.* Vols. 1-46, 1987-1990. Vols, 46-54 as Supplements. Gulf Breeze, FL: Academic International Press

The most authoritative encyclopedia in English in the field. Solid scholarly work based on Soviet and Western sources. No comparable work is available in Russian.

48   Weber, H.B. (1977-) Editor. *The Modern Encyclopedia of Russian and Soviet Literature.* Gulf Breeze, FL: Academic International Press

The only work of this scope in English. Covers authors, literary history and criticism, literary genres, schools, movements, journals and folklore. Combines information from a variety of sources, and some translations from them. An essential source.

49   Stevens, P.D. (1988-) Editor. *The Modern Encyclopedia of Religions in Russia and the Soviet Union.* Gulf Breeze, FL: Academic International Press

One of the latest projects by AIP. It is planned to cover the religious culture of the peoples of Russia and the Soviet Union in 30 volumes or so.

50   Paxton, J. (1983) *Companion to Russian History.* New York: Facts on File Publications

Contains 2,500 brief entries. Also has a gazetteer, atlas, chronology, who's who, and a select bibliography. A basic work for general readers.

51   Jones, D.R. (1977-) Editor. *Soviet Armed Forces Review Annual.* Gulf Breeze, FL: Academic International Press

An annual. Facts, analysis, documentation, bibliography and historical background relating to Soviet forces.

52   Pollard, A.P. (1977-) Editor. *USSR Facts and Figures Annual.* Gulf Breeze, FL: Academic International Press

A wealth of data on all facets of political, social and cultural life in the Soviet Union: chronologies, events, statistics, etc. Based on a variety of official, private and international sources. An annual.

Biographical Dictionaries

53   *Biographical Dictionary of Dissidents in the Soviet Union, 1956-1975.* (1982) compiled and edited by S.P. de Boer and others. The Hague: Nijhoff

Almost 3,400 dissidents – the criteria for this title are closely specified – are listed. Biographical data and dissident activity are given.

54   Davies, R.W. (1990) *Soviet Government Officials, 1922-1941: A Handlist.* Birmingham: University of Birmingham, Centre For Russian and East European Studies

Provides data on senior government officials in institutional, chronological and alphabetical sequences.

55   *Directory of Soviet Officials, National Organizations.* (1981-) Washington, DC: CIA

One of a useful series of irregularly published official personnel directories. Data include addresses, appointment dates, organisational structures etc. Other titles listed in *CIA Maps and Publications Released to the Public, 1971-1985,* Washington DC: Public Affairs Office, 1985: 18-28.

56   Helf, G. (1987-) *A Biographic Directory of Soviet Regional Party Leaders.* Munich: Radio Free Europe Research

Similar in arrangement to Rahr (58). The August 1988 issue is in two parts. Part 1, RSFSR oblasts, krais, and ASSR; Part 2, Union Republic oblasts and ASSR.

57   Mann, D. (1989) *The Supreme Soviet: A Biographical Dictionary.* Washington, DC: Center For Strategic and International Studies; Munich: Radio Free Europe/Radio Liberty

Describes the organisation of the Supreme Soviet followed by brief biographies of its members.

58 Rahr, A.G. (1989) *A Biographic Directory of 100 Leading Soviet Officials,* 4th edn. revised with some additions. Munich: Radio Liberty Research, Radio Free Europe/Radio Liberty

Lists highest ranking government and party officials. Includes basic biographical data, career details, publications, awards, etc. Systematically updated.

59 *The Soviet Biographic Archive, 1954-1985.* (1986) Alexandria, VA: Chadwyck-Healey

Consists of 2,812 microfiches. Lists more than 50,000 individuals from a wide range of public life. Entries are arranged according to the Cyrillic alphabet. Data are based on the holdings of Radio Free Europe/Radio Liberty and the Hoover Institution. It is continued by *Public Figures in the Soviet Union: A Current Biographical Index, 1984-.* This is a bi-annual cumulative index to press and other sources of biographical data.

60 *Soviet Biographical Service.* (1985-) Minneapolis, Minn: J.L. Scherer

Organised by broad areas of activities such as party, government, culture, sport. Covers all walks of life. In addition to biographic data, included references press statements about individuals. A loose-leaf service which is continuously updated and cumulatively indexed. A very useful service in times of change.

61 *The Tauris Soviet Directory: The Elite of the USSR Today.* (1989) compiled by R. Cichero. London: Tauris

Family backgrounds, education, careers, addresses, publications, offices, etc. of 2,000 prominent individuals. Wide coverage but emphasis is on personnel in the top of the economic, administrative and political hierarchies.

62 Vronskaya, J.A. (1989) *Biographical Dictionary of the Soviet Union, 1917-1988.* London: K.G. Saur

Brief biographies of 5,000 notabilities from all walks of life. A useful index groups entries by vocation.

63 Weeks, A.L. (1991) *The Soviet Nomenklatura: A Comprehensive Roster of Soviet Civilian and Military Officials,* 3rd. edn. Washington, DC: Washington Institute Press

Previous edition in 1987. This version updates data to April 1, 1989. Compiled from Soviet sources. List of persons associated with Soviet Party, government and military bodies.

64 Chainikov, S. (1990) Editor. *Who's Who in the Soviet Government.* Moscow: Novosti

Sponsored by the Information Department of the USSR Council of Ministers. Intended for the general public. Brief biographical data and interviews with individuals to highlight official plans and objectives. English text.

65 Lewytzkyj, B. (1984) Editor. *Who's Who in the Soviet Union: A Biographical Encyclopedia of 5,000 Leading Personalities in the Soviet Union.* München; New York: K.G. Saur

Covers all fields of activity. Also lists recently retired and deceased individuals, as well as those relieved or dimissed from office.

66 Schulz-Jorge U-J. (1990) Editor. *Who's Who in the Soviet Union: Political and Military Leaders.* New York: K. G. Saur

In two volumes. Volume 1 – chronological survey of leading officials in the Party, the state, the KGB, and the armed forces. Volume 2 – biographical entries for 2,000 individuals.

Directories

67   *Neformalniye: A Guide to Independent Organizations and Contacts in the Soviet Union.* (1990) Seattle, WA: World Without War Council

Lists over 500 grassroots organisations with names, addresses and telephone numbers of leading figures or contact persons. Intended for scholars, journalists and special interest travellers to the Soviet Union.

68   Rose, C. (1988) *The Soviet Propaganda Network: A Directory of Organizations Serving Soviet Foreign Policy.* London: Pinter

Factual profiles of organisations contributing to Soviet propaganda. Data include names, addresses, origins, aims, organisation and membership, office holders, finances, etc.

69   *A Scholar's Guide to Humanities and Social Sciences in the Soviet Union: The Academy of Sciences of the USSR and the Academies of Sciences of the Union Republics* (1985), Compiled by R. Mdivani and others. Armonk, NY: M.E. Sharpe

A directory of institutions. Gives addresses, directors, history, areas of research, structure, publications, contacts, recent publications, etc. An official publication giving very official information.

70   *USSR: Yearbook.* (1964-) Moscow: Novosti

An annual almanack chronicling events and providing factual data about most facets of life.

71   *Vsia Moskva. All Moscow, 1990/1991: The Database of Moscow.* (1990) Moscow: Vsia Moskva; Marburg: Blaue Horner Publishing House

Published in English and Russian versions. A straightforward city directory, but valuable because it provides information not available in such accessible form previously.

Machine-Readable Bibliographies and Data Sources

BIBLIOGRAPHIC DATABASES

72   *Current Digest of the Soviet Press.* (1949-) Columbus, OH: Current Digest of the Soviet Press

Contains selected translations and abstracts from 40 newspapers and 65 magazines from all Soviet Republics. Published weekly, indexed quarterly and annually. Available in print, microfiche and online on DIALOG, KNOWLEDGE INDEX and NEXIS.

73   *Daily Report: Soviet Union: Index: Foreign Broadcast Information Service.* (1952-) Stamford, CN: Newsbank

Supplies English-language translations of Soviet broadcasts, newspapers and some journal articles. Online since 1970.

74   *Index to U.S. Government Periodicals.* Chicago: Infordata International Inc.

Provides subject access to 180 major government periodicals. Available online through BSR and WILSONLINE and on CD-ROM as part of WILSONDISC.

75   *Magazine Index.* (1977-) Menlo Park, CA: Information Access Corp

Covers 435 magazines from US, Canada and the UK. Microfiche and online.

76   *National Newspaper Index.* (1979-) Foster City, CA: Information Access Corp.

Indexes major US newspapers as well as selected newswire services. Monthly.

NON-BIBLIOGRAPHIC DATABASES

77 *Biography Master Index.* Detroit, MI: Gale Research

The standard guide to biographical sources. Gives names of biographees, dates of birth and death and details of the source publications that include biographical information. Over 3,400,000 entries drawn from more than 700 source publications. Available in print form as *Biography and Genealogy Master Index.*

78 *Guide to Resources and Services.* (1977-) Ann Arbor, MI: Inter-University Consortium for Political and Social Research

Social science machine-readable data in the form of surveys, census records, election returns, and other records maintained and distributed for research and teaching purposes. Data received from over 130 countries.

79 *SOVSET.* Washington, DC: Center For Strategic and International Studies

Computer network for Soviet and East European studies, established 1984. Links more than 500 leading specialists worldwide. Available for computer conferencing and electronic mail. Data library service offers access to a number of electronic sources, for example *PlanEcon Report, Eastern Europe Newsletter, Radio Liberty Daily Report, Le Monde Soviet Politics.* Accessible through Compuserve, Tymnet, and Telenet.

DATABASE DIRECTORIES

80 Maraccio, K.Y. (1989) Editor. *Computer-Readable Databases: A Directory and Data Sourcebook.* Detroit, MI: Gale Research Inc.

Comprehensive directory of databases and CD-ROM services.

81 *Database Directory.* (1989) White Plains, NY: Knowledge Industry Publications

International coverage. Published with the support of the American Society for Information Science.

82 *Directory of Online Databases.* (1990) Santa Monica, CA: Cuadra Associates

'Describes a total of 4,615 databases available through 654 online services' (Preface). Coverage is international.

83 *Fulltext Sources Online: Bibliodata for Periodicals, Newspapers, Newsletters and Newswires.* (1988) Needham, MA: BiblioData

Full text services are increasing in numbers and in subject coverage. Guides such as this record the developing field. Several entries are listed under the Soviet Union.

84 Hall, J.L. (1986) *Online Bibliographic Databases: A Directory and Sourcebook,* 4th edn. London: Aslib

More selective than its American counterparts. Covers 250 principal English-language databases. Provides the usual cluster of related information about producers, suppliers, useful references, etc.

85 *Information Industry Directory, 1991* (1990) 11th edn. by B.J. Morgan. Detroit, MI: Gale Research Inc.

A comprehensive international descriptive guide to more than 4,500 organisations, systems and services involved in the production and distribution of information in electronic forms.

86 Tenopir, C. (1989) *Issues in Online Database Searching.* Englewood: Libraries Unlimited

A collection of previously published articles useful for gaining an understanding of current problems and potential of various electronic forms of publication.

Index